CISTERCIAN STUDIES SERIES: NUMBER ONE HUNDRED AND TWO

THOMAS MERTON:

Monk and Artist

CISTERCIAN STUDIES SERIES: NUMBER ONE HUNDRED AND TWO

THOMAS MERTON:

Monk and Artist

By Victor A. Kramer

Cistercian Publications
Kalamazoo, Michigan

Originally published as *Thomas Merton* in the Twayne
United States Authors Series, Nbr 462.

© 1984 by Twayne Publishers, a division of
G.K. Hall & Co., Boston

Chapter Ten, 'An Afterword: Scholarship and Thomas Merton'
© 1987 by Cistercian Publications, Inc.

Available in Britain and Europe from
A.R. Mowbray & Co., Ltd
St Thomas House Becket Street
Oxford OX1 1SJ

Available elsewhere (including Canada) from
Cistercian Publications Inc
WMU Station
Kalamazoo, Michigan 49008

The work of Cistercian Publications is made possible in
part by support from Western Michigan University through
the Institute of Cistercian Studies.

Library of Congress Cataloguing-in-Publication Data:

Kramer, Victor A.
    Thomas Merton, monk and artist.

    (Cistercian studies series; no. 102)
    Rev. ed. of: Thomas Merton © 1984
    Bibliography: p. 207
    Includes Index.
    1. Merton, Thomas, 1915–1968 — Criticism and
interpretation. I. Kramer, Victor A. Thomas Merton.
II. Title. III. Series.
PS3525.E7174Z73   1987   818'.5409   87–6418
ISBN 0–87907–602–X (pbk.)

For Dewey Weiss Kramer

Contents

About the Author

Victor A. Kramer received the A.B. degree from Saint Edward's University in 1961, and the M.A. from the University of Texas at Austin in 1963; his Ph.D. was awarded by the University of Texas in 1966. He has written extensively about American literature and literary criticism and is the author of *James Agee* (1975), and joint editor of *Olmsted South* (1979). He has edited issues of *Studies in the Literary Imagination* on the "Harlem Renaissance" (1974), "Contemporary Literary Theory" (1979), and "Religion and Literature" (1985). His numerous essays and reviews have appeared in more than a score of journals. He is co-author of *Andrew Lytle, Walker Percy, Peter Taylor: A Reference Guide* (1983), editor of *American Critics at Work: Examinations of Contemporary Literary Theories* (1984), and co-editor of *Conversations with Walker Percy* (1985). He has been a member of the faculty at Marquette University, and was Fulbright Senior Lecturer at the University of Regensburg, Bavaria in 1974–75. At present he teaches at Georgia State University in Atlanta.

Preface to Expanded and Revised Edition

This reprinting of *Thomas Merton* has appeared, in large part, because of encouragement of those who enthusiastically read the book when it first appeared. Reviewers, monks, friends, scholars (some all these things at once) saw valuable qualities in the book which make it a useful tool for observing the "interior Merton" through analysis of his writing. I am thankful for the critical comments which have stressed this, and as I have written the new final chapter for the expanded version I have tried to bear in mind that it is Merton's interior journey which is most important.

The "Afterword" surveys all recent books about Merton and, as well, posthumous books by him which have appeared in the last several years. My concern has been to demonstrate that Merton's multi-faceted ability is becoming clearer as scholars accumulate more systematic evidence about the unity of his dual vocation. Interestingly, such an understanding of Thomas Merton/Father Louis has been to a significant degree made possible by the steady growth of primary works as well as biographical and secondary material. I am therefore in continuing debt to other scholars and to the prodigious spiritual and artistic energy which generated Merton's writing.

In particular I want to thank three of Merton's brother monks who have encouraged me. Abbot Flavian Burns, who served as Merton's last Abbot; Brother Patrick Hart of Gethsemani Abbey in Kentucky; and Father Thomas Francis Smith of Our Lady of the Holy Spirit Abbey, Conyers, Georgia, have all been helpful critics. Many other monks also have been critical in the best sense and this is true of many Merton scholars, especially Rev. George Kilcourse, Sister Elena Malits, and Dr. Robert E. Daggy, all of whom have provided constructive suggestions over a period of many years. I wish also to thank Dr. Rozanne Elder of Cistercian Publications for her careful editorial suggestions as this book was being revised.

1986   *Victor A. Kramer*

Preface

This study is about a man of letters who chose to be a monk, and about how his writing speaks to all men of the modern world. To be both a cloistered priest and a writer may seem contradictory, yet it must be recognized that Thomas Merton was always an artist. He decided to become a monk, and through his writing perfected two roles which were mutually supportive. Ironically, Merton's literary career developed in large part because he sought to ignore that he even had such a career, especially during his earliest years within the monastery. We now understand that he always needed to write—just as other men breathe—but that his writing was part of a dual movement toward both accepting the world and paradoxically moving toward greater solitude. Through continual use of language Merton defined his relationship to God, and he also celebrated the mystery of living. Writing did not necessarily make it easier to provide answers about the mystery of life; indeed, in some ways it made it even harder. Yet if his answers sometimes became more oblique, the questions became increasingly intriguing as he perfected his talent. Journals, autobiography, poems, and essays written throughout an extremely prolific career provide a map of both spiritual and literary development, movements which were sometimes not what the writer himself might have predicted. The lesson, however, is a simple one; in his autobiography Merton, perhaps simplistically, recognized it as a paradox: "man's nature, by itself, can do little or nothing to settle his most important problems. If we follow nothing but our nature, our own philosophies, our own level of ethics, we will end up in hell."[1] To become a successful writer Thomas Merton, or Father Louis, his name as a monk, had to give up any ambition to be so; however, not surprisingly, a careful reading of the entire body of his writing reveals that he learned to give up a consciousness of himself precisely through the exercise of writing. One of the major concerns of this book is with the development of Merton's literary abilities. His writing is the record of a going beyond mere artistry, yet Thomas Merton, who was Father Louis, was able to do this because he became convinced of the unimportance of self, and the mystery of the universe as a whole, which he sought to confirm through writing.

Early in life Merton sensed that his vocation would be that of a man of letters. It took years for him to find out exactly how. He noted in a journal entry of late 1941 that he sensed he must go beyond the kind of peacefulness which he enjoyed as a college teacher at St. Bonaventure's, "[a] quietness which does not belong to me, and cannot. For a moment I get the illusion that the peace here is real, but it is not. It is merely the absence of trouble, not the peace of poverty and sacrifice. This 'peace' cannot be enough for me any more."[2] To go beyond a quiet which was merely the absence of trouble meant finally to commit himself to life in the Abbey of Gethsemani.

Retrospectively, it is clear that Merton conceived of his vocation as fundamentally that of a writer—a monk striving to find God through language. His life as a cloistered religious, however, was nevertheless in a basic way, paradoxical; by accepting the silence of the monastery he found himself one of the most vocal priest-poets in the history of the church. Merton realized the peculiarity of such a career. In his preface to *A Merton Reader* he notes: "I have had to accept the fact that my life is almost totally paradoxical."[3] What the mature writer knows is that God chose to place him in a monastery, but since he was first a writer, and a monk second, God allowed him to work his way closer to the Divine through the writing. Such wisdom clarifies an insight which the young Tom Merton had on 27 November 1941, just a few days before he became a monk: "If God wants me to write, I can write anywhere."[4]

Clearly, as a monk Merton never desired to relinquish fully all hopes to be a successful writer; but it is significant that as a young monk he was willing to cease writing if that appeared to be God's will. Reflecting upon his paradoxical career the mature Father Louis realized that in a strange sort of way it had ultimately become possible for him both to do the writing and to give it up as well:

If the monastic life is a life of hardship and sacrifice, I would say that for me most of the hardship has come in connection with writing. It is possible to doubt whether I have become a monk (a doubt I have to live with), but it is not possible to doubt that I am a writer, that I was born one and will probably die as one. Disconcerting, disedifying as it is, this seems to be my lot and vocation. It is what God has given me in order that I might give it back to Him.[5]

While the writing was a way for Merton to strengthen his personal relationship to God, it was also an overt way to lead others on a similar journey. An interesting fact was that if this monk's writing was to be for a public and not for private edification, Father Louis had to cultivate the work habits of a conscientious man of letters. To lead others, therefore, meant revisions, drafts, letters, and plans, projects and deadlines. At times this seemed to divert him too much from his religious life, but we must recall that for many years as a young monk Merton/Father Louis only had six or eight hours per week to devote to writing.

It is good to think of all of his writings as journeys. This is another paradox which should be recognized—when one agrees to stay put (the vow of stability) one can really begin to travel.[6] The habit of writing allowed Father Louis to move far beyond a concern with self, yet the only way to accomplish this was to begin with an examination of self. When that is accomplished, then one transcends self. Just as with Thoreau's apology within the opening pages of *Walden* for the subject matter he knows best (himself), Merton's literary strategy often builds on paradox. As a contemplative, Father Louis was drawn back into the world of writing, and galleys, and proofsheets. Such a journey with the pen became a model for others. Yet all this also brought quiet. Standing back from the entire career definite patterns stand out, for Merton was a lover of both life and art. He knew that both reinforced the other. The dual career as artist and contemplative eventually became wedded parts of one spiritual journey. Through study of the development of the writing we can make a similar journey with Thomas Merton/Father Louis.

The plan of this study keeps the chronology of Merton's career in mind, but the books which possess literary merit are best understood when seen as part of larger patterns which were developing in Merton's life. Thus, in the opening chapter an overview of the life is provided, and in the two chapters which follow examination of early works of prose and poetry reveal how Merton structured his art. In the fourth chapter books of a devotional nature which range from the historical and biographical to the personal, such as meditations and journals, are treated. In the middle chapter several later books of poetry are examined as they reveal Merton's own development toward more experimental writing. The sixth chapter treats books which approach a range of problems in the world, but through varieties of prose which clearly demonstrate Merton's developing literary talent and his increasing manifestation of an awareness that as Father Louis, the contemplative, he had a responsibility to craft his writings so that opinions about the contemporary world were clearly expressed. In the remaining chapters of this volume Merton's fascination with the East, and the literary benefits he derived from such an interest and his exuberant development of new varieties of "antipoetry," are traced. The final chapter is an analysis of some of the most important writings which were posthumously published.

The unifying thread among the separate chapters of this study is Merton's writing as it reveals his dual vocation—monk and writer. Through successive stages Merton developed ways as artist to treat greater areas of concern. Father Louis lived a life of prayer, but through the writing published under the name of Thomas Merton he made more and more connections beyond his solitude. The writing demonstrates that it was a solitude for others. Because Merton was such a prolific writer, and because he wrote on such a wide variety of topics, many different approaches have already been made to his work by other scholars. My research has profited from the many studies of Merton completed since his death, and I will acknowledge my debts to many writers in specific places.

I am especially thankful that the work of Marquita Breit, Frank Dell I'sola, Raymond Bailey, James T. Baker, James Finley, John Howard Griffin, Brother Patrick Hart, the Reverend John T. Higgins, the Reverend Frederick J. Kelly, the Reverend George Kilcourse, Sister Elena Malits, Dennis McInerny, the Reverend Henri A. Nouwen, Sister Therésè Lentfoehr, Edward Rice, Gerald Twomey, and George Woodcock has so well prepared the way. Recently still other books by William H. Shannon, Ross Labrie, Richard Cashen, and Daniel J. Adams have helped me to refine my developing insights. The biographical investigation done by Monica Furlong has assisted me in understanding Merton, as is the case also with the photographs taken by him and recently gathered by James Forest and Deba Patnaik. When we have a completed authorized biography still more details will become available. Eventually more of the uncollected materials and correspondence will be published.

The manuscript materials and other primary documents at the Thomas Merton Studies Center of Bellarmine College have proved to be of great benefit throughout this study. To have access to Merton's correspondence, notebooks, photographs, and other materials has allowed me to support this investigation with significant primary documents. Dr. Robert E. Daggy, curator of the Merton Collection, has provided specific help in many ways over the years.

I am deeply appreciative of the assistance I have received from all these sources.[7] Especially I appreciate the assistance of Brother Patrick Hart and the monks of Gethsemani Abbey, Trappist, Kentucky; and the Monastery of the Holy Spirit, Conyers, Georgia. My emphasis on the literary career provides, I hope, a valuable way of approaching Merton, writer and monk, a man of letters for a wide audience.

Victor A. Kramer

Decatur, Georgia

Acknowledgments

From the Thomas Merton Legacy Trust permission has been granted for use of selected manuscript and tape-recorded materials now located in the Thomas Merton Study Center of Bellarmine College, Louisville, Kentucky.

The frontispiece portrait was provided through the courtesy of the estate of the photographer, John Howard Griffin.

From *Exploration* permission has been granted to incorporate parts of my article *"The Geography of Lograire:* An Introspective Journey."

From the *Journal of the American Academy of Religion* permission has been granted to use parts of my article "Merton's Art and Non-Western Thought."

From *SEASA '79 Proceedings* permission has been granted to use parts of "Thomas Merton's Concern about Institutionalization, Bureaucracy, and the Abuse of Language."

From *Studia Mystica* permission has been granted to revise and incorporate paragraphs from my article "Thomas Merton's Published Journals: The Paradox of Writing as a Step Toward Contemplation."

From the *American Benedictine Review* permission has been granted to revise and incorporate parts of my article "An Autobiographical Impulse: The Early Prose of Thomas Merton."

From New Directions Publishing Corporation permission has been granted to quote from the following books:
Collected Poems of Thomas Merton, © 1977 by the Trustees of the Merton Legacy Trust; *New Seeds of Contemplation,* © 1961 by The Abbey of Gethsemani, Inc.; *Seeds of Contemplation,* Copyright 1949 by Our Lady of Gethsemani Monastery; *Figures for an Apocalypse,* Copyright 1948 by New Directions Publishing Corporation; *The Tears of Blind Lions,* Copyright 1949 by Our Lady of Gethsemani Monastery; *Emblems of a Season of Fury,* © 1963 by the Abbey of Gethsemani, Inc.; *The Strange Islands,* Copyright 1957 by the Abbey of Geth-

semani, Inc.; *The Behavior of Titans,* © 1961 by the Abbey of Gethsemani, Inc.; *Gandhi on Non-Violence,* © 1964, 1965 by New Directions Publishing Corporation; *The Wisdom of the Desert,* © 1960 by the Abbey of Gethsemani, Inc.; *Zen and the Birds of Appetite,* © 1968 by the Abbey of Gethsemani, Inc.; *The Way of Chuang Tzu,* © 1965 by the Abbey of Gethsemani, Inc.; *Raids on the Unspeakable,* © 1966 by the Abbey of Gethsemani, Inc.; *Cables to the Ace,* © 1968 by the Abbey of Gethsemani, Inc.; *The Geography of Lograire,* © 1968, 1969 by the Trustees of the Merton Legacy Trust; *The Asian Journal,* © 1968, 1970, 1973 by the Trustees of the Merton Legacy Trust.

Materials from the following sources are reprinted by permission of Farrar, Straus & Giroux, Inc.:
from *Secular Journal* by Thomas Merton, © 1959 by Madonna House; from *Thoughts in Solitude* by Thomas Merton, Copyright 1956, © 1958 by the Abbey of Our Lady of Gethsemani; from *The Living Bread* by Thomas Merton, Copyright 1956 by The Abbey of Our Lady of Gethsemani; from *The New Man* by Thomas Merton, © 1961 by The Abbey of Gethsemani; from *Disputed Questions* by Thomas Merton, Copyright 1953, © 1959, 1960 by The Abbey of Our Lady of Gethsemani; from *Seeds of Destruction* by Thomas Merton, © 1961, 1962, 1963, 1964 by The Abbey of Gethsemani; from *Love and Living* by Thomas Merton, © 1965, 1966, 1967, 1968, 1969, 1977, 1979 by the Trustees of the Merton Legacy Trust.

Materials from the following sources are reprinted with the permission of Doubleday & Co.:
from *My Argument with the Gestapo,* © 1969 by The Abbey of Gethsemani, Inc.; from *A Thomas Merton Reader,* edited by Thomas McDonnell, © 1974 by the Trustees of the Merton Legacy Trust; from *Conjectures of a Guilty Bystander,* © 1965, 1966 by The Abbey of Gethsemani; from *Contemplation in a World of Action,* © 1965, 1969, 1970, 1971 by the Trustees of the Merton Legacy Trust.

Harcourt Brace Jovanovich, Inc. has granted permission to reprint excerpts from *The Seven Storey Mountain, The Sign of Jonas, The Waters of Siloe,* and *No Man Is an Island.*

Chronology

1915 Born at Prades, France, 31 January, son of Owen Merton, artist from New Zealand, and Ruth Jenkins, artist from Ohio.

1916 Moves to the United States. Lives in Maryland and New York, at Flushing, Long Island, and at Douglaston, Long Island (with mother's family).

1921 Mother dies.

1922 Goes to Bermuda, attends elementary school.

1923 Returns to Douglaston.

1925 Goes to France with father.

1926 Enters Lycee Ingres, Montauban, France.

1928 Goes to England.

1929 Enters Oakham School (Rutland, England).

1931 Father dies.

1932 Acquires higher certificate and scholarship to Clare College, Cambridge.

1933 Visits Italy; summer in United States; enters Cambridge in fall. Studies French and Italian.

1934 Gains second in Modern Language Tripos, part 1, Cambridge. Moves to New York.

1935 February, enters Columbia University.

1937 Editor of 1937 *Yearbook,* art editor of Columbia *Jester.*

1938 Graduates from Columbia with B.A. Begins work on M.A. thesis: "Nature and Art in William Blake."

1939 M.A. Columbia. Teaches in University Extension.

1939–1941 Teaches English at St. Bonaventure University New York. Contributes to *New York Times Book Review* and *New York Herald Tribune,* as well as to literary magazines.

1941 10 December, enters Abbey of Gethsemani (Cistercians), Kentucky.

1944   19 March, makes Simple Vows. *Thirty Poems.*

1946   *A Man in the Divided Sea.*

1947   19 March, makes Solemn Vows.

1948   *Figures for an Apocalypse; Exile Ends in Glory; The Seven Storey Mountain; What Is Contemplation?*

1949   26 May (Ascension). Ordained at Gethsemani by Archbishop John A. Floersh of Louisville. *Seeds of Contemplation; The Tears of the Blind Lions; The Waters of Siloe.*

1950   *Selected Poems* (first English edition); *What Are These Wounds?*

1951–1955   Master of the students (Magister Spiritus), Gethsemani.

1951   *The Ascent to Truth.*

1953   *The Sign of Jonas; Bread in the Wilderness.*

1954   *The Last of the Fathers.*

1955–1965   Master of Novices, Gethsemani.

1955   *No Man Is an Island.*

1956   *The Living Bread; Praying the Psalms.*

1957   *The Strange Islands; The Tower of Babel; The Silent Life.*

1958   *Thoughts in Solitude.*

1959   *The Secular Journal of Thomas Merton; Selected Poems of Thomas Merton.*

1960   *Spiritual Direction and Meditation; The Wisdom of the Desert; Disputed Questions.*

1961   *The Behavior of Titans; The New Man; New Seeds of Contemplation.*

1962   *Original Child Bomb; Clement of Alexandria; A Thomas Merton Reader.*

1963   *Breakthrough to Peace.* Receives Medal for Excellence, Columbia University. *Life and Holiness; Emblems of a Season of Fury.*

1964   *Seeds of Destruction.* Receives Honorary L.D., University of Kentucky.

1965   Retires to hermitage. *Gandhi on Non-Violence* (editor); *The Way of Chuang Tzu; Seasons of Celebration.*

1966   *Raids on the Unspeakable; Conjectures of a Guilty Bystander.*

1967   *Mystics and Zen Masters.*

1968   *Cables to the Ace; Faith and Violence; Zen and the Birds of Appetite.* 10 December, dies at Bangkok, Thailand, where he was invited to attend a meeting of Asian Benedictine and Cistercian abbots, monks, and nuns.

1969   *My Argument with the Gestapo; Contemplative Prayer; The Geography of Lograire.*

1970   *Opening the Bible.*

1971   *Contemplation in a World of Action; Thomas Merton on Peace.*

1973   *The Asian Journal of Thomas Merton.*

1976   *Ishi Means Man.*

1977   *The Monastic Journey.*

1977   *The Collected Poems of Thomas Merton.*

1978   *A Catch of Anti-Letters* (by Merton and Robert Lax).

1979   *Love and Living.*

1980   *Thomas Merton on St. Bernard.*

1981   *Day of a Stranger; The Literary Essays of Thomas Merton.*

1983   *Woods, Shore, Desert*

1985   *The Hidden Ground of Love,* The Letters of Thomas Merton on Religious Experience and Social Concerns; *Eighteen Poems.*

1987   *The Alaskan Journal of Thomas Merton.*

Chapter One
A Pilgrim's Movements

Cities that stood, by day, as gay as lancers
Are lost, in the night, like old men dying.

The Night Train

From France to Kentucky

Thomas Merton's life was a spiritual pilgrimage, one whose course he could not foresee. This metaphor of an unpredictable journey suggests a recurring pattern in the life of a priest-poet which proved full of surprises[1]. Born in 1915 in the Pyrenees of southern France, Merton's many travels were first within France and England, and later between the European and American continents; during his childhood he lived in many places, and eventually during the 1930s he found himself a student at Columbia University. In December 1941, after seven years in New York City, he entered the Cistercian Abbey of Gethsemani located in the hills of Kentucky, and that monastery became his permanent home. He was then twenty-seven years old.

The decision to become a monk might have seemed the end of Merton's journey in the world, but in terms of the spiritual and literary career, it was his real beginning. In twenty-seven years as a cloistered monk he sought to know himself and God's will through continual and systematic investigation of ways to be both contemplative and writer. Ultimately each activity reinforced the other, because while Merton decided to enter the monastery, he would never forget that he was by temperament an artist. Son of artists, and a man who while in college at Columbia had decided to make a career of writing, he gradually developed ways to combine his artistic talent with an intense desire to move closer to God.

A basic pattern present throughout all of Merton's literary career is his awareness of the power of language, and correspondingly its limitations if used poorly.[2] Such concerns recur so regularly in his writing, that they serve as basic motifs. In a related way, he often suggested that while language could express much, he also knew that many aspects of experience would never be expressed through

1

language or images. This is especially true when a writer attempts to use language to suggest what it means to be alone, pray, meditate, contemplate, or give one's life over in love for God.

Merton's memories of his formative years—adolescence and college—provided most of the narrative within his famous auto-biography, *The Seven Storey Mountain.* Through such a structure he dramatized his early years, a time which he later considered to have been largely turmoil. Those turbulent years are the foreground of many pages in the well-known autobiographical book, Merton's account of conversion which brought him early and wide recognition. His youthful years contrasted with the peace and quiet which the young monk had found as part of his new vocation at the Abbey of Gethsemani. Merton's youthful years had included many unusual experiences: travel, sometimes separation from family, and the years of education in France, England, and later New York City. These were the years when the young Merton gradually recognized his developing vocation as writer, but they were also a time of intense personal difficulty.

In retrospect, we can see it was indeed fortunate that Merton's early life developed in the rather complicated manner in which it did, yet it must be admitted that a fictionalized account of his adventures which led up to the commitment to be a Cistercian monk would seem almost too improbable. Yet what could be more fortunate of circumstances than for Thomas Merton to have been born in the south of France just at the beginning of World War I, the son of parents who possessed high ideals about life and art? And what could have been more fortunate for American letters than for Merton's life to have been shaped during the years between the World Wars and before he decided to become a monk? He absorbed aspects of his mother's Quaker strength and his father's cosmopolitan wanderlust. He crossed the Atlantic several times, wandered in Europe, finally finished his education at Columbia University, and taught for two years before he made the decision to enter Gethsemani. The structure for a good story is here, and these facts brought special pressures to bear on the formation of this man whose range of prolific writing seems to have grown because of such a diverse background. We now see it is no accident that in mature years Merton was actively interested in photography, music, drawing, and calligraphy.[3] Each of these are additional facets which reflect his temperament.

The fact that his father, Owen Merton, was from New Zealand and that Ruth Jenkins, his mother, was an American from Ohio, and that they should have met in Paris, is one symbol of the complexity of Merton's talents and interests. (That Merton's first abbot should have come from the same town in Ohio as his mother, and that the abbot should have been knowledgeable about printing and bookmaking, is one more complexity in the web which makes Merton's career a special one.)[4] Tom Merton's remembrances of his earliest years with parents and grandparents, and his reconstruction of those years in *The Seven Storey Mountain,* emphasize the strength which he gained from his father who returned to France with his son when the boy was only ten years old. Merton re-creates his father as representative of the dedicated artist within a society where art is little honored; he realized his father possessed strength, discipline, and courage to pursue his art.

The period in France when the boy was entering adolescence was extremely significant in Merton's formation. Of those years he later recalled both good and bad aspects, for example, children who could be extremely cruel to one another, but also people of devout Catholic practice who provided a strong remembrance for him many years later. Thus, his recollection of a stay in the village of Murat with the Privat family exemplifies how "this going to Murat was a great grace,"[5] and also shows how Merton later was able to recognize that all events work together to the good. He remembers that once, when the question of the validity of protestantism came up in conversation with the quite conservative Privats, they were so firm in their Catholic faith that they did not even begin to argue with the young boy. The ring of Monsieur Privat quietly speaking, "Mais c'est impossible," remained clearly fixed in his mind, and serves as one part in the framework of his continuing journey:

> Who knows how much I owe to those two wonderful people? Anything I say about it is only a matter of guessing, but knowing their charity, it is to me a matter of moral certitude that I owe many graces to their prayers, and perhaps ultimately the grace of my conversion and even of my religious vocation. Who shall say? (*SSM,* 58–59)

Such an experience remained, for Merton, one small example of God's grace at work, yet in ways often impossible to understand until long after the event.

Childhood was for him unconventional, sad, and in some ways unpleasant; he lost his mother when he was only six years old, and he was fifteen when his father suddenly died of a brain tumor. Owen Merton had only begun to be recognized as an artist of note when he became seriously ill. Suddenly young Merton was all alone at a relatively early age. Even worse, he later indicated, he mistakenly imagined himself to be free to do what he chose, and it took him "five or six years to discover what a frightful captivity I had got myself into" (*SSM*, 85).

After his father's death he attended the Oakham School in England from 1929 to 1932, and then won a scholarship to Clare College, Cambridge. The year at Cambridge, however, proved to be a severe disappointment because of what he considered to be its decadent atmosphere.[6] We might conclude that his memories of Cambridge are colored by the tone of life experienced while *The Seven Storey Mountain* was being composed within a Cistercian monastery; the *Seven Storey* account of Cambridge reflects a pious seriousness. In the autobiography Merton structures those crucial years of his coming into adulthood as a symbol for many who attempt to live in the absence of God. Upon reflection he realized that God's presence had always been available, yet he, and he implies many like him, lamentably chose to ignore it.

Circumstances, which included not attending classes, led to Merton's getting into trouble, and to eventual separation from Cambridge. Monica Furlong's biography of Merton provides many details about these months. When his godfather informed him that it would not be wise to stay on at Cambridge, the young Merton also quickly came around to the idea that it would be more sensible to move back to America to live with his grandparents. This was the first of many abrupt reassessments which changed the course of his whole life, and ten years later, the writer of *The Seven Storey Mountain* realized that it had been fortuitous that at that time he should have gone to New York City. In his opinion, there was something fundamentally wrong with the atmosphere of the England he had been experiencing. The decision to live with the grandparents on Long Island and the transfer to Columbia College was invigorating: "Compared with Cambridge, this big sooty factory was full of light and fresh air. There was a kind of genuine intellectual vitality in the air" (*SSM*, 137).

During the years between 1935 and 1938 Merton made several friends who shared his literary interests; he also informs us that he ran the cross-country (without training), and flirted with the Communist party. More important, he got involved with various literary projects, and pursued serious study which changed the course of his life. His acquaintance with Daniel Walsh, who taught at Columbia and introduced the young Merton to Thomistic philosophy, and his friendship with Mark Van Doren at Columbia, were crucial steps in his intellectual and artistic formation. During this same period both his grandparents died, his grandfather in the fall of 1936, and his grandmother in the summer of 1937. With these additional losses Merton found himself very much alone. Being an undergraduate at Columbia was, he recalls, in many ways genuine fun, but (in his words) a lot of that fun was only drunken foolishness. By 1938 he sensed that he needed much more if his life was going to make any sense at all.

It is significant that the second major division of *The Seven Storey Mountain* begins with an examination of Merton's life at this time, a time which he considered to be an extremely low point. Without either parents or grandparents, and close to the end of his undergraduate career, Merton reports that he realized he needed a way to make better sense of living. What raised him up out of this second period of darkness was his reassociation with things related to the Catholic church. That gradual reassociation with things which, he said, he had not even thought about much since when he and his father had lived in St. Antonin, France, eventually brought him into the church. Thus, early in part 2 of *The Seven Storey Mountain* he reports how, walking down Fifth Avenue in February of 1937, he saw a book displayed in Scribner's bookstore window. It was Gilson's *The Spirit of Medieval Philosophy*. Attracted by the title, he purchased it; later he realized how that decision was another crucial moment in his life. (How he structures the remembrance of this event contributes to the success of the autobiography, and will be discussed in the next chapter.) Merton's conversion is, of course, the centerpiece of the autobiography. His accounts of attending mass, his reading and becoming "more and more Catholic," his decision to become a Catholic, his baptism—each is a carefully delineated episode. How he chose to use aspects of these years in various literary works (poems, journals, essays, fiction) will play a part in much of this subsequent investigation.

Under slightly different circumstances it is possible that Merton might have continued graduate study in a rather conventional manner, and become either a professor or a writer. His master's thesis, "Nature and Art in William Blake," gives an indication of early abilities, and suggests how he might have combined his developing interests in mysticism and literature within a secular academic career. His proposed doctoral subject was about Gerard Manly Hopkins. But conversion to Catholicism made it increasingly difficult to think just in terms of an academic life, or just a writing career. Religious questions were becoming increasingly important; finally religious vocation became the dominant question of his life.

Merton realized that Columbia University played an important role for him "in the providential designs of God," for it was there that he was brought together with friends, a "half a dozen . . . in such a way that our friendship would work powerfully to rescue us from the confusion and the misery in which we had come to find ourselves" (SSM, 178). Such confusion, partly, he said, due to their fault, and partly due to the fact of "modern society," was changed through a friendship which developed at "the level of common and natural and ordinary things." Friendships with people like Bob Lax, Ed Rice, and Mark Van Doren that began during these years were never to cease. Interestingly, Merton's wry recollection of the summer of 1939, which he spent with his student friends at Olean, New York, is a vague foreshadowing of the life he would find himself leading after he became a monk. He, Lax, and Rice lived together in a cottage which belonged to Lax's brother-in-law, and, with a great deal of ambition, each proceeded to produce literary works. All three were writing novels, yet in Merton's account that summer was mostly a matter of growing beards and getting in trouble.

Back in New York during the academic year following, he decided he should enter the Franciscan Order, but then concluded that this was not to be his vocation. By late summer in 1940, he decided to become a lay Franciscan, and had purchased a breviary so that he could begin saying the Divine Office daily. By the fall he had taken a job teaching at St. Bonaventure College. Another year was to pass before he would decide to become a Cistercian. It was fortunate that Merton developed associations with the Franciscans at St. Bonaventure while he lived in Olean, and that he was able to teach there during the year 1940 and 1941. Apparently, St. Bonaventure was just what he needed as a transition to a more rigorous way of life, something which he had only dreamed up to this time. The patterns of small college life at St. Bonaventure provided an extremely useful atmosphere for Merton, who had become used to Columbia and Greenwich Village: "It amazed me how swiftly my life fell into a plan of fruitful and pleasant organization . . . under the roof with these friars . . ." (*SSM*, 304). Thus, while in early 1940 he was sure that he would become a Franciscan priest, when those plans were foiled (because it was unclear if he really had a vocation) through being on a Catholic campus, he was gradually led elsewhere. During the period 1940–41, when he taught English at St. Bonaventure, Merton continued to seek a way to devote his life to both God and writing. Such steps were important in the formation of the incipient contemplative-writer. The atmosphere at St. Bonaventure was extremely valuable. One short sentence in *The Seven Storey Mountain* sums it up: "as the months went on, I began to drink poems out of these hills" (*SSM*, 304). Merton's love of the quiet at St. Bonaventure was a step toward the monastic life. It was a retreat at the Abbey of Gethsemani during Easter of 1941 that led him to make the single most important decision in his life—to give up teaching—within circumstances which he really loved—and to enter the Cistercian monastery just a few days after World War II had begun.

As we can see, Merton's life immediately before he chose to enter the Abbey of Gethsemani was extremely full. He was in the process of deciding how he might best spend his life, as writer, priest, or professor, or in some combination of these many activities. In *The Seven Storey Mountain* he provides abundant information about these active months, a time which he called "more productive" than all of the years which preceded it. It was such a fruitful period because the young writer had begun a systematic quest for a more religious life, and was also channeling considerable energy into the making of poems and the writing of prose. His months of decision in 1940 and 1941 were full ones; in retrospect it is clear that they functioned, on a minor scale, as a model for the later extremely productive Father Louis.

The Monastery as Refuge?

The decision to go to Gethsemani was made in harmony with the rhythms of Merton's life; he had spent the years and months preceding that eventful December in consideration of what he might best do. Then he suddenly realized that he had to give himself up into the silence of the Cistercian monastery.

This was a crucial new beginning for him; he realized that "Liturgically speaking, you could hardly find a better time to become a monk than Advent . . . you enter into a new world at the beginning of a new liturgical year. And everything that the Church gives you to sing, every prayer that you say . . . is a cry of ardent desire for grace, for help . . ." (*SSM,* 379). In Merton's view, he was soon convinced that he had been given a grace simply in being a part of these particular surroundings. He recalled how he felt in January of 1942 as he was working in the fields, and suggested this through a line from one of the gradual psalms: "*Montes in circuitu ejus, et Dominus in circuitu populi sui* (Mountains are round about it, so the Lord is round about His people from henceforth, now and forever)" (*SSM,* 385).

The young monk came to feel so comfortable at Gethsemani in its regular routine that he was soon able (in at least one part of his mind) to lose any desire even to write verse. One passage in *Seven Storey Mountain* recounts the fact that while a new member of his community Merton had discovered that in the interval after the night office, between four and half-past five on feast days, when his mind was "saturated" with the peace of the liturgy and as dawn was just breaking, poems seemed to come almost by themselves. However, he wryly qualifies: "that was the way it went until Father Master told me I must not write poetry" (*SSM,* 390). Merton explains how he came to use the same time for reading and meditation, and how that "was even better than writing poems." Such a matter-of-fact report of his acceptance of the directive from the master of novices is clearly emblematic of how he sought to live during his earliest years at Gethsemani.

But, of course, what we also recognize is that in reading, meditation, in following the rule, and acting upon the direction of his superiors, Merton quietly prepared himself for much more writing. His life and skill as a writer and a contemplative were building together. Becoming a monk at Gethsemani in 1941 was in some ways like stepping back into nineteenth-century France, and the contrast with the hustle and bustle of activities in New York City as compared to this new quiet, was never to be forgotten.

He had known for a long time that he wanted to be a priest, but only after the Easter retreat in the spring of 1941, and his observation of the beauty of such an austere way of life, could he make his decision. That choice was both deliberate, in that he had long been concerned about how best to live his life for years after his conversion, yet abrupt, in that he was not absolutely sure what he would do until just before he made the decision to become a Trappist. A postcard sent to Mark Van Doren, dated 9 December 1941, indicates something of his frame of mind on the very day he left St. Bonaventure for Kentucky; interestingly, in that note we find no indication that Merton had definitely decided to stay with the Cistercians; rather as he prepared to leave St. Bonaventure, he gathered up accumulated manuscripts, and penned a quick note to his friend and teacher asking him to keep them, a strategy that left open the possibility of returning to writing.[7]

The next communication which Van Doren received was written only five days later, a hand-written copy of the poem "Letter to My Friends," with a note appended. Merton's note announced: "I have been tentatively accepted into the community," yet in a few short lines, added at the bottom of the second page, more words about his various books, notebooks, and the manuscript for the novel, *Journal of My Escape from the Nazis,* were added. About the novel Merton wrote: "I make you a present of it."[8] His novel had been making the rounds of publishers, and it would be another ten years before the author would again even look at the manuscript. In December 1941, he was clearly making a break from an earlier part of his life; yet what must also be observed is that while this was a complete change, it was a change which allowed him to stay in contact with a group of friends with literary interests; and eventually much of the material which he entrusted to Van Doren at this crucial moment was published. It is significant that the second "Letter," dated "St. Lucy's Day," was a poem; there Merton reflects upon his contentment in becoming part of the monastery, a house of God, and metaphorically "Nazareth, where Christ lived as a boy." This was the house where he now hoped to grow in spiritual awareness, a special home in close harmony with its surroundings

> Where fields are the friends of plenteous heaven,
> While starlight feeds, as bright as manna,

All our rough earth with wakeful grace.[9]

Such was the beginning of Merton's new life, a life which promised little time for the aspiring writer of just a few days earlier.

The acceptance of monastic anonymity meant that there was a definite possibility that none of the schemes which Merton had conceived for literary work would ever be realized. But two facts are of significance: First, the atmosphere of his monastery, which might in some ways seem like a fortress to someone unfamiliar with it, was no refuge, but rather a place of nourishment, and its very atmosphere proved to generate poems. Second, by virtue of the vow of obedience, the young monk readily came to be recognized as a man gifted with language. Not much time passed before he was being asked to do various "writing jobs."

Merton embraced the routine of the monastery, and within a few years he was engaged, once more, in many projects. Clearly, at first he had little time for any private writing, but the discipline of the monastery proved a great boon both for his spiritual life and in his development as writer. Acting under the vow of obedience, but with at first only a few hours per week, Merton embarked on what would become the most fruitful career of any priest-poet in the history of American letters. While he would never write the proposed doctoral dissertation on Gerard Manly Hopkins, his whole life and writing career built toward a combination that would finally rival the career of all priest-poets!

Merton's literary career falls into distinct stages, and the first part includes all the years before Gethsemani. Subsequent stages correspond with the development of his religious life. He spent the first several years at Gethsemani in seclusion and in formation with a minimum of contact with the outside world. During this time he was obligated to many writing jobs, but he also wrote poetry and an autobiography. He pruned down the manuscript for the autobiography, and soon found it a best-seller. In an entry for 1 May 1947 within his journal *The Sign of Jonas* he lists twelve different writing projects in which he was currently involved. His decision to go into the quiet of Gethsemani resulted, then, in a life quite different than he first thought might be the case. As he prepared to make his solemn vows, he was involved in many different projects, and that pattern was to continue. Already then, however, a second stage in Merton's life and career was drawing to a close. Through

The Seven Storey Mountain he provided an overview both of his secular life and his early years as a monk. With its publication it became possible for his work as monk and writer to enter another stage and to develop in still other ways.

It might have seemed that he could make a career of "religious" writing, yet Merton realized that during those early years he was apparently trying too much to be in control of the various projects in which he was engaged. Simultaneously he was learning as another phase in the career opened and he began to write about it, that his existential experience, not history or biography or abstract "religious" experience, would remain fundamental. Thus, while he wrote about his earlier life in *Seven Storey Mountain,* he had already begun to live beyond it; and so as he became more sure of his experience of the monastic life and prepared for his ordination, his desire to write about that life became less a matter of historical, devotional, or theoretical interests and became instead a matter of communicating how he, as a separate person, yet bound up in the community of all men, experienced God. Merton sensed after a few years in the monastery that he had to let go of trying to control his life, and therefore he had to stop thinking of his various writing tasks as "his" projects. However, as the career developed in scope, it was through such projects that he assumed greater responsibilities and also became more intrigued with the fact that his life was one in which contemplation was the most basic element. All of these experiences led him back to still more writing so he could inform the world of the peace and happiness which he had found. His joy is already reflected in the early poems entitled "Three Postcards from the Monastery." He writes as though he is amazed at the atmosphere he was experiencing and that he must write about it in comparison with what was left behind: He and his brothers are in a different world:

> The smoky choirs
> Of those far five-o'clock trombones
> Have blown away. Our eyes
> Are clean as the September night.[10]
> (*CP,* 153–55)

Other significant moments in Merton's early monastic life and literary career are outlined in the journal *The Sign of Jonas,* a record of five years from the time when the autobiography was finished into the early 1950s. During these years, as Merton's public reputation was developing, he was becoming known both as a poet and prose writer. This was, as well, a period when Merton apparently had doubts about problems concerning how to combine contemplation and poetry—doubts about whether such a combination was even possible. Such questions continued well into his mature career—into the late 1950s. Eventually he came to grips with the fact that he definitely had a dual vocation and, therefore, a responsibility as a contemplative and as someone who must also write from a contemplative point of view. Above all, what Father Louis learned through a continuing production of meditations, poetry, essays, journals, and letters was to combine questions about himself with questions of, and for, the world. In doing so he finally ceased asking questions about the precise nature of his vocation, and instead began to live; perhaps these years became the busiest of his entire life.

The Monastery as Place of Instruction

During the years from 1941 to late in that decade Merton prepared for the priesthood and was ordained on 26 May 1949. Gradually Father Louis assumed more duties within the monastery, first as teacher, then as master of students from 1951 to 1955, when he was named master of novices. These were years of considerable change for him and his monastery, partly because of changes in the mood of the country following World War II, but also perhaps partially because the success of Merton's own writing led large numbers of men to enter Gethsemani. This decade of preparation led to an even more intense period of complex activity for Merton which was to include both more writing and more immediate contact with other men in the monastery.

Merton continued to write poems and to keep a journal, but he became involved in many other types of writing as well, sometimes historical, sometimes theological. He himself was seldom pleased with the results of the writing which was done on command, under the rubric of a vow of obedience, because his heart seemed to be more in projects which were creative and personal. He also had to learn that his gift as a writer was not, apparently, going to develop into the systematic production of books about theology. His book *The Ascent to Truth,* written during this period, is his only book which is a systematic theological treatise. Published in 1951, it is a more than competent study of the doctrines of John of the Cross; but in comparison with other writings about mysticism and contemplation produced later, it lacks force precisely because it is so systematic. This book was completed in 1950, just before he became master of studies. Those duties continued into 1955, at which time he assumed additional responsibility.

His duties for ten years after he became novice master at Gethsemani were demanding, yet the output of his writing was greater during these years than during the initial magnificent outpouring of the late 1940s.

One might think of a novice master as someone who would be content with passing on traditional knowledge of monasticism. But Merton's urge to write and to experiment allowed him to produce considerable original work during this period. His teaching and his reading obviously stimulated his work with a pen. We also see his poetic skill developing; and we see Merton producing books on questions of silence, on meditation, and about monasticism. He also was drawn to more literary experiments as his studies brought him into an awareness of the relevance of historical and mythical figures in understanding contemporary Christianity.[11] We also see him raising more and more questions about the world; and finally within this extremely productive period we see Father Louis (no longer the pious Merton of *Seven Storey Mountain*) turning more toward the East.

Obviously, Merton was a man of tremendous energy and discipline and thus it was possible for him to accomplish an enormous amount. Despite his daily responsibilities for teaching and spiritual formation, these years were also productive in writing and in contacts made through reading and correspondence which allowed Merton to understand better both the nature of the monastic life which he led and its relationship to the wider culture. Here then was a monk who originally had sought seclusion from the world, but who found himself more and more speaking to issues which were very much a matter of the relationship of contemplative questions and religion to the modern world.

During this period up to 1965 he wrote on a wide range of subjects, and we can also see that the stylistic variety of his writing expanded. Perhaps more searchingly during these years than others he felt compelled to ask questions about the nature of the secular world (maybe because of the large number of novices which that world was sending to the hills of Kentucky?). Such questioning led ultimately to one of the most intriguing of many circular patterns in Merton's career—a movement wherein the quiet of the contemplative world led him back to questions of how best to use what he had gained for the benefit of others; was he, he began to ask, an innocent or a guilty bystander.[12] Was the contemplative life enough? Was there a way through language to remind man of his basic needs?

It is surprising to realize that Merton wrote so much during these extremely active years; but we see that the more he taught and thought, the more connections he sought to make. He simply could not remain quiet on issues which, to him, were important for both the whole church and mankind. Questions about liturgy, race relations, the relationship of monastic life to the life of the church as a whole, war, myth, and materialism all became subjects of a continuous inquiry. Merton's years as novice master therefore provide a period of demarcation in his literary career because during those years, as he became more involved with the daily activities of novices, he simultaneously came to a fuller awareness that separation of spirituality from questions about the world was not only not desirable, but hardly even possible. Books such as *Disputed Questions, The Behavior of Titans, Seeds of Destruction,* and *Conjectures of a Guilty Bystander,* are indications that Father Louis was convinced that he had a responsibility to draw more and more connections.

The Hermitage: Solitude and Action

The final three years of Merton's life are the culmination of over twenty years of preparation as a monk. He was given permission to live in a hermitage on the grounds of the monastery, and found there a degree of the solitude he had often longed for earlier. It was also during these final three years of his life that his concerns with various Eastern traditions intensified and when most of his books about the East were published. These years were also a time when he began again to write a considerable amount of poetry (sometimes a variety of antipoetry), considered in chapter 8.[13] He was, as well, continuing to write about many public questions—issues such as racial conflict and the war in Vietnam.

These three years might be called the years of the hermitage, but one must remember that this was a very special kind of monk— one who relished his solitude, but at the same time one who required a briefcase to carry his mail from the monastery back to his concrete block hermitage.[14] He nurtured his solitude; of that fact there is no doubt; but he continued to write, to read, to plan, to correspond, indeed, to talk with many of the visitors who sought him out. He also regularly continued to give talks to novices (and other members of the community) at least once a week. Many of these informal Sunday afternoon conferences are preserved on tapes that provide an invaluable record of the diversity of his interests.[15] They range in subject from rather technical questions about monastic life, education, and Cistercian history, to commentary about modern literature. The last three years of Merton's life were, therefore, spent in the semiseclusion of a hermitage at Gethsemani, but Merton did not cut himself off from the community. He returned to the monastery on a regular basis, often for one meal each day. He delivered the Sunday talks on subjects which ranged from history and questions about the spiritual life to questions about poetry—its meaning and differences from other uses of language. He spoke on William Faulkner and Rilke. He read his own poems. He clearly loved to teach and talk about a wide range of subjects; even more so he clearly enjoyed his students. His sense of humor and wit is reflected throughout the recordings. Photographs taken during these years reflect the joy which he experienced at this time. The collection entitled *Geography of Holiness,* edited by Deba Patnaik, provides evidence of Merton's use of the camera to develop a contemplative attitude.

As hermit Merton was paradoxically cutting back his connections with the world, but in other ways he was extending other connections. The solitude provided in the hermitage made it possible for him to avoid what he considered to be distractions within the routine of a large monastery, and as well the distractions which resulted from visitors who could more easily meet him at the monastery. Enforced solitude allowed much additional time for thinking and writing. The poetry, correspondence, and essays of these final years therefore manifest Merton's appreciation of his new found quiet, but also paradoxically his realization that such solitude strengthened ties with the world.

From Kentucky to Asia

During the final months of his life Merton spent some weeks in California and then made an extended trip to Asia. He had been invited to address a conference of Asian religious superiors, and he combined that trip with investigations for a more secluded hermitage, perhaps in California or even in Alaska. Preceding his departure for Asia he sent the manuscripts for several new books to editors, a gesture reminiscent of that day before he left for Gethsemani twenty-seven years earlier when he sent his manuscripts to Mark Van Doren. When he suddenly died, various books were in the hands of his editors. These, and subsequent volumes, demonstrate the type of thinking and writing which preoccupied Father Louis during the final period of his life. [16]

As has been established, Merton was no ordinary hermit. While he lived alone in a hermitage he remained in contact with enormous numbers of people. One significant example of this was his editing of four issues of the magazine, *Monk's Pond*. Another example was his serious involvement in the peace movement and resistance to the Vietnam War. The trip to Asia was the culmination of his earthly life; that journey's many connections—people, thoughts, places, books—reflect the wide range of his interests. His final full weeks in Asia—observing airports, holy men, art objects, trains, temples, landscapes, and ordinary people—are symbolic of what he had already accomplished with a wonderfully active pen for three decades. His actual going to Asia is a reminder of the fact that, in a sense, he had already encompassed the whole globe with his thinking, and encountered the living God in his contemplation. (Posthumous writings such as those in *Contemplative Prayer, Contemplation in a World of Action,* and *Love and Living* confirm this.)[17] His meetings throughout the trip with various religious leaders including the Dalai Lama, were the physical fulfillment of spiritual journeys he had begun much earlier.

His posthumous *Asian Journal* is a specific record of readings, thoughts, and movements during the final weeks of his life. Thus just as Merton strengthened his ties with the world after he was allowed to become a hermit, evidence in the *Asian Journal* shows that he was able to focus more clearly on spiritual matters precisely because he was able to travel. *The Asian Journal,* while not a finished composition, reflects its writer's constant enthusiasm as he becomes more aware of the value of looking, seeing, observing a world so very different from the West.

Merton's death took place on 10 December 1968 while he was attending a religious conference of Benedictine and Cistercian superiors of Asia in Bangkok, Thailand. It was sudden, accidental, and mysterious. He was found alone in his room late on the afternoon after which he had delivered a talk on "Marxism and Monasticism." He had apparently touched the exposed wire of an electric fan.

He died twenty-seven years to the day after he had entered the monastery at age twenty-seven. A poem he wrote in a notebook some years earlier, in retrospect, seems prophetic:

> O the gentle fool
> He fell in love
> With the electric light
> Do you not know, fool,
> That love is dynamite?
>
> Keep to what is yours
> Do not interfere
> With the established law
>
> See the dizzy victims of romance
> Unhappy moths!
>
> *(CP,* 671)

Chapter Two
An Autobiographical Impulse

For even as I killed You,
You made Yourself a greater thief than any in
Your company.
Stealing my sins into Your dying life [.]
The Biography

Plans and Novels

During the late 1930s Merton made the decision to live well as a Christian, but, as has been indicated, he also realized that he must find a way to use his skills as a writer. The question he faced was, what would be the best combination? As late as the fall of 1941 he had not yet even ruled out the possibility of going to Harlem to work with the poor. Yet it was certain he had doubts about the benefits of such a radical commitment. In November of 1941, he wrote his friend Mark Van Doren:

so much of the work in Harlem seems to me to be from the point of view of whatever it is I want, so much wasted effort: standing around for several hours just so that your presence may keep order among some children . . . or maybe arguing about how to mimeograph something . . . it all seems ordered in some scheme of references that would be more significant to somebody else than to me: and the same standing around, the same apparently wasted time, could be very fruitful for me in some other context. In other words, I have to seriously consider whether my vocation is not contemplative rather than active. . . .[1]

Other letters to Van Doren written during the two years before he finally left for Gethsemani are of special interest because they make it clear that while he was willing to give up a potential career as a writer, should that be the will of God, he remained excited about the prospects of writing. Besides various details about poems, reviews, journals, masques, and novels in progress, as well as thanks to Van Doren for advice about work underway, these letters include Merton's admission, as early as October 1939, that academic work was no longer of much interest: "I'm not paying any attention to my dissertation now. In fact I am more interested in medieval Latin courses and medieval philosophy courses than in English courses. . . . I may start finding out a lot about the language of analogy in Bonaventure and Hugo of St. Victor. . . .[2] During the year following, 1940, Merton first decided to become a Franciscan priest, then abruptly decided against such action. In another letter to Van Doren, on 25 August, he outlined his state of mind which included the desire to teach at a Catholic college "and tak[e] my chance with fellows who never heard of a book."[3] Significantly, in the same letter he provided a funny report about the progress of his one-year-old novel which "pretty soon . . . will have been to every publisher in the world"; he also expressed his appreciation to Van Doren for mentioning his name to James Laughlin as a possible contributor for a New Directions Publishers collection of poems.[4] In other words, throughout this period of abrupt change in his life, as he moved further away from the secular world, he also clearly kept open the possibility of a career as a writer.

Such behavior is not surprising if we remember that as a child Merton was writing novels when he was all of twelve years old. As a student at the Lyceé Ingres at Montauban, he recalled, he was engaged in the manufacture "of a great adventure story . . . never finished"; and he also noted that he did finish "at least one other [novel] and probably two, besides one which I wrote at Antonin . . . all scribbled in exercise books, profusely illustrated in pen and ink . . ." (*SSM*, 52). By 1946 he could laugh at such childish enthusiasm, but he also seemed to realize that he was never to lose that youthful excitement about writing.

A similar observation has been made by others who knew him. In a moving remembrance of the Tom Merton of the late 1930s, Naomi Burton Stone, his agent and editor, wrote of the circumstances under which she met this "blond young man [who] never appeared to doubt for one minute that he was destined to be a successful author." She referred to the three early books which she had seen and relates how she became furious when she learned that Merton had chosen to enter a Trappist monastery, but added: "as the world knows now, his faith in his gift was well founded, and my lamentations proved unwarranted."[5]

Stone's description of the two novels which Merton brought to her when she was working in the book department of Curtis Brown Ltd., a literary agency in New York, is valuable because it helps us to appreciate subsequent development. Both books were autobiographical. Her recollection of one of the novels, *The Man in the Sycamore Tree,* is that it "was a wild and wonderful story, often

extremely funny."[6] This was one of the completed novels which
Merton destroyed in December 1941.

Another novel, *The Labyrinth,* was also a book with a heavily
autobiographical base. Merton's own account of the composition of
The Labyrinth during the summer of 1939 provides insight into
circumstances under which the book was produced, as well as into
other work produced during this period when he, Ed Rice, and Bob
Lax were living together and "writing novels." Merton's opus eventually ran over five hundred pages. It was first called *Straits of Dover,*
then *The Night Before the Battle* (in a letter to Van Doren he described
the book as having its origins in "intellectual autobiography").[7]
Covering the period from 1929 to 1939, it treated some of the same
ground that *Seven Storey Mountain* would. In the published autobiography Merton recalls that he had

found the writing of [*The Night Before the Battle*] easier and more amusing
if I mixed up a lot of imaginery characters in my own story. It is a pleasant
way to write. When the truth got dull, I could create a diversion with a
silly man called Terence Metrotone. I later changed him to Terence Park,
after I showed the first draft of the book to my uncle, who abashed me
by concluding that Terence Metrotone was a kind of acrostic for myself.
That was, as a matter of fact, very humiliating, because I had made such
a fool of the character. (*SSM,* 241)

Naomi Burton Stone also remembers that she very much wanted to
sell both *The Labyrinth* and *The Man in the Sycamore Tree,* and that
while young editors shared her enthusiasm "older and wiser (and
perhaps later sadder?) heads always seemed to prevail." *Sycamore
Tree,* which the young Merton had so hoped might be published,
was also a work which resembled *Seven Storey Mountain* and other
early prose written in the years immediately before Merton became
a Cistercian. But, as was to prove to be the case in subsequent stages
of his life and writing, once something was written, Merton often
was quickly moved to go beyond it.

By the fall of 1939 his activities included daily mass and
communion along with the daily writing and revising of the novel
which was then making the rounds of publishers. Eventually he
would joke about the peculiarities of that somewhat experimental
book "handed back to me politely by one of those tall thin, anxious
young men with horn-rimmed glasses who are to be found in the
offices of publishers" (*SSM,* 207). In his *Secular Journal,* a diary for

the period from October 1939 to late November 1941, he provides
a record of some of his concerns about the vocation of writer; in a
February 1941 entry he jokingly comments about the unpublished
novel which

has just been rejected by Macmillan. Since then it has been to Viking,
Knopf, Harcourt Brace, then to the agent Curtis Brown, who sent it to
Modern Age, Atlantic Monthly Books, McBride and now Carrick and
Evans' "No" has not yet reached me.

So many bad books get printed, why can't my bad book get printed?[8]

Within the total context of his life at that time the journal entry
is significant because it demonstrates how important it seemed to
the aspiring writer to be published, yet it also demonstrates that
his religious life was becoming much more important and that he
realized it would be no great loss if *The Labyrinth* never got published.
The *Secular Journal* has an interesting history in that it also was
written during these same years before Merton became a monk and
would remain unpublished for a long time. Finally appearing in
1959, it provides an overview of the activities of a young writer
who was slowly coming to a realization about what he could best
do with his life.

A Secular Journal

Just as the novel *My Argument with the Gestapo* would not be
published until some thirty years after its composition, twenty years
passed before it seemed the appropriate time for publication of
Merton's record of the days preceding his entrance into the Abbey
of Gethsemani. He had made a gift of that manuscript to Catherine
de Hueck Doherty, founder of Friendship House in Harlem, when
he had entered the monastery. In 1955 he received a letter from
her which reminded him of his original intention when he had given
the manuscript with the hope that any profit might go toward her
Catholic Action work. When he looked at this early manuscript he
decided it might still be of value for some readers; it reflected some
of the first steps in his spiritual journey. It is also valuable as the
record of the initial stages in his literary career.

In the preface Merton indicates that the manuscript did receive
some editing; however, he noted that he purposely avoided changing
the "artless spontaneity of the original." He said he wanted to keep

"its somewhat naive essence," and only correct its more intolerable defects. He also points out that his views and aspirations, held with such severity at that time, had "softened . . . with the passage of time and with a more intimate contact with the spiritual problems of other people" (*SJ,* ix). Father Louis obviously thought that the general thrust of the book remained important and that it might inspire others to follow on a quest like his. *The Secular Journal,* as published, is valuable precisely because Merton let it stand as it was written twenty years earlier, so that it remains a document which shows us how a young writer sought to make sense of his world, as well as, indirectly, a record of a young artist as he pays careful attention to the world which surrounds him.[9] The mature writer realized that the book's real value was precisely its immaturity. In retrospect, Merton admitted that it seemed almost arrogant in tone, yet it was the honest record of a younger Merton's concern about fundamental questions, and an indirect record of his acceptance of the vocation of writer.

The Secular Journal is arranged in five parts, each representing a step in the spiritual journey of the writer. The entries give a picture of the writer slowly trying to make sense of his world. They begin on 1 October 1939 and run for approximately two years, ending on 27 November 1941. One of the most interesting threads which runs throughout the book is the writer's concern about art and especially writing by poets and prose writers. His first entry, as has been indicated, is about William Blake, and Blake is mentioned again in the last entry. To an important degree, through an awareness of the work of others, Merton's insights developed as they did during this period. His thoughts about Dante, Graham Greene, Pascal, Lorca, Rilke, Kierkegaard, Bloy, George Elliot, Joyce, Huxley, and many others fill these pages. Why he was attracted to writers interested in theological questions such as Blake, Dante, Joyce, and Graham Greene is obvious, and through his references to them we can trace the development of his interests. Similarly, his analysis of strange newspaper articles and bad travel books, such as T. Philip Terry's guidebooks to Mexico and Cuba, reveal his definite skepticism about the printed word.[10]

It is significant that the first section of *The Secular Journal* is the more heavily literary part of the book, in contrast with the second part, which is about Merton's visit to Cuba in April 1940. The first portion is about a writer's respect for language and art; the second is about the contrasting experience of life in Havana, and, above all, Merton's joy in "the complete interpenetration of every department of public life . . . the overflowing of the activities of the streets into the cafes . . ." (*SJ*, 74).

What Merton first focuses upon in his *Secular Journal* is a world where things so often seem to be taken out of context. The entry about the art exhibit at the 1939 New York World's Fair reveals Merton's pleasure in looking at paintings by Fra Angelico (*The Temptation of St. Anthony*) and Breughel (*The Wedding-dance*), yet he writes mostly about the misconceptions he often heard expressed by other viewers, misconceptions often derived from assuming that a painting was to be learned, or understood. A point Merton stresses about his appreciation of the paintings is that they suggest worlds beyond language; modern man is so given to affixing labels and expressing opinions that it has become difficult for him to realize that there are whole areas of experience beyond the apparently measurable. In *The Secular Journal* we see how a young writer, literally sorting out what was of importance for him, could laugh at a society which has not yet progressed to such a level of insight.

Fascination with language remains fundamental. More precisely, Merton is often concerned with man's abuse of language. For example, on 18 April 1940 he meditates about a society which seems to have lost its respect for traditional values, a society which is "worshipping frustration and barrenness." Especially in Germany and Italy, he notes there seems to be so much talk about peace, life, and fertility; but, he says, "the people who yell loudest about all these things are clearly responsible for the worst war that was ever heard of, and are also busy putting out of existence in lethal chambers everybody that has gone crazy as a result of this kind of thinking (gone crazy, that is, without getting into the government)" (*SJ*, 89). Related concerns about abuses of thinking and language brought Merton to the composition of an imaginary journal which remains today as his only extant novel.

The third part of *The Secular Journal* follows the Cuba meditations and is, in large part, an analysis of materials read. Here we see Merton as he tries to achieve distance both from the activities of his life and from what he reads, especially in newspapers. His reports of reading—stories of Germans desecrating a church in Poland; Mann's *The Magic Mountain;* questions of morality; Theresa Neumann; Bloy; popular opinion; Kierkegaard on the "Dark Night of the

Soul"—indicate his wish to penetrate beyond common unexamined beliefs. He can also be very funny when he examines his own ambitions and beliefs, as, for example, he reports his attempts to write or to find a publisher.

The fourth section, a record of his Easter Retreat at Gethsemani Abbey in the spring of 1941, begins: "I should tear out all the other pages of this book, and all the other pages of anything I've written, and begin here. This is the center of America . . ." (*SJ*, 183). And when he returned back home at Douglaston, Long Island, the world seemed odd: "How different," he wrote, "to hold on to what I had down there . . ." (*SJ*, 208).

The final section of the journal provides a picture of the young writer continuing to look at the contemporary world, but becoming still more concerned with questions of who he is. So much of what he actually recorded in the *Journal* seems to be a record of man's ambition. By 3 September 1941, and prompted by a reading of the *Imitation of Christ,* he writes:

> The measure of our identity, or our being (for here the two mean exactly the same thing) is the amount of our love for God. The more we love earthly things, reputation, importance, ease, success and pleasures for ourselves, the less we love God. Our identity gets dissipated among a lot of things that do not have the value we imagine we see in them, and we are lost in them: we know it obscurely by the way all these things disappoint us. . . . (*SJ*, 243)

The publication in 1959 of *The Secular Journal* permitted its recognition as a valuable work that records all the matters foremost in Merton's mind as he moved toward the most crucial single decision of his life. Through the *Journal* we also understand why he continued to expend considerable energy on fiction which dealt with matters related to his intellectual interest. During the summer of 1941 he wrote another novel, which at that time he called *Journal of My Escape from the Nazis.* In a way, that fanciful novel, written in the form of a journal, is a continuation of the same inquiry conducted in *The Secular Journal,* yet it too was destined to remain in manuscript for decades, and to be published posthumously.

An Argument With the Gestapo

Three novels were destroyed by Merton when he decided to enter the monastery, but he preserved one manuscript, *Journal of My Escape from the Nazis.*[11] Not surprisingly, correspondence with Mark Van Doren early in the years at Gethsemani indicates that Merton was hopeful that the remaining novel might be published. It was a favorite of his, and a quarter of a century later it was published with a new title, *My Argument With the Gestapo.* The novel is a funny, witty, crazy work, a book unlikely to have found a publisher in 1941, just as America was entering the war. Thirty years later Merton realized that it would have value for readers trying to puzzle out the meaning of the modern world, not just the horrible world-wide cataclysm of World War II. However, it was only at the end of his life that Father Louis knew that this novel would be published. It pleased him to see that his ideas of 1941 still had value for readers in the late 1960s. The book is also of value because, like *The Secular Journal,* it implies much about Merton as artist.

The novel reflects Merton's reading of Joyce, his love of languages, and above all his meditation about the dilemma of living in the modern world, as well as drawing upon his own experiences in Europe. The book, written during the summer of 1941, describes an imaginary visit to the England and France which Merton had known during the preceding ten years. The novel is structured so that its "argument" grows out of a dissatisfaction with a world which puts immense amounts of energy into trivial unimportant things, while most of the significant questions go unasked. It is ultimately a novel of foreboding because the author realizes so many in the world have little desire to raise significant questions—especially as long as insignificant answers remain. Above all the novel is a writer's argument with a world that can go to war so easily.

The impression made by this journey-journal is that the writer-hero (who is suspect precisely because he is a writer) has seen beyond the superficiality and veneer of contemporary civilization. To explain this, however, he must first return to the world of superficiality so that he can begin to explain what is beyond. So much of life imagined by the writer in England seems to be only a matter of a void filled by activities, yet activities which he realizes are often meaningless. What happens, he questions, if enormous numbers of people (British and German) are willing to fight to the death for such triviality and meaninglessness?

My Argument is the imaginary record of the movements and thoughts of a young writer (who very much resembles Thomas Merton) as he wanders about London, spends a night in an underground station during an air raid warning, and meets various people whom he had earlier known. These persons seem singularly unable to provide help for him as he tries to puzzle out the meaning of the life he observes in London at this curious moment in history. The writer spends most of his time with two figures, one is simply called "B," a girl with whom he earlier had been very much in love. She is now matter-of-factly doing her job as an air raid warden. The other character is the mysterious "Madame Gongora," who provides a room for him and his typewriter, and a window from which he makes further observations of London. Madame Gongora is a bizarre, almost surrealistic, figure who is weighted down (supported by?) all of the superficial things which are so often associated with civilization. Her house is crammed full of objects of culture, but they seem to have little meaning. The writer has a delightful time providing catalogs of her drawing room. Its windows have been blown out by bombs and are boarded up and the room is full of objects moved to the lower floor when the roof burned. Such chaos symbolizes the fragmentation of the entire culture, a culture which does not seem to know where it is or why it is as it is.

The writer is caught in the midst of death and finds himself completely surrounded by events of which he can make little sense. Hints from the past suggest vague meanings, but nothing ever becomes completely clear. He sits at his typewriter while Madame Gongora, "amid the heterogeneous lumber of the living room," "reads the poems of Paul Valery."[12] He then imagines the churches in another part of the city, but these are churches empty of people, as so many of the people are empty of belief. The writer imagines that he sees buildings which are ill. He also recalls incidents from earlier days in London when things seemed to make more sense. Once, for example, when he was fourteen, and enjoying his reading ("in French, too") of *The Count of Monte Cristo,* Mrs. Frobishe had asked him if he had ever read *The Jungle Book* by Rudyard Kipling, and proceeded to provide a meaningless lecture about duty. Such a remembrance only seems to point up the fact that so much of what occurs in the present is so because of the unthinking actions of others.

As the narrator-writer tries to piece together what has and is happening he begins to sense that he is being watched. But why? Little seems to make sense; he asks himself why he is being followed?

Similarly, when he tries to talk with his old friend "B" she maintains that when she is in uniform she cannot fully remember who she is. Duty for her takes over. She does not seem to realize that her visitor really cares for her. Instead, she continues her work, and we understand that these two people can never really be reunited; the novel drifts forward. Along the way, Merton has a good time making fun of German, French, and English peculiarities. His hero sometimes writes an odd Joycean language molded from all the major European tongues. All of these people, as imagined, seem caught up in an irrational web of action and language. Within the book only the writer seems to realize that sense will never be made of things with either a rational or a patriotic approach to the madness everywhere apparent.

One of the craziest incidents in the novel occurs when the narrator is apprehended by French police who try to understand his strange journal. Of course, they can make little sense of it. The resultant interrogations are hilarious, and they are so primarily because it is simply assumed that if anything is written, it must be of a political nature or at least make definite sense. To face the fact that the journal is only a private memoir is more than the French authorities are able to do. At the end of the novel the writer entrusts his manuscript to a Mr. R, who has been asked to deliver it to an agent in America. Mr. R. assumes it must therefore be a pornographic novel. He, too, cannot understand a book that is apparently neither pro-British nor pro-German. Merton makes fun of the fact that men are so conditioned to expect certain things to happen. The book is entertaining, a delight, precisely because of the pleasure which is to be derived in its reading.

In *My Argument with the Gestapo* Merton produces an imaginary journal which reflects his knowledge of European culture and which raises fundamental questions about the nature of language in modern Western civilization. The novel employs a narrative, but more important it is a record of a writer asking fundamental questions about how language is used, misused, and why. Such themes indicate Merton's interest in the nature of language and the responsibilities of a writer. What he often imagines (about English, French, and German events) is a perverse misuse of language. More often than not, when language is used in the book, it is tied only to the immediate moment, or to man's attempt to control the immediate. Merton's writer seems to be moving toward the conclusion that the reason for keeping a journal, or any kind of writing, is to find that one's relationship to others (something more than the mundane and trivial activities of day-by-day living) should lead to something beyond visible life.

The ending of the book with an extended reference to William Blake is symbolic of a method Merton will come to employ throughout his subsequent career. Little has been resolved within this novel; yet the writing and enjoyment in reading has been a help. When the manuscript is ultimately entrusted to "the hands of a maniac who believes he understands world affairs, political rights and wrongs," Merton implies that he entrusts his book to us, but his novel (any book) cannot provide definitive answers, only hints:

Yet here is the typewriter and a pile of new paper, white, untouched.

I think suddenly of Blake, filling paper with words, so that the words flew about the room for the angels to read, and after that, what if the paper was lost or destroyed?

That is the only reason for wanting to write, Blake's reason. (*MA*, 259)

We might say that for similar reasons Merton saw a value in writing this novel. Much of what he does within the imaginary journal is to point out the craziness of a world wherein we accept so much without thinking. This is true of all the characters encountered within the narrative. Indirectly, the novel serves as a commentary about why Merton finally chose to become a Trappist. He finally concluded that he had to get down to a life which was not cluttered by nonessentials.

The Seven Storey Mountain

The most famous account of the decision to enter the Abbey of Gethsemani is the well-known autobiography. This was the book which made Merton an internationally respected writer, and it did so in just a matter of a few years. [13] It was a book which proved to be appropriate for the milieu of the late 1940s. Very "Catholic," somewhat pious, yet carefully written, it caught the eyes of many— Catholic and non-Catholic.

Since it is an overview of his entire life, and the first piece of sustained autobiographical prose which he published while a monk, it both provides an extraordinary view of his earlier life and suggests something of his methods as a writer at Gethsemani. The book was well received throughout the general press, and among Catholic circles it was very popular.[14] The title of the autobiography alludes to Dante's *Purgatorio,* and the implication is that the writer is thankful that metaphorically he has reached the stage of purgatory. The general tone of praise implies an appreciativeness that Merton's life has worked out as it has, and a thankfulness for the quiet of Gethsemani. This is done by building gradually, as indeed Merton had done in his life, a matter of carefully molding the narrative step by step. Therefore *The Seven Storey Mountain* is a carefully structured work divided into three basic parts. Merton's plan is to demonstrate to his reader how his life had been in great need of God's grace, and how that grace was slowly revealed to him. The beauty of the book as autobiography in the Augustinian mode is that so much comes unforeseen. Merton wants readers to perceive that God's plan is not man's. In terms of this literary structure, it is convenient that his life was as it was. Everything in the first section of the book builds toward the conclusion of part 1 where Merton as a young man felt horribly alone and afraid. It is as if everything he had done, especially after his parents were dead had led him up to a "blind alley"; on the surface at Columbia University he seemed to be a great success, but he insisted "scarcely four years after [he] had left Oakham and walked into the world that [he] thought [he] was going to ransack and rob of all its pleasures and satisfactions," he had accomplished just that, only to find himself "emptied and robbed and gutted."[15]

Part 2 contrasts with the conclusion of the first main section where the young Merton had felt lost. In the second division he recalls his growing familiarity with the church, conversion, and then eventually his gradual acceptance of the idea of possibly becoming a priest. In terms of the structure of the book everything in part 2 leads to the crucial moments recalled when he went to the Jesuit Church of St. Francis Xavier on Sixteenth Street in New York City to tell someone he wanted to be a priest.

The final major part of the autobiography traces Merton's journey by way of various side trips—his desire to be a Franciscan; the visit to Cuba; the wish to be a Camaldolese; his teaching at St. Bonaventure—to the retreat that proved the destination at Gethsemani during Holy Week in April 1941. All of this makes a wonderful, tightly woven story.

What makes the book so effective, though, is that Merton tells such good stories throughout it. A letter from his editor Robert Giroux to Mark Van Doren, for example, urges Van Doren to read the various "stories" in the book.[16] Because Merton is a successful storyteller he can hold his reader moment by moment; and thus while the book is a carefully planned spiritual autobiography, it is at the same time a successful collection of episodes set in France, England, Columbia, Olean, St. Bonaventure, and finally Gethsemani. Readers can picture Merton's grandfather with all his luggage in Europe, or Bramachari standing in Grand Central Station when he visited Columbia, or the classes Merton taught at St. Bonaventure, as well as the details of setting in the monastery of Kentucky because these events never remain vague. They are always made vivid revelations through which Merton lets us see the grace of God working in that specific situation.

The arrangement of materials in *Seven Storey Mountain* also allows the writer to interweave narrative with commentary. Little by little we see this life unfold, and events which seemed to have little significance at the time take on a greater significance within the overall structure. The episode about Merton's acquisition of Gilson's *The Spirit of Medieval Philosophy* illustrates the method: at first Merton was genuinely interested in the book; then he was furious and felt tricked when he saw the "imprimatur"; and gradually, he reports, over months and years he came to an understanding of the significance of that book and its relationship to his subsequent life. Merton would later realize that the fact of his walking past that particular bookstore display on Fifth Avenue on that day was a crucial event in his life.

Many times throughout *Seven Storey Mountain* Merton builds around the realization that something had happened to him which he could not at the time fully understand. For example, his account of his appendectomy, and his awakening in the hospital, and preparing for communion, illustrates how he uses such facts to further the narrative.[17] Still another of those moments when something crucial takes place (and thereby changes one's life) is recounted in an experience in which Merton participated in Havana. He was attending Mass, as he had done many times before, but somehow the particular combination of being in a particular church when the creed was spoken with a great deal of enthusiasm by children, "a joyous affirmation of faith," was a situation where the stage was prepared for what he described as being "suddenly illuminated . . . blinded by the manifestation of God's presence" (*SSM*, 284). Also, his account of suddenly knowing that he must seek out a priest to discuss his own desire to enter the priesthood is another one of these crucial moments recalled. He explains how he had been compelled to act, but at that time he could not fully understand why he was doing so. As has been pointed out, that episode functions as the culmination of the second major movement of the entire book.

Seven Storey Mountain is a carefully executed version of the autobiographical account which Merton had tried earlier to fictionalize in the novel *The Labyrinth*. The autobiography, somewhat self-consciously at times, outlines the steps which brought the writer to his present vocation—a combination of contemplative and writer-spokesman. It can be read as a straight narrative; yet to appreciate fully why it functions as it does we must also note not just its title, and organization, but its rhetorical dimension. Merton's careful control of all of these elements allows him to arrange the narrative to reveal states of mind and to induce readers to be encouraged because of the spiritual journey which he relates. His rhetorical strategy assures his readers that God's plan will bring each of us to our best place in God's time. He does this by cultivating a tone of near amazement because everything is finally working out. Of course, in terms of the success of the book as a book, what this really means is that *he* is able to work it out with his pen, yet without compromising its honesty. Later books by Merton never achieved this same tone, probably because he grew to see that his interior life, and the communication of that life, was immensely more complicated than he earlier thought.

Once Merton had made his Easter Retreat at Gethsemani it was clear to him that his vocation pointed toward the Trappists. He wrote:

Back in the world, I felt like a man that had come down from the rare atmosphere of a very high mountain. When I got to Louisville, I had already been up for four hours or so. . . . And how strange it was to see people walking around as if they had something important to do, running after busses, reading the newspapers, lighting cigarettes. (*SSM*, 332)

He then knew he had to go back into that "rare atmosphere." Yet once he became a monk he also knew that he had "brought all the instincts of a writer with [him] into the monastery." He noted: "I knew that I was bringing them, too. It was not a case of smuggling them in" (*SSM*, 389). Such a quiet colloquial tone reassures the reader. Merton, the writer, lets his reader know everything is now all right.

In other places his language can be much more formal; then it seems almost as if the reader is praying with the writer-contemplative. We are drawn into the very quiet which the writer has found so rewarding. All of this is to say that the language Merton employs varies according to the mood of particular places in the volume. Sometimes anecdotal; sometimes ironic; sometimes amusing; sometimes a direct address to God; Merton provides a combination of many different styles. That combination has a way of reassuring the reader that it is possible to move from the world to the monastery as he did; and indirectly it is Merton's way of reassuring the reader that the links between world and monastery remain strong ones.

All of the language in *Seven Storey Mountain* strains to be heard. Merton relies upon diverse types of rhetoric and imagery to suggest different moods. His careful use of rhythm and images, along with the ability to tell good stories, contributes to the overall impact of the book. Thus, while the book is a narrative, and sometimes includes whole pages of exposition, it is also finally orchestrated by a poet, someone who loves language. The sections about Merton's brother John Paul, carefully interspersed throughout the text, and moving toward John Paul's own conversion and death at sea, culminated by Merton's elegy as the last part of the book, are an excellent example of this successful integration of many different ideas and methods into a successful whole.[18]

The Seven Storey Mountain may be the most famous single religious autobiography of this century. It is ultimately successful because it is so carefully written, and has a dramatic and spiritual appeal. The appeal of Merton's book grows from his ability to relate his life in a way which strikes chords for so many in the twentieth century. Merton's quest is one which his readers also want to make, yet his movement toward God into silence is one which he admits he himself is only beginning to understand. As the text of the autobiography ends, he hears God saying: *"I will lead you into solitude. I will lead you by the way that you cannot possibly understand . . ."* (*SSM*, 422).

Chapter Three
A Desire to be a Poet

How shall the seeds upon those furrowed
papers flower?
The Poet to His Book

Literary Friends

It was fortunate that Merton made several acquaintances at Columbia who shared his literary interests, for after he entered the monastery he continued to maintain regular contact with those people, most especially Robert Lax and Mark Van Doren. All his effort spent as an aspiring writer could not be forgotten; and it is therefore not surprising that a study of Merton's relationship with Van Doren reveals that his early books of poems were published, at least in part, through the former teacher's efforts.[1] It should be observed, however, that this was not a matter of suggestions urged upon Merton, or of his engineering things which might lead to publication. Rather, matters took a natural course. Merton early knew that he had a gift as a writer; during his first years as a monk the question was how best to use that gift.

Merton was before anything else a writer; he relishes this fact throughout *Seven Storey Mountain,* as well as in prose which preceded the autobiography. One cannot minimize the important effect of monastic formation upon his literary career, but one also comes to realize that throughout the career the ability to write strengthened the ability to see, understand, indeed, to live the monastic existence, as well as the reverse. Merton's early prose and poetry is therefore significant both as crafted work and as inspiration to readers, and also as evidence of how artistic and spiritual interests coalesced. He became a true contemplative, while retaining all of the instincts of a literary person, and without ever losing an awareness of basic questions about the uses of his literary talent. All of his writing became a seed bed and a testing place, a foundation for other ideas and more art, as well as a process in his own spiritual development. In a paradoxical way, therefore, it seems to have been necessary for Merton to write so that he could become more quiet, while his poems are the record of an artist-contemplative who never forgot that language was his most valuable instrument; yet unlike many literary artists, Merton also realized that writing was only a means, not an end.

He had left for the monastery with a traditional gesture of destroying the manuscripts which he considered profane. But just as important in terms of the development of his career is the fact that he saved many poems, a journal, and a completed novel. That was just good planning! We can now clearly establish that, as artist, he realized much of his earliest work had value even if it would take ten or twenty years for some of that material to be published. Such foresight was fortuitous. It was also fortuitous that he had made friends with men like Van Doren and Robert Lax, friendships which endured throughout his life. (Proof of his friendship with Lax is seen in the recently published volume of their letters.)[2] A letter of Lax's about Merton to Van Doren written after a visit to Gethsemani at Christmas of 1943 helps us to appreciate more particularly the conditions under which Merton's unusual career was to develop and as well how friends, who realized he possessed special gifts, remained concerned. Lax's words indicate much about the general atmosphere of Gethsemani at this time, and how Merton had apparently happily adjusted to this new place:

Of all the monks he looks the most pious, but like he sounds in the poems, really religious, not deceived or acting. . . . Next day it is more like Merton. Pontifical Mass with the Abbot sitting on throne, one choir religious holding Pontiff's hat, Merton holding a shepherd's crook . . . all proper and with a polish that looks like acting, which is right for the ceremony. . . .

Really good talk too. . . . He's very much himself, all full of jokes, writing the lives of some saints, which in spite of the serious topic sounds like his funny writing and there are a lot of good anecdotes translated, which other people would have missed . . . his insights are new and good, sounding like the great ones.[3]

Such a report makes it clear that the young monk had definitely found a place where he felt comfortable.

The hope to be a writer was clear to Merton much earlier, and one of the best indications of this is the correspondence between him and Van Doren. Perhaps in an unconscious way this aspiring writer realized that Van Doren would recognize the value of his literary abilities; it must have been for such reasons that Merton had hurriedly sent his manuscripts to Van Doren on the very day he had left to go to the monastery, along with that note which did not even indicate where he was going, or why.

Additional letters written to Van Doren during Merton's first few years at Gethsemani clarify aspects of his developing role as writer. Clearly Merton was happy to be in the monastery, and it was natural to express that happiness through writing. In later stages of the career writing became a way for Merton to clarify doubts and raise issues, part of a continuing pattern wherein he sought ways to combine abilities as writer and contemplative. In his correspondence with Van Doren it was possible for him to affirm that such a combination was possible. For Merton it was never a matter of suddenly changing; it was more a matter of combining patterns which had been important before he went to Gethsemani. His entire literary career might finally best be described as a mode of combining a gift for literary vocation along with a contemplative need. In a preceding chapter it has been shown that one value of the *Secular Journal* is that it allows us to observe early examples of Merton's parallel interests, a vocation which always remained a combination of the contemplative and the active—by means of writing.

Reviews, Plans, and Early Poetry

While still a graduate student at Columbia Merton was busy writing poems and fiction and hoping to attain recognition as a writer. In those years when he wished to become a successful writer, he also reviewed a wide range of books. Some of those book reviews have been reprinted in *A Thomas Merton Reader* and *The Literary Essays of Thomas Merton*. The fact that Merton was willing to reprint two of his early efforts in the *Reader* indicates something of his opinion about these early pieces. His decision was to include reviews of Nabokov's *Laughter in the Dark* and John Crowe Ransom's *The World's Body*.[4] What he stressed about both of these books was his interest in the particulars of style; he recognized the value of an artist's close attention to individual words; thus he admires both Nabokov's ability to execute meaning in a minimum of words and Ransom's skill in explicating the particularities of individual poems. Such concerns with particularities reflect Merton's own interests in language and hint about the nature of his earliest poetry. Those first lyrics, *Early Poems* (1940–42), like *The Secular Journal* and the novel already discussed, waited many years before they were published. Now, as part of the *Collected Poems, Early Poems* provides significant insight into an aspiring artist who loved words, wit, and successful phrases, but an artist who finally had to choose between himself and ambition.

Merton's poem entitled "The Strife Between the Poet and Ambition," part of this early gathering, could serve as a model for the collection as a whole:

> Money and fame break in the room
> And find the poet all alone.
> They lock the door, so he won't run,
> And turn the radio full-on
> And beat the poor dope like a drum.[5]

Merton acknowledges that he did have the skill to produce competent verses (and prose), yet the question remained—would it be worth it to do so? Was there something more important than proof of a technical competence and a facile use of language? Clearly there was, and throughout *Early Poems* we see the young artist working hard to demonstrate his wit and cleverness, but we also see him trying to demonstrate how crazy the world seems to be. In such a manner we can see connections between these early poems and the novel, *My Argument.* Merton's earliest poetry is witty and intellectual and shows how he labored to execute pieces that were technically right. In the years that followed, and as his literary career developed, Merton moved away from such a self-conscious variety of writing. This is not to say that his later work ceased to be witty—rather, it ceased to be so formal and dependent upon accepted literary traditions. Already in this early collection Merton's dissatisfaction with convention is evident.

While these earliest poems reflect Merton's reading, and indirectly his love of the church, its saints and legends, the most prominent theme is the young poet's dissatisfaction with a world he felt he must turn away from. Thus, the sixteen poems which constitute *Early Poems* (1940–42) are witty and inventive, but their overall tone is sad because the poet so often chooses to focus on unpleasant aspects of contemporary life, a world which had taken a turn for the worse during the 1930s and which he now feels is empty. The first two selections—"The Philosophers" and "Dirge for the World Joyce Died In"—are characteristic of the gathering; significantly, those poems treat problems the poet faces when he attempts to use language.

The world imagined in *Early Poems* seems to be one of false courtesy, a veneer made possible because of materialism. Only occasionally does beauty in the world poke its head through to be celebrated. A nine-line poem, "The City's Spring," is unusual because it does suggest that there can be beauty in a world where usually there seems to be none. Each of its groups of three lines builds upon the idea that while spring remains a time of joyous rebirth, it is difficult to see beauty in a modern city; nevertheless, "flowers and friendly days are in." This short poem is printed in immediate juxtaposition with "Dirge for the City of Miami," and the placement of the poems is clearly intentional. The first stresses that beauty may still come at unexpected moments. The second, longer and in no way lyrical, is a song for the lost inhabitants of the city of Miami who never beheld the beauty of their surroundings in lush Florida; "Miami" seems ironically to echo Wallace Stevens. Merton's poem does not sustain a uniform tone; and sometimes it seems almost childish in its attempt to suggest the loss of innocence of its imagined characters. A common bond in both of these poems is the implication that man, no matter the degree of his degradation, will never completely separate himself from the effects of nature:

> The weary thief, the limping whore
> Lie down upon the windy shore:
> ....
> While all the downcast palms recall
> The tears that Magdalen let fall.
> (*CP,* 8)

Themes to which the young poet most often returns in *Early Poems* are death, loss, and confusion. The "Hymn of Not Much Praise for New York City" exemplifies this emphasis, as do two longer poems: "From the Second Chapter of a Verse History of the World" and "Hymn to Commerce." In "Hymn of Not Much Praise for New York City" Merton imagines a city full of crazy monsters ("The elevators clack their teeth and rattle the bars of their cages," *CP,* 19); he sees little in a large city that offers good.[6] His city seems to be a zoo; inhabitants seem to be satisfied with a horrible situation—"Stupefied forever by the blue, objective lights" which fill their "infirmaries" which are the restaurants, and "clinics," which are schools and offices.

The funny long poem "From the Second Chapter of a Verse History of the World" is a mixture of myth and fantasy. In it the Minotaur announces that there was a time when young girls were sacrificed to the monster who sat on the throne of Aegean Minos, but as the narrative unfolds we have the uncanny feeling that this poet is telling the story of Columbia College, and of the sacrifice of Manhattan's beauties:

> Arms full of cornflowers, grouped in their sororities,
> With honor students slightly to one side
> The fairest wights of all our wienie roasts
> Are off to picnic with the Cretan brute.
>
> (*CP*, 16)

The poem "Tower of Babel" develops the idea that mankind seems to be stupefied by his own creations, especially by contorted language. This poem is introduced by four lines called "The Political Speech," and the suggestion is that history moves forward (unfortunately) through the "misuse of words." As man builds his tower of Babel, the primary function of language is only to designate the machines in which he has faith. Then the machine proceeds to destroy the very things which it produces. The horror is that man is seemingly incorporated in such a forward movement; what is forgotten is that he will be destroyed in the process: "Insofar as man is more important than God . . ./Words also reflect this principle" (*CP*, 21). In such a world, words can have little meaning. They are simply a way of moving back and forth, "Created by the history which they themselves destroy." Such is the crazy world which man has made. (This poem also contains the seeds of a verse play of the same title which was published in *The Strange Islands*.)[7]

Early Poems provides glimpses of a side of Merton not so easily visible in his first published volume, *Thirty Poems* (1944). The wordplay of the opening poem, "The Philosophers," can be interpreted as a statement about the misuse of language and the abuse of art, as well as a commentary about war in the twentieth century. Keat's "Beauty is truth" is twisted in Merton's poem to become "Body is truth, truth body" and "Beauty is troops, troops beauty," and we are quickly made to see how perverted the present era's use of language has become. The setting of this poem is a public park, but the speaker informs listeners that he cannot get any sleep because of the mandrakes who keep talking about the meaning of life. Through such a crazy poem Merton suggests that both sensuality and war are an immense distance from Truth and Beauty. Merton's decision to place this poem at the head of this retrospective gathering indicates his fondness for it. The world which Merton imagines throughout his early poems is one whose inhabitants exist in a kind of living death. This was a world which had once produced Joyce, but which had now become so disappointing for the young poet that ultimately he can only sing a "Dirge for the World Joyce Died In." Death is the most prominent motif in these poems. "Two British Airmen" and "Dirge for the City of Miami" are representative; they lament a loss of idealism now innundated by materialism, selfishness, and greed. The poem about Miami resembles Eliot's early poetry, as well as Auden's; the lives imagined within it have lost *all* dignity:

> Never did the drunkard think
> To taste such bitterness in his drink
> And there the gentle murderer stands,
> And sadly, sadly wipes his hands:
> There the forger and the thief
> And the bank robber bow in grief
> While up and down the perjurer goes[.]
> *(CP, 9)*

This ludicrous world makes it impossible to take its inhabitants seriously. In such a setting the poet perceives ever more clearly that he will have to make a decision between serving a mediocre world and the world which is beyond it. His "The Strife Between the Poet and Ambition" is an important statement because it reflects some of the problems which Merton himself confronted as aspiring writer. He certainly realized that he could produce a modicum of "successful" poetry. Yet he also realized that it was perhaps still more important not to write. Ambition tells the poet he had better write fast: "Tomorrow, tomorrow. Death will come/And find you sitting dumb and senseless/With your epics unbegun" *(CP,* 10). The poet, however, seems to realize that it might be as well to be silent. We can understand the development of Merton's career as a whole more

clearly through reading those early works. They are a reflection of
the two parts of him (the desire to write and the desire to be silent)
which continued to be important throughout the 1940s. The real
question implied is, can one prudently spend time writing poems
at all?

Thirty Poems

Merton chose to be a monk within an order where silence was
the rule. When he first became a monk even writing letters with
any kind of regularity was impossible. But as we have seen he did
write, and while he entertained doubts, he did continue to perfect
his skill as a poet. His first published volume of poems was carefully
chosen to reflect his decision to be a Cistercian. The book's prayerful
artistry is almost a model of what one might expect of a young
monk, a reflection of his decision to be a contemplative. The collection is carefully planned; and while many of the poems were actually
written before December 1941, it is nevertheless a book which works
well to mirror the happiness which this young monk felt.

Sufficiently a curiosity when published in 1944 (a young Cistercian who writes!), perhaps it was recognized as a strong voice in
"Catholic" poetry partly because it seemed to reflect the strength
of the institution.[8] Its real strength, though, is in the lyric voice
of the young artist. As poet he seemed to have found an ideal subject
matter. Just a few years later, as we see toward the end of this
chapter, he was to feel somewhat differently.

Thirty Poems is arranged to minimize the actual monastic experience. (Mark Van Doren, instrumental in arranging for its
publication, also did some editorial work with the manuscript.)[9]
The themes in this first gathering are predictably fervent, but they
are also carefully written and highly disciplined poems. Often echoing
Merton's reading of Eliot and the Metaphysicals, his poems are
highly compressed works which expand outward toward the contemporary world.[10] Thus "The Flight into Egypt" and "Prophet" work
together to reverberate as a commentary about the twentieth century:

> Through every precinct of the wintry city
> Squadroned iron resounds upon the streets;
> Herod's police
> Make shudder the dark steps of the tenements
> At the business about to be done.[11]

With this poem as a backdrop, "Prophet" makes good sense; retreat from the madness of a world which apparently has no use for the desert. Who is this "prophet?" Perhaps a saint or a monk who is now a traveler in "the holy desert":

> Honeycomb, beggarbread eater,
> Lean from drinking rain
> That lies in the windprints of rocks. . . .
>
> *(CP,* 28)

In *Thirty Poems* we find evidence that Merton has begun to stop arguing with the world (as he does in so many of the poems which precede this book). His concern is much more with celebration. Celebration of having found a way of life which allows a new perspective on the world is, perhaps, the core of the book's accomplishment.

Not surprisingly, some of the poems use as settings the Trappist Abbey of Gethsemani where Merton had come to find peace. Many of his lines unite themes which were important during the author's years as a contemplative. The comfort of nature and the pleasures of silence and prayer contrast with earlier times when God was ignored or denied. The subject of one poem is how an ordinary morning in the abbey is such a time of wakefulness and promise while the poetic speaker cannot easily forget the loss suffered by so many who turn their backs on God's dawning. The poem opens:

> When the full fields begin to smell of sunrise
> And the valleys sing in their sleep,
> The pilgrim moon pours over the solemn darkness
> Her waterfalls of silence,
> And then departs, up the long avenue of trees.
>
> *(CP,* 45)

This is a specific reference to the road leading to the front entrance of the Abbey of Gethsemani; the implication is that given the special circumstances of life in a monastery this speaker hopes his daily activities will be appropriate praise of God. But he fears that many activities of men, by day, will remain dubious at best. Light comes but many remain in darkness. The poem continues:

> The stars hide, in the glade, their light, like tears,
> And tremble where some train runs, lost

> Baying in eastward mysteries of distance.
> Where fire flares, somewhere, over a sink of cities.

The poem then becomes a prayer of thanksgiving that the poet, still haunted by his own past darkness, will be illumined:

> Now kindle in the windows of this ladyhouse, my soul
> Your childish, clear awakeness:
> Burn in the country night
> Your wise and sleepless lamp.
> ....
> Wake in the windows of Gethsemani, my soul, my sister
> For the past years, with smokey torches, come,
> Bringing betrayal from the burning world
> And bloodying the glade with pitch flame.

Admittedly, these conceits are often extreme; nevertheless, they are effective. Merton conveys the paradox of finding himself so happy and full of light, although he has given up much of what the world considers to be illuminating. Other poems in this first book are castigations of a world left behind, such as "Dirge for the Proud World" and "Death" ("Where are the merchants and the money-lenders/Whose love sang in the wires between the seaports and the/inland granaries?" *CP*, 38) Still others are statements of faith. "The Vine" is a consideration of the fact of the mystical body; "The Holy Sacrament of the Altar" is a consideration of the Divine Presence "Who loves us so, He won't outshine our winking candles!" (*CP*, 50). A poem which combines many of the basic themes in the volume is "An Argument: Of the Passion of Christ." It celebrates the fact of the passion and man's redemption; it also meditates about all those who rebel against God's gift to them:

> There is no ear that has not heard
> The deathless cry of murdered God:
> No eye that has not looked upon
> The lance of the crucifixion. . . .
>   (*CP*, 53)

The dominant mood of *Thirty Poems* is wonder and awe that Christ has been found by this poet. At the same time, there seems to be a just barely controlled rage that men could so waste their energies and lives in the pursuit of the worldly. Therefore, in "The Night Train" Merton considers that it is possible to awaken too late; he imagines that it is possible to

>   . . . weep the deaths of cathedrals
>   That we have never seen,
>   . . . .
>   At once the diplomats start up, as white as bread,
>   Buckle the careless cases of their minds
>   That just fell open in the sleeper:
>
>   For, by the rockets of imaginary sieges
>   They see to read big, terrible print,
>   Each in the other's face. . . .
>
>   (*CP,* 31)

Merton reminds his reader that it is possible to find ourselves in November having missed all of the summers: "And though we seem as grave as jailers, yet we did not come to wonder/Who picked the locks of the past days, and stole our summer" (*CP,* 33).

The excellent "For My Brother: Reported Missing in Action, 1943" is perhaps the best example of how Merton unites many different themes basic to this collection. He knows that he and his brother are united in Christ who died for all men:

>   . . . Christ weeps in the ruins of my spring:
>   The money of Whose tears shall fall
>   Into your weak and friendless hand,
>   And buy you back to your own land. . . .
>
>   (*CP,* 36)

Gradually, as this poem develops, its images about loss are changed to paradoxical images of gain.

A Writer in a Divided Sea

When Merton's second book of poetry, *A Man in the Divided Sea,* appeared in 1946, many of the same themes reappeared which had first informed *Thirty Poems.* The second volume is a collection produced during the first seven years after Merton's conversion. In his author's note Merton states that the poems "are printed more or less in the order in which they were written."[12] Thus, the opening part of the volume has a history similar to *Thirty Poems*, both apparently composed between 1938 and 1941; later poems were written during approximately the first four years Merton lived in the monastery. In these ambitious poems Merton sometimes writes in a self-conscious and rather calculating manner. Thérèse Lentfoeher's study of Merton's poetry makes it clear that he was consciously building a style of his own. However, the occasional angry strain seen in the first books becomes more visible, perhaps caused by too much concern about a world "left behind."

More than anything else Merton's second collection of verse demonstrates that he had found his home at Gethsemani. Two years had passed since his first volume of poems had appeared, and while sometimes in *A Man in the Divided Sea* Merton appears to be straining too hard to find startling images which will surprise his readers, on the whole, the book functions well. It is balanced by poems which are devotional and meditations about the culture, as well as by lyrics which are personal. The collection seems to be set somewhere between the land of bondage and the promised land. Merton's metaphors are often meant to suggest his wonder and surprise that man is given a chance to escape from Egypt, while his tone of urgency remains strong; in some of the poems the speakers seem so concerned with man's mistakes as to forget that the peace of God's grace has been found. What is especially striking about the somber side of this book is how it contrasts with the later career when Merton discovered that many aspects of the world were to be celebrated. Of course, he could not come to that conclusion without first removing himself from an evil world he lamented; thus some of this earlier poetry is a symbolic movement away from that world, while it also contains the seeds of Merton's compassionate movement back toward the world outside the monastery. The title, *A Man in the Divided Sea,* suggests the tone of the book and the definite sense of urgency which informs most of these poems. Merton's allusion is to God's mercy toward His chosen people as they fled Egypt— but what he also implies is that the poet remains in between the world of bondage and a land where he can accept the trust which has been promised to him. It suggests further that Merton the poet cannot so easily turn away from the world. The significant thing, of course, is that he did persevere in the contemplative life, and that the life and the writing which followed eventually led him back again to concerns with the world. Study of this collection reflects the poet's commitment to a religious life, and a trust that God will free him from the world. But little could the writer of these years realize that his vocation would lead him, while within the monastery, nevertheless definitely back to concerns with the world. Significantly, *A Man in the Divided Sea* contains the first steps of that movement.

Some of these poems are specifically about the difficulty of life in bondage, and about the false lives of many who live in contemporary America. There is an uneasiness of tone which permeates this subject matter, an uneasiness which reflects the poet's concern. "Poem: 1939" is characteristic. There the poet fears that time is running out: "Towns dry up and flare like tongues/But no voice prophesies." This poem, arranged as a group of quatrains, succinctly suggests the speaker's horror of a contemporary man who attempts to live independently of a Divine presence. The poem foreshadows the approaching world war, and suggests man's selfishness. Man, himself, is responsible for his own death. War and violence can only bring destruction, but the image of conflagration also stresses the possibility that God may come; the Holy Spirit will descend on mankind if he will properly prepare himself. In a related poem, "The Man in the Wind," the implication is that while man is called to silence, to a peace which he finds in God, he remains so busy with his own interests that he cannot see: Man's "five senses, separate as their numbers" constantly move in separate directions, with the result that "Captain April's mind, leaning out of its own/amazing windows,/Dies in a swirl of doves" (*CP,* 63).

Other poems in the book deal still more harshly with man's imperfect sense that he should prepare; ironically, Merton says, modern man does not even seem to know for what preparation is to be made. So much of his action appears to be simply a waste. "The Oracle," "Tropics," and "Ash Wednesday" all deal with this subject. Merton, who was disturbed by man's overemphasis on materialism and disregard for things of the spirit, indicates such disturbance through a castigation of the world. "Ash Wednesday" (a title perhaps chosen with Eliot's poem of the same title in mind?) contrasts seeker and sleeper, believer and disbeliever. A "naked traveler" starves in his apparent madness. This reference is to a prophet in the desert and how inevitably such a "lone traveler" will be slain. But today's sleepers who make no spiritual journey are "slain" as well "by the stillness of their own reflection."

Additional poems, apparently written because Merton was still very much concerned with the distractions and the often futile actions of the city, suggest similar ideas. "Tropics" ends: "the prisoners of the state/Do not cease their labor:/Collecting the asphalt fragments of the night" (*CP,* 65). Yet with such a poem one is also reminded of Merton's later fascination with modern-day cargo cults, which he uses as a subject for meditation in his long poem *The Geography of Lograire.* There the same subject matter is rather more generously and complexly beheld.[13] If this early Merton writes about selfishness, greed, and arrogance, and paints the secular world as a mirror of those aspects of man, what he later came to learn was that he had earlier only seen fragments, and he realized that such partial knowledge was not an accurate reflection of the world, but rather his own subjective response. Interestingly, other poems within this volume, in a kind of mosaic, foreshadow much of what the more mature poet later wrote.

One of the most characteristic aspects of this collection is seen in the tension of the poem "Some Bloody Mutiny." Merton simultaneously creates a meditation about man's arrogance and weakness and also indicates that, though divided, man is drawn in two directions. "Heaven is given/To ingrow in [our] flimsy cage of structures" (*CP,* 69). Men should, therefore, learn to be self-effacing; when they do so, life comes. Merton writes that the problem is that "We time our Easters by the rumpus/In our dancehall arteries." Importantly, his poem is no lamentation; and within it, and others of this period, we have a clear reflection of Merton's humor, which suggests his compassion for man's weakness.

The collection contains three poems called "Aubade." Printed closely together, they form a unit. The one on Harlem suggests the abuse, and metaphorically, crucifixion of those in any secular city. The second, "Aubade—The Annunciation," is completely different; Mary accepts her role. Interestingly, the time designation which Merton uses in this poem is that of the monastery where he himself has found peace: "When the dim light, at Lauds, comes strike her window,/Bellsong falls out of Heaven with a sound of glass" (*CP,* 83). This poem is full of paradoxical images which suggest the amazement and awe which Merton imagines Mary must have felt:

Speech of an angel shines in the waters of her thought like diamonds
Rides like a sunburst on the hillsides of her heart,

And is brought home like harvests,
Hid in her house, and stored
Like the sweet summer's riches in our peaceful barns.

(CP, 84)

Such must have been that morning of a new era which man, today, has forgotten to appreciate. How much man has forgotten is seen in the third poem of the group, "Aubade—The City," a poem where people are captives of the city. They seem to sense something wrong: "Cries of defiance/As delicate as frost, as sharp as glass,/Rise from the porcelain buildings/And break in the blue sky." Ironically, what these people fear is the coming of light which is a threat to their "hiding places" *(CP, 86)*. In the poem that follows, the speaker realizes that such men are in peril because they will not submit to a power greater than themselves; he also prays that he be made "poor enough to bear [his] priceless ransom" *(CP, 87)*, meaning his birth into Christianity. The tone of this poem and in fact of the whole first part of this book, is a harsh, stern cry of warning, a plea for man to come to his senses.

In other poems, written, more than likely, during the earliest years at Gethsemani, Merton implies that he had found peacefulness. "Advent," "Carol," "How long We Wait," and "A Letter to My Friends" all suggest a great deal about Merton's developing life, and a closeness to God which he implies all could experience. In the first, advent is sung as a time when God pours "darkness and brightness" upon "our solemn valleys." In "Carol," the contrast between the peace of the nativity and the "unnumbered children of the wicked centuries" *(CP, 89)* is stressed. The third poem, "How Long We Wait," is about those who wait and accept a life for God; questions are raised about how long it is possible to continue waiting "with minds as dim as ponds" *(CP, 90)*. The speaker implies that it need not be long, but the question is raised at the end of the poem: "O earth, when will you wake in the green wheat,/And all our Trappist cedars sing." This is another specific reference to the landscape of Gethsemani. The speaker's question seems to be why cannot more men become attuned to the harmony of their natural world. If they could, then a life in Christ would make good sense.

It is also significant to note that whereas many of the earlier poems in this collection deal with classical figures (often figures preparing for the coming of a hero) and treat false preparations (often those in modern cities), beyond the mid-point of the collection Merton lavishes attention on subjects which have their roots in the New Testament: "Cana"; "Wine for old Adam, digging in the briars!"; "The Widow of Naim"; "St. Paul"; and many other saints—Lucy, Thomas Aquinas, Alberic. Merton apparently had found happiness in the Christian lore which he was absorbing day by day as a young monk; such satisfaction would eventually lead to the composition of many related poems. Others here deal with the particular atmosphere of Merton's Kentucky monastery and its surrounding landscape. His "Song for the Blessed Sacrament" is done, therefore, in terms of the fields and birds which surrounded Gethsemani. The poet's love of that terrain and the specifics of Gethsemani was changing the course of his life. Toward the end of this collection it was already possible for him to write a poem which clearly welcomes inevitable death:

> Sing your new song in the winepress where these bloody pence
> Weep from the skin of our Gethsemani,
> Knowing that we must die to break the seed our prison
> And spring like wheat from the wet earth. . . .
>
> (*CP*, 113–14)

And, as might almost be expected, one of the finest poems in this group is a meditation about the Trappist cemetery. There the poet suggests that simple lives, wherein so much was hidden, have much to teach. These Cistercians no longer need even hear "the momentary rumors of the road/Where cities pass and vanish in a single car" (*CP*, 116).

Finally, toward the end of the volume poems like "Trappists, Working" and "After the Night Office—Gethsemani Abbey" treat the beauty which the young monk found in the quiet of the monastery. The first is a short, tightly executed, and highly rhythmic poem which suggests the pleasure to be derived from physical labor. (Merton would often refer to physical labor in his later years, in entries in journals like *The Sign of Jonas* and *Conjectures of a Guilty Bystander*.) The second poem is about the simplicity of life at Gethsemani. "The weak walls/Of the world fall/And heaven, in floods, comes pouring in" (*CP*, 109). In the poem about the Trappist cemetery Merton emphasizes the peace which he sensed within the monastery. He realized that he was still on his way, but he knew he was making the right journey:

> . . . we, the mariners and travellers,
> The wide-eyed immigrants,
> Praying and sweating in our steerage cabins,
> Lie still and count with love the measured bells
> That tell the deep-sea leagues until your harbor.
>
> (*CP,* 117)

Merton, always a traveler, draws insights from specific experiences. The monastery itself is like a silent ship carrying him toward—he knows not where. In the same vein is "The Biography," a verse sketch for his autobiography; it is a confession and poetic compression of material Merton was to handle in prose in *The Seven Storey Mountain.* In that poem he refers to his year as a student at Cambridge, and states in cartological terms similar to his sometimes abstract descriptions of other men of the world that "my life is written on Christ's Body like a map." With every wound, paradoxically, Christ was the greatest thief of all. "Stealing my sins into Your dying life/ Robbing me even of my death" (*CP,* 105). Merton knows he was born "Now not in France, but Bethlehem." Thus he echoes the words of Paul.

These early poems provide a record of the poet's love of nature, of solitude, and of the contemplative vocation—all aspects of a life which, in maturing, would lead him back to concerns with the world. Together, the poems trace a clearly marked movement away from the world, but paradoxically toward it as well. Thus "A Whitsun Canticle," like "The Biography," is a song of praise for the Spirit of God that has changed Merton's life. Importantly, the images are not abstract ones: "You are all the prudence and the power/That change our dust and nothing into fields and fruits" (*CP,* 121). Some poems in this collection are straightforwardly "religious," such as "Song for the Blessed Sacrament," "The Word—A Responsory," and "The Dark Encounter." Together all these poems stand as a document of Merton's developing spiritual and literary career. We perceive changes in his poetic style within this book as he moved away from the highly intellectual and compressed idiom of poetry which he admired in Eliot, and toward a poetry which was more

personal and direct, a poetry based more upon his attachment to
the land and the simple rhythms of living experienced at Gethsemani.

Figures for a World Left Behind

Figures for an Apocalypse, the next step in Merton's poetic career,
is a book which more than any of the preceding collections seems
to emphasize two themes. It stresses the fact that time is running
out, and that modern man needs to realize the significance of the
approaching day of judgment. And yet this is finally only part of
what Merton chooses to emphasize, since the bulk of the volume
continues to celebrate the peace and holy quiet which he has found
at Gethsemani. Merton's poetry in this volume continues to give
glory to God, and this is accomplished in many tightly constructed
poems in the book; yet simultaneously other poems emphasize the
fact that the poet finds it lamentable that few of those who are still
in the world seem even aware of the urgency of his message. The
sometimes surprising (and unfortunate) result is that these poems
can often become strident. [14] Merton himself wondered as he prepared
this book for the press if perhaps writing poetry had ceased to be
of much use to him. [15] Writing and publishing poetry was a far
different kind of activity from the life he sought as a contemplative.
Nevertheless, he reasoned that perhaps through poetry he could
provide glimpses for readers of a world beyond their secular one.

Figures contains three basic varieties of poetry: first, a group of
poems which is self-consciously about Merton's reconstruction of
life in the world; second, another group which is focused on the
contemplative life; last, a group specifically religious in nature,
dealing with subjects which apparently have been a help to Merton
(the poet) in forming his contemplative life. His title poem for this
volume establishes the tone and serves as the somber introduction;
Merton clearly felt it was important to stress his apocalyptic vision.
The title poem, which is composed of eight sections, begins with
a plea to the "Beloved," the Bridegroom to come down to the
world. [16] The poet knows that when the Lord does appear at the
Second Coming he will do so by making an end to the present world
of sin "Splitting the seven countries/With the prism of [His] smile."
The second section of the poem commands all "rich women" to
come to their windows and "weep for the bangles on your jeweled
bones." The end clearly seems near. Part 3 is for Merton's friends—

"(Advice to my Friends Robert Lax and Edward Rice, to get away while they still can)"—and suggests that they must flee the city:

> It is the hour to fly without passports
> From Juda to the mountains,
> And hide while cities turn to butter[.]

Section 4 contains the apocalyptic vision and is based on the Apocalypse 14:14. The poem which follows, "Landscape, Prophet and Wild-dog," is a crazy vision of a false prophet (Marx?) attacked by a mad "wild-dog." Merton implies the secular prophets have not been able to deliver what they had promised; the rhetoric of the 1920s and 1930s brought only war. The end of civilization now seems inevitable.

Section 6 is called "In the Ruins of New York," and is a vision of a future when man's evil works are gone, the city destroyed.

> There shall be doves' nests, and hives of bees
> In the cliffs of the ancient apartments,
> And birds shall sing in the sunny hawthorns
> Where was once Park Avenue.
> And where Grand Central was, shall be a little hill
> Clustered with sweet, dark pine. . . .
>
>   (*CP*, 145)

In the poem which follows, "Landscape: Beast," Merton provides another Apocalyptic picture of those last "waiting to . . . hear the seven voices of the final blasphemy."

The effect of the total poem is to provide a picture of the world which will be lost, and inevitably will be judged by an angry God. This is an Augustinian vision of the City of Man. The final section of the poem, called "The Heavenly City," is a vision of the unearthly city. God comes and delivers man from the earth. Comparison might be made between this verse drama and the later "The Tower of Babel" which appeared in *The Strange Islands*. The poems which follow suggest that the poet felt he had, in a sense, begun to find that heavenly city at Gethsemani. The poem which Merton prints immediately following his title poem is called "Landscape: Wheat-fields," and everything about it is designed to emphasize a contrast with the barren landscape which he imagines throughout the "Apocalypse."

One important accomplishment of this volume is the poet's ability to show readers that he is extremely happy in his role as Cistercian. His "Two States of Prayer," the third poem of the collection, emphasizes this fact. There are two ways to pray: In "Wild October" prayer can be like "thousands in the far, forgotten stadiums," but, to continue the analogy, after trees have lost their leaves and we find ourselves in stark December awaiting rebirth, a cleaner and purer state of prayer exists. (However, this poem sometimes seems to be trying almost too hard for successful images.) Poems such as "Three Postcards from the Monastery" (already discussed), "Song: Contemplation," "Spring: Monastery Farm," "Evening: Zero Weather," "A Christmas Card," and "Winter Afternoon," successfully indicate that the poet had made his monastery home the base for good poems. And even if the imagery is often extreme, such successful poems suggest his new found pleasure.

Nevertheless, *Figures for an Apocalypse* is in some ways a weaker collection of poems than the preceding volume, for it seems to be both more ambitious while at the same time indicative of the writer's doubts; it is a book which displays both the assets and liabilities of Merton's talent. As a collection it is full of allusions (literary, biblical, etc); and it is a book which contains Merton's own castigation of the evil world which he has left behind. It is, however, perhaps too full of Merton's own trying to make phrases and images which will be effective. The final poem of this volume indirectly indicates all of these assets and liabilities. We can admire the poem for its directness and honesty, and we can also appreciate it as an indirect commentary by Merton about the craft of making poems.

"The Poet, To His Book" simultaneously reflects Merton's doubts about the efficacy of what he writes and his hope that the poetry will have good effects for the world beyond the monastery. As envoy, it is a meditation about the good of writing poetry at all; it is also a questioning of what might be accomplished through this new book. This writer has put the poems together and knows that it is now time to send the book forth: "Now is the day of our farewell in fear, lean pages:/And shall I leave some blessing on the half of me you/have devoured?" Merton does not know exactly why he has suffered to produce what he has written; clearly he hopes it has something to do with the working out of his salvation. He therefore questions the book and his act of writing: "Were you, in clean obedience, my Cross,/Sent to exchange my life for Christ's in labor?"

If it is not clear to the poet if these poems are expiation for sins, he is also not certain about how his lines will be apprehended by others.

A basic pattern exhibited in *Figures For an Apocalypse* builds upon Merton's paradoxical realization about the problems of writing. As a monk he has doubts about expressing what he feels, while the sense of having at last found his home is crucial to the effect of the volume. That he included the essay "Poetry and the Contemplative Life" as the concluding section of this book is important. This essay raises serious questions about whether it is possible to publish poetry *and* be a contemplative. In it Merton implies that it may even be necessary, at least for some, to give up the active production of poetry. It was another ten years before this significant essay was revised by Merton and republished in *Commonweal*. The two different versions of the essay, Merton's two ways of dealing with the dilemma of how to combine the life of poet and contemplative, will be discussed in chapter 5 in conjunction with his later poetic career.

Merton's poetic enthusiasm for various worldly subjects, something which he clearly senses has been relatively profitless, diminishes in this volume. In fact, in some ways the entire book, along with its title poem, manifests the poet's realization that castigation of the world is profitless, while, more important, a certain peacefulness is necessary if one is to live. This seemed so much the case that Merton thought it might become necessary for him to cease writing poetry altogether. This possibility is emphasized by his inclusion of the essay "Poetry and the Contemplative Life" as the final seventeen pages of *Figures*.

Chapter Four
Writing and
Meditating for Others

Under the blunt pine
Elias becomes his own geography [.]
Elias — Variations on a Theme

How to Write?

During his first decade as a monk Merton assumed responsibility for many writing projects which were neither autobiography nor poetry. He was proud to be a Cistercian, and a desire to share information about that way of life drew him into many varieties of writing; some of these resulted in books which would later satisfy him, but others produced books which he felt to be less successful. Most of the books of this middle period which were not poetry or autobiography fall into three broad, overlapping, categories: historical; meditative; and those looking outward toward the larger community. This chapter concerns this wide variety of books, which all work together to demonstrate the writer's increasing awareness of contemporary man's needs.

Merton produced successful historical pieces, but his most effective writing proved to be works which looked not backward, but focused rather on man's situation in the present, his relationship to others, and his need to find his true identity. Such an awareness of man's needs and his continuing journey is basic to all the books treated in this chapter, yet also during the period from the late 1940s to the 1960s a considerably different kind of book emerges. Importantly, this is so because Merton himself was developing into a somewhat different kind of person during this period, and we see this development in the groups of books studied here. As he himself became surer of historical continuities, he was able to cease his preoccupation with history, even as he became more aware of the needs of people beyond the monastery; he was also able to place his own meditative writings within a more inclusive framework with connections far beyond his Cistercian life.

The Waters of Siloe (1949) is an example of a successful project which he himself might not have even chosen; it is a history of the

Cistercian Order from its inception in the twelfth century down to the present. Merton traces the ideals of the founders who had sought to return to a strict adherence to the Rule of Saint Benedict, and he then charts the course of development of the order as it grew and declined. He then focuses especially on hardships faced in the eighteenth and nineteenth centuries—hardships overcome at places like Gethsemani in Kentucky. The prologue of *The Waters of Siloe* sets the stage; Merton provides the story of a French businessman who became a lay brother after experiencing a vision of a nun in, of all places, a hotel lobby. She had mysteriously appeared—then just as mysteriously disappeared. Only later did this businessman realize that he apparently had experienced a vision of St. Thérèse of the child Jesus; soon after this miraculous appearance the man decided to become a member of the Cistercian Abbey of Aiguebelle in southern France. Merton informs his readers that other situations, perhaps just as surprising, have led many men to the Cistercian monasteries of the United States.

The history of the development of the Cistercians which follows is forceful, succinct, sometimes romantic, and often inspiring. The title (an allusion to Isaias's symbol of the "waters of Siloe that flow in silence")[1] is alluded to throughout the volume as Merton emphasizes the unusual thirst of men who will give up everything for an austere life. This historical account is both factual and moving; for the most part it is quite detailed, and the writer's ability to incorporate novelistic elements makes the book compelling reading. Specific details about the foundation of Gethsemani Abbey are a good example of how Merton depicts scenes. He does not just provide information; he arranges the facts so that the journey of these particular monks, like so many who make (physical and spiritual) journeys in the book, holds our attention. Readers are made to feel what it must have been like to arrive in New Orleans, to travel up the Mississippi, and to go into a wilderness which would only slowly be developed into the particular monastery in the hills of Kentucky which Merton knew so well.

The concluding essay, "Paradisus Claustralis," is a consideration of Cistercian common life. In it Merton celebrates a life which he personally felt to be almost intoxicating, because as he clearly demonstrates the paradoxical life of monks is a life wherein love of God and others demands self-effacement, but it also brings a peace unknown under any other circumstances. *The Waters of Siloe* provides,

therefore, in addition to an overview of the history of the development of the Trappists, Merton's unique meditation on some of
the basic mysteries of the contemplative life.

Yet for an artist with a mind and heart as active as Merton's,
such a straightforward method only reveals one facet of his interests.
Questions about his own inner struggles, and about what it meant
for him to be a monk, had to be recorded in another manner; his
journal *The Sign of Jonas* offers the best evidence of this fact for this
same period, and it is also perhaps the best way to understand
Merton as a writer during these years. The very title suggests the
fundamental paradox which he felt about his developing career as
writer *and* contemplative. Such personal writing allows Merton a
method which reflects personal doubts, questions, and investigations. In such a journal we also see his doubts about how best to
write. The subject matter for *The Sign of Jonas*, therefore, might be
described as a short history in the life of just one Cistercian.

In *Jonas*, Merton provides a specific record of his development as
a monk, as priest, and as writer for the period from December 1946
to July 1952. The book is deceptively simple in outline, but just
as with *The Seven Storey Mountain*, examination proves it to be rather
carefully orchestrated. These journal entries document Merton's
success as a monk at Gethsemani and show him examining the issues
(literary, historical, contemporary, personal) that he finds of value
in his developing spiritual life. Like Jonas in the belly of the whale,
he saw his life formed by divine providence, but as a writer it
seemed almost a duty to chronicle that mystery in as much detail
as possible. Merton's task as artist became one of organizing a
personal history that was faithful to his actual experiences, but which
also emphasized God's providence and the mystery of an encounter
with God—rather than just a particular writer-monk's actions,
thoughts, and meditations.

The Sign of Jonas is arranged in eight basic parts. Its six major
divisions are united by prologue and epilogue. Part 1 begins exactly
five years after Merton had come to the abbey—toward the end of
the period of simple vows and as he "was making up [his] mind to
take solemn vows and stay in the monastery for good."[2] Subsequent
sections are about the steps taken toward ordination, and the first
years as a priest. Merton also records his personal loneliness and the
spiritual aridity he experienced in 1949 and 1950. The final major
portion of the journal covers a longer time period than any of the

others. In that concluding division Merton suggests how he had found a new kind of spiritual peace during the Christmas season of 1950. The excerpts chosen for the remaining eighteen months or so reflect that newfound peace.

This journal succeeds as a work of art because Merton allows the reader to glimpse the difficulties which the author experienced; a tension is usually apparent, but the writer does not linger with particulars which were especially disturbing to him. Above all, the monk-writer demonstrates that he had to learn to accept appointed tasks as they were given to him. Ultimately the reader comes to perceive that perhaps this writer would never fully understand why he was asked, under the special circumstances of a cloistered life at Gethsemani, to be a writer. *The Sign of Jonas* is especially valuable therefore because, in addition to being a record of Merton's activities during years of preparation for the priesthood and just after, it also treats (sometimes indirectly) the question of literary vocation.

It is clear from his journal entries that he remained ambitious about being a good writer. In *Jonas* he indicates he was dissatisfied with his biography about Mother Berkmans because it seemed too verbose:

I have no objection, I know that I talk too much. It is a vice Cistercian writers have—at least modern Cistercian writers. It means that we do not really know the meaning of silence and that we have not discovered the secret of the contemplative life. (*SiJ*, 54)

It is also clear that Merton admires other writers; without a doubt he too wants to write well. Perhaps the fact that he included such references within the published journal indicates that he felt he had not attained the level of artistic proficiency he desired. References to T. S. Eliot, Rilke, and Dylan Thomas are typical of his self-criticism.

The Sign of Jonas is in some ways a curious book, mainly because it is so clearly the work of a writer. Merton uses the journal form as a way of demonstrating that he has definitely found his vocation as contemplative, without however ceasing to be concerned about his responsibilities as writer. The result is a journal which documents how he found his way toward God through the writing.

There are many levels of concern in *Jonas*. Merton indicates that any writer can focus on different levels of reality; and one of the more important facts of *The Sign of Jonas* is how it reveals this writer sorting out possibilities. Sometimes this is implicit (by the materials included) and sometimes it is explicit. For instance, Merton describes three levels of depth and concern: "the slightly troubled surface of the sea . . ."; "the darkness that comes when I close my eyes . . ."; "[the] positive life swimming in the rich darkness which is no longer thick like water but pure, like air." He noted that at this stage in his life God seems to intend for him to write about the second level, not the first: "I abandon all problems to their own unsatisfactory solutions: including the problem of 'monastic spirituality.' . . . God in me is not measured by your ascetic theory and God in you is not to be weighed in the scales of my doctrine. Indeed He is not to be weighed at all" (*SiJ*, 338–39). *Jonas* focuses on the second level, the depth of darkness that comes when one closes one's eyes to troubles apparent on the surface and this can be seen in the epilogue "Fire Watch, July 4, 1952." In that elaborate prose-poem Merton demonstrates how he felt as he performed the night watch; details about walking from room to room in the monastery suggest the power of God's presence in ordinary things.

The Sign of Jonas is, perhaps most important, Merton's journal of acceptance of a dual vocation, priest and poet, contemplative and writer. It is the record of someone who was gradually coming to the realization that he never had been in control of his life as he moved toward Gethsemani and as he lived there; ironically, he realized, he would never be in control of such a deep mystery. His vocation was to accept what God asked him to do; and what that meant was that he accept the job of writing. The result, however, is that as we encounter both *The Waters of Siloe* and *Jonas,* it is as if there are two completely different facets to the emerging man of letters, Father Louis. One is the man of "projects" who will write successful books, mostly retrospective ones, such as *The Seven Storey Mountain* and *The Waters of Siloe;* the other is a much more private and imaginative Merton who continues to look, question, and wonder—more often than not about himself; he becomes his principal subject. Such is the Merton of *The Sign of Jonas.* This does not mean that he is writing about his personality; it means paradoxically he has to learn to efface himself—at least in some ways—by writing about himself.[3]

Reflections for Others

Two distinct varieties of writing flowed from Merton's pen during this period. On the one hand, he wrote historical studies such as *The Waters of Siloe* and biographies of important Cistercian figures. On the other, he produced much more personal work, such as *The Sign of Jonas,* and meditations about the spiritual life which grew out of his own experiences. Both varieties of writing proved of use for those outside the monastery. As noted, Merton himself retained a rather low opinion of some of the books which he had written, more or less on command, about Cistercian religious figures; yet, interestingly, examination of these books demonstrates his skill as a writer. The fact is that such books, produced because of the vow of obedience, are successful, especially so if we recognize them as growing out of the special circumstances which nurtured Merton at this time. Two books about religious figures written early in this period are *Exile Ends in Glory,* the life of Mother Berkmans, published in 1947, and *What Are These Wounds?,* a life of St. Lutgarte of Aywieres, published in 1950. While Merton himself later had little patience with these books, they do possess intrinsic value, and placed in the proper context they help us to understand the development of his career. These studies are within the traditional genre of lives of saints; yet Merton sought to word them so that they would speak to modern readers. His figures provide models for emulation; through their lives connections are drawn with the present moment.

Mother Berkmans was a nineteenth-century woman called to be a Cistercian nun; born into France of the 1880s, she was raised in an orphanage in Lyons. As a young woman she entered a Trappistine convent at Laval, but that sheltered life soon led to a convent in Japan where she was destined to spend the rest of her life. *Exile Ends in Glory* was published in 1947, and the preface says much about Merton's attitude toward the project. Just as with *Siloe,* and indeed his own journal, he saw this story of a nun's "exile" in Japan as part of a larger continuity.[4] He explains that he feels it is significant that he began this book just as a group of monks were leaving Gethsemani in 1944 to establish a new house near Conyers, Georgia; and as he was putting the finishing touches on the manuscript, still another group of men left Gethsemani for a new monastery in Utah. The story of Mother Berkmans's goodness, devotion, avid interest in the life of St. Thérèse of the child Jesus, self-effacing work in her convent, and finally sickness and death are chronicled within Merton's narrative. It should especially be noted that the book about Mother Berkmans is largely organized around Merton's successful incorporation of passages from her own letters and journal. He lets her words speak. What emerges because of his (editorial) control of the material, which could have easily seemed sentimental, is a picture of a saintly woman who was also in many ways an ordinary person. The implication is that others can choose to be like her.

The other book, *What Are These Wounds?*, about the mystic Saint Lutgarde, can hardly be said to be about an "ordinary" person, yet as Merton indicates in the preface to this book Lutgarde's appeal is in the reality of her life:

The charm of St. Lutgarde is heightened by a certain earthy simplicity which has been preserved for us unspoiled in the pages of her medieval biography. She was a great penitent, but she was anything but a fragile wraith of a person. Lutgarde, for all her ardent and ethereal mysticism, remained always a living human being of flesh and bone.[5]

Merton's study of St. Lutgarde was first undertaken at the wish of the abbot of Gethsemani as an anonymous pamphlet in 1945. There was at that time no English translation of the standard work about her life written in the fifteenth century. The project eventually developed into a full-length book, and *What Are These Wounds?* finally appeared in 1950. More than likely it would ordinarily have been published anonymously, but the publisher wanted to make use of the then famous name of its author. Merton's comments in his preface, again, indicate much about his basic attitude toward the book and his hopes that it inspire others. St. Lutgarde's life is a model for that side of life associated in Cistercian monasteries with penance and separation. He insists that his readers understand, however, that "the love that embraces penance and hardship for the sake of Christ is never merely negative. . . . The fire of love that consumed the heart of St. Lutgarde was something vital and positive. . . . It was this love that Christ came to cast upon the earth and which Dom Frederic [Dunne] did so much to enkindle in the Cistercian . . . monasteries of America." Merton importantly insists that his admittedly pious chronicle must be seen as part of a continuity which lives down to the present moment. The same thing must be said of his book *Seeds of Contemplation* (1949), a collection of reflections about the inner life which he wrote during the same period. In the two biographies as well as in *Seeds of Contemplation* we again see that Merton could produce two quite different kinds of books.

In *Seeds* Merton stresses that basic Christian insights cannot change, yet this is an altogether different book than his "authorized" biography of a medieval figure. Significantly, within the revised version of *Seeds of Contemplation* he made the point that he certainly never intended for the book "to be popular." It was immensely so. He also noted that he realized that some readers had been misled, and that such a book "can easily be misunderstood."[6] What he stressed was that all seeds had to be nurtured within a contemplative way of life which allowed them to grow. He implied that aspects of life in the monastery might be adapted to secular life.

If the success of *Seeds of Contemplation* was somewhat surprising to Merton, we can now understand why a book like this was successful, for when it was published his name was recognized as that of a famous writer because of *Seven Storey Mountain*. Merton knew that being on the best-seller lists hardly made him an expert on the spiritual life, and he cautioned his readers, "Above all, remember that in this book the author is talking about spiritual things from the points of view of experience rather than in the concise terms of dogmatic theology or of metaphysics. . . . Many of the things said in this book could be said much better by somebody else, and have been said better already by the saints. The author has tried to say them in the language of the men of our time . . . (*SC*, 7–8).

The well-known author of *The Seven Storey Mountain* could maintain that "this is the kind of book that writes itself almost automatically in a monastery" (*SC*, 8), but many of his readers realized, of course, that this was very much Merton's book. These meditations provided an avenue for the reflective and meditative side of Merton to flourish. Thus while he might maintain that the book's commercial success was surprising to him, we understand that it contained all of the elements which would work to its success. Somewhat predictable perhaps, it is a book which grew out of years of thinking and meditation. Merton's comments about subjects as diverse as faith, tradition, understanding, renunciation, and contemplation appear throughout the book; yet what binds these parts into a whole is Merton's careful use of metaphor and examples so that the reader's attention is held. It must be noted, though, that Merton was not particularly satisfied with the book because it seemed to be almost too introspective, and worse, even smug. His comments in the revised edition indicate this, and thus a dozen years later, in 1962, a completely different version of the book was published.

New Seeds of Contemplation is not a new edition of the preceding book even though it retains "the full substance of the former work."[7] It is rather a broader consideration of the same ideas. In contrast to the earlier book, the new volume shows Father Louis's developing skill as a writer who continued to combine personal reflection along with an expanding awareness of the world. While abandoning little of the first book, the perspective of *New Seeds* is much wider and contrasts with the earlier version in many ways.[8] The fact that titles were changed to provide a different emphasis is significant; even more important are the many sections added which change the tone of the book as a whole. Whereas the earlier book seemed to grow out of an isolated monastic experience, in the expanded version there are many more conscious connections between monastery and world. The opening chapters of *New Seeds* are especially important, since they reflect change in emphasis which the writer incorporates throughout the entire book. Sometimes this is done by a simple rearrangement of chapters, or through the addition of a new chapter heading, but usually the change in emphasis is achieved through the addition of new material.

Perhaps the principal difference between these two books is to be found in the way Merton added material for the later version to reflect his concern for a lonely and troubled world. Two important facets of Merton's personality are reflected in both versions of the book, but the contemplative who could turn away from the world is more prominent in the first. The Merton who saw a responsibility for the world (if not in it) is much more clearly reflected throughout *New Seeds*. While *Seeds of Contemplation* is a valuable guide to the spiritual life, *New Seeds* is that as well as a demonstration of connections which must be made between man's spiritual life and life in the world. Thus a chapter which was at first called "We Are One Man" is retitled "Union and Division," and in the rewritten version Merton seems more aware of the fact that modern life can so easily separate men from each other. Following this part of the book Merton also added material about solitude, and especially its need today "when the collectivity tends more and more to swallow up the person in its shapeless and faceless wars" (*NS*, 53).

The chapter "Humility Against Despair" is also representative of the kinds of expansion and revision which went into the new version. Merton's decision to add to this part of the book reflects his concern for the dilemma of modern men who can so easily fall into despair; the writer reminds us that "in every man there is hidden some root of despair because in every man there is pride that vegetates and springs weeds and rank flowers of self-pity as soon as our own resources fail us" (*NS*, 180). He reminds his readers that they need not rely solely on their own resources. Despair comes because man tries to stand alone; yet man cannot stand alone, and humility allows him to realize this. Humility, then, is the answer: "the surest sign of strength" (*NS*, 190). And with humility, Merton is convinced, man also learns that he must be subject to suffering before he becomes a contemplative: "Contemplative experience is not arrived at by the accumulation of grandiose thoughts and visions. . . . It is a pure gift of God" (*NS*, 185). To receive that gift, Merton reminds us, we have to contemplate the fact that we should not try to be a success alone.

The concluding chapter of *New Seeds* is a further indication of basic changes which Merton has brought to the entire book. He added a section called "The General Dance," a meditation about man's need to enter into the harmony of the universe. There he makes clear that he realized he can give readers only hints about how to move closer to God; ultimately "the presence of God in His world as its Creator depends on no one but Him" (*NS*, 295). But Merton also realizes that if we truly believe in the Incarnation, we must be prepared to see the mystery and presence of Christ in *all* persons. Man finally has to accept the fact that he will never completely "understand" the glory of God; yet Merton insists in the new concluding chapter of *New Seeds* that trivial concerns of individual human persons have little bearing on life itself: "No despair of ours can alter the reality of things, or stain the joy of the cosmic dance which is always there" (*NS*, 297). Merton stresses that we must learn to forget ourselves on purpose. Ultimately, this is the direction of his entire literary career, because it was the combination of Merton's gifts as an artist and his love of the contemplative life which allowed him to pursue his dual career. The next book to be discussed within this chapter, written approximately midway between these two quite different versions of *Seeds of Contemplation*, helps us to see how his own life in the monastery, but also thinking and writing about it, assisted Thomas Merton/Father Louis to develop as he did.

Reflections about the Psalms

Father Louis wrote no more pivotal book during this middle period than *Bread in the Wilderness*. It is a defense of, a meditation on, and praise of, the Psalms. This book is of significance for several reasons. It helps us to see why Merton remained so interested in basic questions about life in a monastery, a life centered around prayer, and prayer based specifically on the Psalms. Also, this book helps us, again, to understand that monastic life is experienced as part of a living continuity. Still more, it reveals Merton's understanding of the Psalter as a fundamentally unifying force in the life of both monastery and church, and also within his own imagination.

The essays of *Bread in the Wilderness* constitute a meditation on the Psalms and their use in a monastery, always as tied in with the life of individuals day by day. Still another function of this group of essays is as a defense of the Psalms as poetry, and a statement of man's need for such poetry. As had been indicated, by the time *Figures for An Apocalypse* was published Merton found it difficult to synthesize questions about poetry and contemplation. Here he stresses that the Psalms are (as texts, and as sung in the choir) a means of literally leading us back to Paradise. They so function because they are themselves a kind of Paradise. Through such assertions Merton means that love of God is not merely suggested, but communicated to us through these very poems: "The Mystery of the Psalter is above all the mystery of God's will: the history of Israel is a history of trial and suffering not so much because of the enemies of God's people, still less because Israel was forsaken by God, but because, of all things, Israel kept forsaking God by disobeying His will and mistrusting His Providence."[9] Through the Redeemer the prevarication of the chosen people is answered, and its problems, the problems of all men—both in and outside the monastery—are solved. Thus through the use of the Psalms the Christian can be assured that he will be delivered.

Merton assures us that there is nothing mysterious about the use of the Psalms in a monastery. He insists, in fact, that the mythical opposition between "liturgical prayer" and "contemplative experience" . . . was unknown to the Fathers [of the Church]. For them "liturgy" and "contemplation" blended in a spontaneous harmony since both were expressions of the basic need for God and both contributed to the fulfillment of that need. For after all "liturgy" turns into "contemplation" as soon as our prayer ceases to be a search for God and turns into a celebration by interior experience. . . . (*BW*, 6)

A real value of *Bread in the Wilderness* is that it once more exhibits two sides of Merton: the writer who was analytical and observant, and the monk who was drawing sustenance from the living atmosphere of his choir. Thus Merton leads his reader to an appreciation of the Psalms, yet he also acknowledges these are only "steps to contemplation." All of this is to say man needs poetry (and it is not going too far to say that Merton is here working out a justification for poetry, and, indeed, also for the making of new poems). *Bread in the Wilderness* is therefore a consideration of the beauty of the Psalms as both poetry and prayer. This analysis of the significance of the Psalms suggests how Merton personally came to justify his own need for prayer and poetry. Through these essays we see clearly how Father Louis's appreciation of the Psalms helped to both refine an aesthetic sense and extend his appreciation of what it meant to be part of a contemplative tradition.

Through a careful reading of *Bread in the Wilderness* we come to appreciate several things about the development of Merton's career (literary and spiritual); we also see that he was building still more links with the world. An appreciation of the Psalms might reinforce anyone's prayer, he suggests. The Psalms are at the center of the contemplative life of the monastery and appreciation of what they provide could be of benefit to anyone. In the essay "The Problem: Contemplation in the Liturgy" Merton outlines how a genuine praying of the Psalms leads to finding God. It is not, he urges, a matter of the monk's life being a matter of obligations, so that the Psalms are chanted only out of a sense of duty; on the contrary, the vigorous obligations of life in a monastery, which include regularly chanting the Psalms, exist for the sake of the monk. It is like the difference, he says, between praying and saying prayers. The reason for anyone being a monk is not to say prayers, but rather to pray. Praying is something which should come naturally. Real appreciation of the Psalms could, he argues, be bread for anyone who finds himself in wilderness.

While it may be somewhat of an exaggeration, we can assert that during this period something analogous was surely happening to Merton the writer. As we saw in our survey of many of the entries in *The Sign of Jonas*, Merton had earlier sought to *be* a writer out of a sense of duty; eventually he came to learn and accept the simple fact that part of his life included the act of writing. Disciplined and regular use of language brought him closer to what he realized was most important. For Merton this could occur within the choir as the Psalms themselves permeated his life, or outside the choir because of the rhythm of a community life which naturally included writing.

Solitude and Community

To be part of a community and yet to be alone is a theme sounded in many of the books which Merton wrote; and it is this idea which unites all of the books considered in this chapter, whether objective like the histories or subjective like the meditations. The very title *No Man Is An Island* implies what Merton continued to emphasize, while of course he stressed that to find out how one is united to others, each person must first find himself. In terms of Merton's career we have seen that he could write history or biography, and, as well, how he could produce successful meditations; yet he also realized that the significance of this versatility remained rather theoretical since ultimately what was important was confronting one's true self. His inquiry, *Thoughts in Solitude*, therefore stands as a qualification of some of the points emphasized in earlier books.

Examination of *No Man Is An Island* can profitably be done in conjunction with *Thoughts in Solitude* because the two books (like other pairs studied in this chapter) complement each other. They stand, again, as examples of two concerns within this writer, and are quite different in tone and effect. *No Man Is An Island* (1955) functions as a kind of sequel to *Seeds of Contemplation*, and in some ways is even more fundamental. It consists of meditations in the traditional Christian mode about the spiritual life while stressing man's relation to his fellowman. Merton reminded readers that: "We gain only what we give up, and if we give up everything we gain everything. We cannot find ourselves within ourselves, but only in others, yet at the same time before we can go out to others we must first find ourselves. We must forget ourselves to become truly conscious of who we are."[10] The themes stressed in *No Man*

Is An Island are those of love, not just of God, but of others; hope, not just for one's self, but for others; the effect of persons and events, not just on one's self, but upon all: "To live exclusively for myself, I must make all things bend themselves to my will as if I were a god. But this is impossible" (*NM*, 24). This is a book, therefore, about giving, sharing, speaking the truth, and acceptance. In *No Man Is An Island* Merton provides meditations about these fundamental spiritual questions. His tone stresses man's basic needs. Thus the essay "Sincerity" deals with the need to strip away all forms of hypocrisy, and in the chapter that follows, entitled "Mercy," Merton stresses that God left sin in the world in order that there be forgiveness, yet there can only be forgiveness of others if we choose to act.

No Man Is An Island is a useful book, yet it is often a theoretical consideration of basic questions about the spiritual life; Merton has obviously worked to filter out his personality. A much more personal step in his understanding of himself, as well as of the contemplative tradition, is his book *Thoughts in Solitude* (1956), a collection of notes written in 1953 and 1954. In Merton's words these "notes" are "not a recipe for hermits."[11] What he has to say "has a bearing on the whole future of man and of his world" (*TS* 14). What he sought to clarify for readers is the fact that only with an increase of solitude was he himself able to appreciate certain aspects of the spiritual life. His implication is that in a world where so much emphasis has traditionally been placed on the "reality" of what can be seen and measured, Merton must now make us aware of the value of the valueless, the desert.

A basic lesson he seeks to teach in *Thoughts in Solitude* is that we must come to know our own "nothingness"; in fact, that very nothingness is good. It is a "positive entity since it comes from God." He goes on to say a "proud man loves his own illusion and self-sufficiency. The spiritually poor man loves his very insufficiency. The proud man claims honor for having what no one else has. The humble man begs for a share in what everybody else has received. He too desires to be filled to overflowing with the kindness and mercy of God" (*TS,* 44–45). But to come to such a realization it is first necessary for men to realize that they are not self-sufficient. Merton thus reminds his readers that

The spiritual life is first of all a *life.*

It is not merely something to be known and studied, it is to be lived. Like all life, it grows sick and dies when it is uprooted from its proper element. (*TS*, 46)

It is therefore fundamental for man to be alone in his nothingness before God. Merton reminds us through these solitary meditations that if man is to cultivate a spiritual life at all, then the only way for him to do so is to crucify his own life; or as he puts it, "The solution of the problem of life is life itself" (*TS*, 78). But real life begins when one can accept solitude.

Thoughts in Solitude is a book which functions like Thoreau's *Walden*. Its second main section, "The Love of Solitude," is a meditation on the fact that man can begin to live when he accepts his own solitude. This is like Thoreau saying that man must not be encumbered, yet Merton stresses that encumbrance is not merely a matter of external surroundings. It is a matter of attitude, a question of the individual realizing his "inalienable solitude" and seeing "that he will never be anything but solitary." *Thoughts in Solitude* comes alive because throughout it Merton lets these meditations grow out of his personal experience, and the joy which he derived from being alone. Thus he reminds us that it is only through silence that man can come to respect language (*TS*, 114); and it is only through the silence of God, not just in ourselves but also when respected in others, that we become aware of our developing relationship to others (*TS*, 88). Merton urges that "a man knows when he has found his vocation when he stops thinking about how to live and begins to live" (*TS*, 87). If we spend too much time thinking, then perhaps we have not yet found our true vocation—which is to confront ourselves. When we can be at ease in solitude with ourselves, then we have begun to live. Once again, such insights provide evidence about the way Merton himself was developing, as a solitary monk, as an artist, and even more important as a compassionate man.

"Existential Communion"

As a further example of Merton's continuing ability to write books which reached out to ever wider audiences, this final section considers two other volumes which might at first be seen to have little in common. One is about the sacrament of the Eucharist; the other is about man's need to find his true identity. Interestingly however, Merton's working title for the second book was "Existential

Communion."[12] Both of these collections of essays are evidence of Merton's increasing focus on connections which the contemplative could make with the world—connections which reflection, meditation, and contemplation necessitated. These two books demonstrate his conviction that theory divorced from the context of a living situation is of little value.

Each of these books reveals deeper levels of Merton's concern about contemporary man. *The Living Bread* was published in 1956; *The New Man* appeared five years later. Both studies might be described as treatises on traditional aspects of Christianity in the modern world; both are much more than this because they exhibit the writer's gift for taking the traditional and phrasing it in a way capable of holding the attention of a contemporary audience. Belief remains crucial; one is reminded of Flannery O'Connor when she wrote about the Eucharist: if it is only a symbol then to hell with it![13] In the prologue for *The Living Bread* Merton emphasizes his own realization that men pray because they believe they might become men of prayer and also that they "may become men of charity, peacemakers in the world, mediators between God and men, instruments of the divine priesthood. . . ."[14] Merton reiterates themes treated in other books discussed in this chapter, and he again reminds man that too often he attempts to be self-sufficient. He then stresses that contemporary man must somehow learn to share. Merton reminds his readers that materialism has not provided answers, for materialism tends only to separate man still further from other men. Mass-societies which promise a better life, but forget spiritual aspects, are likewise doomed. He believes that the Eucharist could help man to satisfy many of his most basic needs. He writes:

The meal of a Christian family is not so much a mere satisfaction of bodily needs as the celebration of a mystery of charity, the mystery of the Christian home. . . . It is Christ who feeds those present and brings them all the other blessings without which life would be impossible. . . .

[But in] our day . . . the individualism of the bourgeois nineteenth century has corrupted its way into totalitarian submersion of the individual in the masses, this healthy natural consciousness of the convivium—the sharing of a common life and interests by a small group . . . has yielded to the vast, amorphous anonymity of the mass meeting. . . . Men are not asked to contribute anything but servile conformity. . . . What is true of the totalitarian states is true to a lesser degree, but true, nevertheless, of the great capitalist democracies. . . . (*LB*, 127–28)

It is in just such circumstances that the continuing mystery of man's need to share, and the sacrament of the Eucharist, might well be recognized. Merton stresses that men need to be reminded that their lives are to give *and* to share, not to be malformed and distorted because of external pressures. While his fundamental theme in this book is the traditional sacramental one, we see Merton emphasizing this in terms of the contemporary world's needs. Men are what they are; but he points out (through books like *The Sign of Jonas, New Seeds of Contemplation, Thoughts in Solitude,* and *The Living Bread*) that men are not able to admit they have become strangers, even to themselves. Merton stresses that outward identity is not genuine identity. Outward identity is caught up in an individualism which has forgotten about sharing.

The Living Bread is a traditional explanation of the sacrament of the Eucharist, but Merton is aware that if that book is to be effective he must make his points clear for those who live within a system of alienation and distortion. He does this by maintaining a double focus: one theme stresses traditional beliefs fundamental to the church, another stresses the divided and selfish actions of men as they attempt to live without sharing. *The New Man* is an extension of many of these ideas, while at the same time being considerably broader in theme because it is a conscious step to evaluate the drift of all Western culture.

In *The New Man* (1961) Merton takes as his basic concern contemporary man's spiritual identity, and by examining what seems to have gone wrong with Western man and a society, he traces what makes it so difficult to confront one's true self. *The New Man* charts mankind's fall and his redemption in Christ. It is a series of meditations wherein Merton outlines Western man's fatal insistence on emphasizing—overvaluing—the false self. Hence the book is important as a study about identity and false identity; while it too is conventional in its theological framework, it is an essential step forward in Merton's investigation of modern man's inauthenticity.

Merton wants his reader to realize that man has been called out of darkness, but that is no easy lesson to learn. Merton has to remind man who seems to be built in the image of Prometheus that to learn such a lesson one must first admit one's nothingness; to live through such a dark night means men must have hope in things other than themselves. Merton's job in this book is to find images to which contemporary man will attend. He reminds men that what is wrong is that unknowingly they are at war with themselves. Men do not want to recognize that they cannot be self-sufficient.

Merton's chapter, "Promethean Theology," outlines what he believes is wrong with Western man. Also noteworthy is the fact that in this opening for the series of essays which make up *The New Man,* Merton was, as well, working out ideas which he perfected in other more poetic forms elsewhere. Many of the ideas of this book are developed in prose-poems published in *The Behavior of Titans* (1961).[15] Other ideas examined in these essays (just as in *Jonas, Bread in the Wilderness, Thoughts in Solitude*) are sketches for the poems and literary essays which will follow in books such as *Raids on the Unspeakable.*

Merton's theme in *The New Man* is that man has been redeemed, and that he must not make the mistake of trusting in illusions that he himself or society will provide redemption. Man has to realize that by pride he is cut off from God, and cut off from others. From a spiritual point of view it is therefore a

disaster for a man to rest content with his exterior identity, with his passport picture of himself. Is his life merely in his fingerprints? Does he really exist because his name has been inscribed in Who's Who? Is his picture in the Sunday paper any safe indication that he is not a zombie? If that is who he thinks he is, then he is already done for, because he is no longer alive, even though he may seem to exist.[16]

In *The New Man* Merton seeks ways to bring his readers out of such darkness. Of course, he realizes that much in modern society makes it difficult even to admit that man experiences any lack of light.[17]

In the group of eleven books considered in this chapter we see Father Louis/Thomas Merton gradually developing a more outspoken means of warning mankind about complacency and self-satisfaction. In the earliest group of books Merton's focus tended to be on the past, or on reflections about his spiritual problems and exercises: as he matures he becomes much more interested in how what he has learned should be applied to an understanding of the culture as a whole. The key to his growth seems to be that he becomes increasingly aware of the importance of individuals and of the dangers of mass thinking.

Chapter Five
Middle Years and Decisions

As for the liar, fear him less
Then one who thinks himself sincere,
Who, having deceived himself,
Can deceive you with a good conscience.
Sincerity

Poetry and Contemplation

As we survey different aspects of Merton's writing it might seem almost as if he were conducting several different careers at once. One part of him seems to be quietly writing books about meditation for consumption outside the monastery; another part continues to ask questions about the relationship between the spiritual life and the forces which generate poetry; and yet another part of the writer is becoming more actively engaged in raising questions about the church and the world. Through his work as teacher, as master of novices, and as correspondent with many people throughout the world, Father Louis obviously was continuing to look for ways to clarify his own questions about what it meant to be both a monk *and* poet in the modern world. Yet this is not as complicated as it appears, for he definitely saw his life not as divided into parts, but rather as a whole.

The progression within some of the better known prose works provided in the preceding chapter has suggested that unity; in the examination of poetry which follows we shall see how Merton was coming to write verse with a changed focus but poetry in which each stage built on preceding accomplishments. Just as he advised in his prose that man has to get beyond asking questions about how to live so that he can live—that one has to forget self to find self— we see him in his own poetry gradually ceasing to ask questions about how to analyze the world, while he is learning more and more to celebrate aspects of it. Two versions of Merton's essay "Poetry and the Contemplative Life" illuminate his thinking about these issues as he moved toward a resolution of apparent problems of being writer and contemplative. The first version of the essay "Poetry and the Contemplative Life," published as the concluding pages of *Figures for an Apocalypse* (1947), demonstrates how at that time Merton, as a poet, considered himself to be in a serious dilemma. In that essay he systematically demonstrated that poetry, while perhaps often an aid toward contemplation, could also be a hindrance when it comes to the "actual sanctification" of an individual writer. He therefore announced it might be necessary for him to make a choice, "one which will only appal someone who does not realize the infinite distance between the gifts of nature and those of grace"; the contemplative may have to accept a *"ruthless and complete sacrifice of his art."*[1] Merton suggested that it may not be possible for a man to devote attention to both the art of poetry and to a vocation as a contemplative, and he concluded that while poetry can be a help in the movement toward active contemplation, unfortunately when "entering the realm of true contemplation" (109) it can stand as a barrier. If that should be the case, "there is only one course for [such a] poet to take to bring about his own individual satisfaction, *'ruthless and complete sacrifice.'* "

Merton ends the essay by formulating another problem: "What if one is morally certain that God wills him to continue writing anyway?" He implies that in his case he writes out of formal obedience, but he also realizes that there is wisdom in St. Thomas Aquinas's words, "it is more meritorious to share the fruits of contemplation with others than it is merely to enjoy them ourselves." Further, there is no doubt, argues Merton, that the poet is best able to communicate an idea about the "delights of contemplation," something "essentially inexpressible." Merton implies that it is in the light of such ideas that his own poetry could best be understood; yet he also wondered if he would be able to continue as a contemplative and write poetry. Such doubts account for the relatively small production of formal poetry in the decade which followed.

The "Reappraisal" of this dilemma, the same essay revised and published in *Commonweal* a decade later, is a qualification and correction of the earlier version. In his "Reappraisal" Merton explains that during a decade of activity as writer and teacher, he came to reconsider those earlier "confident pronouncements" and realized that it was time to correct and amend some of his "wrong-headed" assumptions. The revised essay emphasizes Merton's belief that it is not necessarily true that if one wants to be mystic or saint he must also give up art: "The most perfect choice is *the choice of what God has willed for us,* even though it may be, in itself, less perfect, and indeed less 'spiritual.' "[2] Merton uses the example of St. John of the Cross as someone whom God chose to remain *"at the same time a mystic and a poet."* The thrust of the revised essay suggests that "contemplation has much to offer poetry," but "poetry . . . has something to offer contemplation" as well. Merton's stress in the second version is therefore on the fact that it may not be an " 'either/ or' choice between 'art' and 'mystical prayer,' " and if a poet is a truly Christian one, he does have a duty to make the mystery of God known to man.

A Quieter Kind of Poetry

When the first version of Merton's essay about poetry and the contemplative life appeared ten years earlier, it was not yet clear how he might reconcile himself to writing. Accordingly, the poetry volume, *The Tears of Blind Lions* (1949), which followed just two years after *Figures for an Apocalypse,* contains yet another variety of poetry and reflects Merton's uncertainty about the utility of writing and publishing poems at this stage in his life. Despite this doubt the general mood of *The Tears of Blind Lions* is calmer than any of the preceding volumes.

Merton's epigram from Leon Bloy suggests much about this collection: "When those who love God try to talk about Him, their words are blind lions looking for springs in the desert."[3] He implies it is quite difficult for him to write of the contemplative life which he has come so to cherish. The opening poem, "Song," is built around water imagery, but this is a water of storm, tears, the water of this poet's interior struggle and disposition. Observers (even within a particular monastery) are unaware of the poet's private topography; they are separated from both his private struggles and his point of view. They, as well, can be seen only dimly, as through a pane of glass; finally one is all alone:

> . . . a glass begins to wrinkle with a multitude of water
> Till I no longer see their speech
> And they no longer know my theater.

> > *(T, 5)*

The presence of others is however of little import. Speaking with them would be of small value. More important is the realization that to be stripped is to see that one does not really need anything. This poem opens with the statement that all external support is gone: "When rain . . . has devoured my house . . . / Silence is louder than a cyclone." Yet because of this spiritual storm, the speaker finds it possible to live "on my own," and thereby also to speak to God: Surprisingly, it then becomes possible to

> Distinguish poems
> Boiling up out of the cold forest:
> Lift to the wind my eyes full of water,
> My face and mind, to take their free refreshment.
>
> (*T*, 5)

The tone of *The Tears of Blind Lions* is clearly established with this opening lyric, a poem which both celebrates the quiet of the contemplative life and stresses the difficulty of making poetry about such experience. If "silence is louder than a cyclone," then to find words to express such a fact does indeed seem to be an insurmountable task.

One way to suggest the contemplative experience is to attempt to be as specific as possible, and many of the poems in this slim collection are successful precisely because they build upon reference to the landscape observed around Gethsemani. Less successful ones are more contrived. "Hymn for the Feast of Duns Scotus," for example, begins with a description of the fields which surround "the borders of my world" (*T*, 6), but except for the opening, this poem remains abstract, even conventional, a hymn in admiration of Scotus's theology. Scotus "burns" the speaker "like a branding iron," and the poet travels toward God: "my life becomes Thy life and sails or rides like an express!" (*T*, 7). But this is almost too much—branding iron, and two modes of travel! By comparison, the impressionistic "In the Rain and the Sun" is very much alive and is less abstract. It is a song which comes from the paradoxical situation of being isolated: "my pen between my fingers / Making the waterworld sing" (*T*, 24). This lyric grows from Merton's own specific contemplation of rain and from the quiet which he experiences within his private place of meditation. He feels as if he is now in "the hap of a slippery harbor." All alone after a difficult voyage he seems to be close to paradise:

> . . . words fling wide the windows of their houses—
> Adam and Eve walk down my coast
> Praising the tears of the treasurer sun. . . .
>
> (*T*, 24)

This poem, or a poem like "Dry Places," are works which seem to have roots in specific experiences. "In the Rain and the Sun" is a plea for God to help the poet: "Sweet Christ, discover diamonds / And sapphires in my verse." "Dry Places" seems to refer to a specific place where iron was mined, and through this image the poet expresses his displeasure with inert materials. The controlling image is the abandoned mine (where "Judas' shadow dwells"). Opposed to such sterility is a life which is to be drawn from contact with the land, a poetry to be made from specific observation:

> Rather than starve with you in rocks without oasis,
> We will get up and work your loam
> Until some prayer or some lean sentence
> Bleeds like the quickest root they ever cut.
>
> (*T, 26*)

Through words, the speaker finds spiritual nourishment, but he reminds us that his nourishment comes not only through words. The speaker suggests that we are nurtured both through farming (nature) and by Christ's wounds (grace). Such nourishment comes unbidden, in unexpected ways. Thus in "In the Rain and the Sun" Merton meditates on his "Cistercian jungle," the enclosure where he has found peace. A similar image of hiddenness is also revealed in "A Psalm," proof of what Merton outlines in *Bread in the Wilderness:*

> When psalms surprise me with their music
> And antiphons turn to rum
> The Spirit sings: the bottom drops out of my soul. . . .

These words echo the Psalter, that form of communal prayer as experienced in a monastery.

Comparison of poems such as these just analyzed with earlier poems which build on specifics about life at Gethsemani demonstrates that this later Merton is more specific in focus. For instance, "The Trappist Abbey: Matins," in *Thirty Poems,* is a prayer and could only have grown out of a specific experience, yet it remains a somewhat self-conscious statement with its many plays on words, and its prudent allusions. It does not fully succeed in giving the feeling that the poet has experienced the peace about which he sings. Similarly, "Evening" of the first volume is related in mood to other early poems which grow out of Merton's enjoyment of the specific place, Gethsemani, but the poet seems to work very hard to stand back from what he observes. It is as though he feels he should not get involved. In the lyrics of *The Tears of Blind Lions* Merton seems to be much more willing to use his own experience; ironically that also means he cannot fully express what he means. Yet we sense through *Tears* that these are things about which he feels strongly. Thus he can write:

> Owning this view, in the air of a hermit's weather,
> I count the fragmentary rain
> In drops as blue as cold
> Until I plumb the shadows full of thunder.
> My prayers supervise the atmosphere. . . .
>
> (*T*, 23)

He is more present, yet paradoxically less self-consciously so.

This kind of writing also represents a tightening of technique that makes this collection stand apart from the abstractness of *Figures*. The lines also tend to be much shorter. It may be that the rhythms of the choir itself are having a good effect upon the way the poems sound.[4]

Through these poems, then, Merton's speaker hopes to suggest the wonder of a contemplative vocation. This is the underlying theme throughout the book, perhaps most obviously manifested in "The Quickening of St. John the Baptist," and "The Reader." Both of these poems help us to understand how during these years Merton was thinking about the contemplative vocation, and how he would write about it, while again it is significant that there are two sides to his picture. In his poem about John the Baptist the ideal of waiting for Christ is sung. A quite different lyric, "The Reader," is about the everyday world of Gethsemani—the atmosphere of the monk's refectory on an ordinary day. "The Reader" suggests the stark beauty of life in the monastery and the strength of the monks who follow that routine. What the reader does at his lectern ("Light fills my proper globe") is of small consequence, yet it is also part of a total harmony. Merton would have us know that the immediate is as important as any abstract ideal.

Some of the poems in this collection continue to be about an imagined world which has turned its back on God. "Christopher

Columbus," for example, is an unusual fantasy which suggests that history could have developed differently than it did. Merton raises the question, what if Columbus had accepted the new continent without trying to exploit it; what if all Americans had been truly Christian? (that is, both active and contemplative?). This poem, which imagines a true "Christopher," caused reviewers to raise their eyebrows because it seemed too fanciful, yet in its way it is a significant poem.[5] It reveals a poetic distancing from the secular world which was so condemned in much of Merton's earlier poetry, for example, as in the title poem in *Figures;* it also looks forward to the same themes in "The Tower of Babel" and to the subject matter of some of Merton's final essays, and even to the poems of *The Geography of Lograire.*[6]

Through lyrics about his own interior life and meditations about the contemplative life, as well as in poems which continue to lament the ways of a secular world, Merton suggests the wonder of what he is experiencing. Just as in previous volumes, the poet of *Tears* writes of a world which has turned its back on God, but in this rather quiet collection he apparently has become considerably less concerned with the fate of the world. This is the mood which generated the calmness of *The Sign of Jonas* and which is exemplified in "Senescente Mundo," the concluding poem of the collection. This poem unites themes which recur throughout the collection, both positive ones about the contemplative vocation, and negative ones which lament man's apparent choice of turning his back on God. Merton indicates that there is no doubt that ours is a "murderous season"; but he also knows that God will deliver us. This poem and the book concludes with a celebration of the mystery of the priesthood; yet, in terms of Merton's career as a writer, it is an allusion to his dual responsibility.

> . . . I hold that secret Easter.
> Tomorrow, this will be my Mass's answer
> Because of my companions whom the wilderness has eaten,
> Crying like Jonas in the belly of the whale. . . .
>
> (*T,* 32)

The Strange Islands

This collection represents seven additional years of poetic work and signals another subtle shift in attitude—mostly because the poet reflected in this collection now feels that he must express both his inward and outward concerns about the culture. Already a decade had passed since Merton had felt himself caught in an impasse when he felt threatened and wondered if it were possible to accommodate a contemplative life and poetic production. With the publication of this volume of poems Father Louis seems to have resolved that seeming contradiction. Now he will lead his reader to an appreciation of a quiet he knows while he will also emphatically write about a world with too little quiet, a world of Babel. *The Strange Islands* therefore reflects the two basic aspects of Merton's deepening concerns as a writer, but he now sees that he can draw his material from a wide range of concerns and that there is no contradiction in praising quiet and lamenting noise.

One of the significant facts about this collection is that it contains both formal poetry, such as the morality play which constitutes its middle section, and meditations about modern culture, as well as lyrics which are extremely personal. At least one of these poems might even have appeared in *The Tears of Blind Lions:* "Sports Without Blood—A Letter to Dylan Thomas (1948)." This poem reflects an earlier stage in Merton's life and his delivery from England's Cambridge where "The times have carried love away / And tides have swallowed charity."[7] This retrospective poem, however, is not an exception to the general pattern of the volume; on the contrary, it reflects a willingness to experiment with technique as early as 1948. Its almost surrealistic images seem to look beyond that earlier moment in his career.

Other poems in this 1957 collection, while thematically related to earlier poetry, possess a change in focus and reflect a concern more with the culture than with imagined people in the culture. The opening poem, "How to Enter a Big City," seems to be such a link. Merton's city is one which most people would probably not want to enter; it is a place of death and futile activity:

> . . . huge clouds all over the sky.
> River smells of gasoline.
> Cars after cars after cars, and then
> A little yellow street goes by without a murmur.
>
> (*SI,* 171)

In this directive about the sterility of large cities, even the wilderness of Kentucky has been changed by too much activity, commerce, and greed: "seas of flowering tobacco / Surround the drowning sons

of Daniel Boone." The second poem of the collection, "The Guns
of Fort Knox," represents still another unnatural disturbance in the
calm of rural Kentucky. The poet realizes that such noise is far from
right and he pleads for silence. He writes about an Army installation
located about twenty miles from Gethsemani; this poem works in
harmony with the one which immediately follows, called "Nocturne."
The third poem of the collection explores the idea that when night
(silence) comes, it "has a sea which quenches the machine / Or part
of it." Merton's arrangement of these three poems as the beginning
of the collection reveals a change in the general direction of his
poetic interests, and implies the basic concerns to be treated in the
collection. As poet, Merton is still clearly repulsed by aspects of
modern culture, especially the contortions of city and war, but he
is now certain that quiet is the answer to men's needs. In quiet of
night men can be made whole:

> Night has tides of rain
> And sources which go on
> Washing our houses when we turn to dream.
>
> (SI, 23)

This lyric foreshadows much of the later writing. Night; silence;
dream; abandonment to God's will—these bring mysterious changes
to lives which earlier could hardly be imagined. "Spring Storm"
suggests this idea; Merton seems to be learning that some things
will not be understood:

> How unsubstantial is our present state
> In the clean blowing of those elements
> Whose study is our problem and our fate?
>
> The intellects go mumbling in the snow. . . .
>
> (SI, 24)

A significant feature of the opening part of this collection and
something which sets it off from his preceding collections is Merton's
willingness to rely upon his own experiences, and even to use the
personal pronoun "I." "Where There is Enjoyment in Bitterness"
is therefore a poem in which the speaker asks to be allowed to
display a side of himself which may even be shocking to some readers.
Merton provides a study of how it might be to be trapped in

bitterness because of false hopes and expectations. Supporting patterns in many of these poems stress the speaker's insistence that to live well one must strip away whatever it is that distracts from the essentials of living. Merton's themes and the style which supports these themes might well be described as a respect for the clean and sparse. It is as if this poet is learning to strip away all ornamentation if it might seem to interfere with what is more important.

"Elias—Variations on a Theme" is an excellent example of this variety of poetry—a getting down to essentials. The poem may be the single most significant one in the collection. Its variations reiterate what is implied throughout: to hear the word of God one must listen to His quiet. Yet this is the single hardest lesson, especially for man who always seems to have something to which he must attend.

The second section of *The Strange Islands* is "A Morality," entitled "The Tower of Babel." For the most part ignored by reviewers, it is significant.[8] It illustrates Merton's desire to return to some of the thoughts which had concerned him in his earliest poetry; it is also another signal of the poet's change in attitude about the world, since it is less concerned with condemnation than with a compassion for man. The verse play contrasts the world as city of man with the city of God. Merton's theme again is that man's illusions must eventually collapse. In this book, and in Merton's career, the verse play seems to be a pivotal work; it looks back to early themes and forward to themes which will become of increasing importance. Above all, Merton concentrates on man's contortions of language which are related to his inordinate love of self. Some men never even realize that there is a city beyond this one because they have so buttressed their tower with illusions. More and more activity, more domination through fear and through artifice, makes it possible for man to have the illusion that he is controlling his destiny; yet all of this will fall as falsity and error finally eat away at the very structure man is trying to build. Men build a selfish city because they have turned their backs on God, yet those who look forward to the City of God seek truth, not their own advancement.

The play is divided into two main divisions. In part 1, "The Legend of the Tower," the opening scene is "The Building of the Tower." Apparent union of purpose is clothed in pride. And even the collapse of the endeavor to construct the tower does not give man pause to think. In Merton's version of Babel men continue by choosing to manipulate truth to their apparent advantage.

The second scene is "The trial." In it Merton reflects on how man distorts the word. Truth and Language are placed on trial; the leader of Babel asserts that he can make words mean whatever he wants them to mean. When Language bears witness to objective truth, Babel will have nothing to do with such facts. In the play Professor, Lawyer, and Philosopher all turn meaning around in the testimony which follows. Falsehood finally speaks: "I am your strength. Without me you fall. I will give you the only words that will serve your purpose" (SI, 61). Which is to say that men seem bent on their own destruction.

In the second half of the play Merton meditates upon the true nature of man. Part 2 is set in "The City of God," and scene 1 is the "Zodiac." Raphael, Thomas, a Prophet, and Children survey the place where once a city stood. Merton's Prophet speaks of the new city that will replace the one destroyed. In this scene mankind is depicted as wandering, lost, and exhausted. The question is how could such outcasts ever, again, become the children of God? For them to be at peace they must somehow realize what is eternal and what is changing. Scene 2, "The Exiles," stresses that for man to obtain peace he must come to the realization that his temporal city is an illusion. The play ends with a chorus (representative of the church) singing the praises of the Eternal Word.

Study of a draft version of this work, which was sent to Mark Van Doren, as well as Merton's own comments about the play, help us to see what he sought to accomplish. He obviously felt that his "morality" play spoke for all men, and especially to contemporary man who has put so much of his hope and energy into the things of the world—only to see them lost.[9] It is significant that Merton felt that a verse play would be an appropriate format in which to express his concern about his contemporary world. Basic is his uneasiness about man's abuse of language, an idea ever more important throughout the remainder of his career.[10] This same attitude is found in early poetry and with increasing frequency in essays produced toward the very end of his life. In the morality play Merton experiments with a method to encompass a meaning that includes both an historical view and his criticism of the contemporary to provide an overview of man's condition. (In some ways such broad concern resembles the view of man provided in Merton's last two books of poems. Both here, and in *Cables* and *The Geography of Lograire,* he attempts to stand back from the drift of all civilization.) In other parts of *The Strange Islands,* his method is less ambitious and more lyrical. Thus, in the concluding section of this volume the short poem "Sincerity" continues to carry related ideas forward, but in a much more concise manner. The poet writes:

> As for the liar, fear him less
> Than one who thinks himself sincere,
> Who, having deceived himself,
> Can deceive you with a good conscience.
>
> (*SI,* 95)

This speaker contrasts the liar's insincerity with the sincerity of God. Merton insists that man must come to recognize things as they really are. This is a basic idea stressed throughout the book—the fact that truth is always to be sought but can be perceived only if man can learn to look carefully, that is, if man can look beyond other men's twistings.

Other poems in *The Strange Islands* are occasional ones which grow out of the writer's personal experiences. "Early Mass (St. Joseph's Infirmary—Louisville)," "To a Severe Nun," and "Elegy for the Monastery Barn" all illustrate that Merton was continuing to develop his gift for finding poetry in places where perhaps others might not look. "Elegy for the Monastery Barn" is a poem which was sparked from seeing an old barn on the monastery grounds go up in flames. The poem's success derives from the fact that Merton is able to retain much of his own spontaneous feeling within it; he catches what happened, and then extends that meaning outward.

The barn in its last moment of splendor seems to call out to those who are watching; it becomes an alluring woman for whom the monks labored; but in its terrible flaming destruction it is also a sign of man's temptation to put too much store in the worldly. It too could be a tower signifying nothing. Beauty is stressed first; this is the initial image, but there is another observation, an unobserved side to this barn, "her solitude." Merton questions: when the moment of destruction came, "Who heard the peace downstairs?" The flames come bringing an end, but this was a sacrament, a reminder of the unity of all things to be consumed, lost, reunited.

Merton stresses that man should flee such beauty; yet it is a symbol of man's ambition and his fate.

> Let no man wait within and see the Holy
> One sitting in the presence of disaster
> Thinking upon this barn His gentle doom!
>   (*SI,* 100)

This barn is lost, but it becomes a symbol of life and man's ultimate deliverance. Its beauty is clearly something to celebrate, yet it also remains something of which we should be cautious.

Selections and Emblems

Merton's *Selected Poems* was published in 1959, and represents a significant moment for Merton as poet because it reflects his opinion about poems produced over a twenty-year period. The process of winnowing poems for a selection may have had the effect of assisting Merton in making more steps in the continuing synthesis that he was now accomplishing in his life. So many of his earlier poems must have seemed to him, in retrospect, the production of someone who had tried too hard to be a poet. By 1959 Merton had ceased to feel such a need; it was simply a matter of fact that he was one. This book therefore signals the end of a phase in his career. Only a few new poems were added beyond those which had already appeared in *The Strange Islands.*

Significantly, in the *Selected Poems* Merton chose to omit his longer, and harsher, poems about the world. Thus the title poem from *Figures for an Apocalypse* is omitted, and many poems which stress what seemed to be wrong with a world left behind are also omitted. Merton probably felt such a looking back was fruitless; the emphasis in poems which he did include is upon particular moments as experienced, not upon generalizations. Merton seems much more interested in short and lyrical works, poems which catch a particular insight. Merton also included the revised version of his essay "Poetry and the Contemplative Life," already discussed. He clearly wanted readers to realize that he had changed his mind; he now definitely felt that use could be made of poetry in the pursuit of God.

We can also see by the additions that were made that Merton felt that an ironic approach could be effective in some poems. His three new poems demonstrate such a change in mood. Thus, "A

Practical Program for Monks" is a humorous poem because it pokes fun at monastic practices; perhaps some "practical programs" are too much so![11] In an ironic way it drives home the point that the observation of externals, while important, is of only minor importance. Other poems, written still later in Merton's career, and included in *The Collected Poems,* such as "CHEE$E," spelled with a dollar sign, stand as evidence of his healthy sense of humor.

The new lyric, "Song: In the Shows of the Round Ox," is a witty treatment about man's insistence on having idols; the poet reminds us of life lost because of the desire to make money. Worth noting is the quiet tone, different than earlier, of the more outspoken poems of condemnation. We see reflected here a poet fascinated by the fact that men are lost in their idolatry; yet we also see a more tolerant and compassionate poet. The same must be said for the third new poem. It is called "An Elegy for Five Old Ladies" and has its basis in a news story: life lost because of a runaway automobile. The subject is a frightening one: but the manner of treatment remains gentle, kind, and compassionate. The perversity of the machine, and not the ignorance of persons lost because of the machine, is the subject. Each of these new poems reflects a change in Merton's manner of expressing his concern.

The 1950s was a period during which Merton had little time to write poetry, but, as we have seen, this did not mean that he ceased writing. As has already been observed in connection with Merton's meditative writing, and we will see in examination of essays about the world which follows, Merton was gradually moving into wider areas of interest, while he was also developing new ways of using language. During these years he was becoming acutely concerned with the state of contemporary society. An example of this is the prose-poem about the atomic bomb published in 1962. Entitled *Original Child Bomb,* it can be considered in connection with the changes in the pieces added to *Selected Poems.* Straightforward in method, this ironic poem is an indictment of contemporary man's misuse of both power and language.[12]

Original Child Bomb is about America's justification of its use of the bomb; this poem suggests that men seek ways to justify actions through the misuse of language, and it accomplishes this simply by enumerating the facts of what happened. The poem signals a change in method; and it serves as a kind of preface to the poetic production which follows wherein Merton sought to remind his readers of their habitual acceptance of untruth. In this poem about the bomb dropped on Japanese cities Merton seems to be stripping his poetic world clean of ornamentation so that man will see what did in fact occur. Genocide on the magnitude of Hiroshima, he stresses, can all too easily be forgotten, even explained away. This stark prose-poem is an example of Merton's reaching out toward a misguided world. Through the poem's horrible facts we are made to confront the fact of man's abuse of nature and language.

Emblems of a Season of Fury (1963) may strike some readers as a radical departure from Merton's earlier collections. However, in many ways it simply extends all the themes already established. The technique is sometimes experimental (but so was *Original Child Bomb*) and, just as during the years which follow we observe many connections between the prose-poetry of *The Behavior of Titans* and the published journal *Conjectures of a Guilty Bystander,* here too we see many connections between the writer's contemplative awareness and his analysis of the world. Merton as poet is also becoming more aware of his responsibilities to take a stand while he is building on writing accomplished in other literary areas. It is not surprising that some parts of this collection are prose. Also, given Merton's widening of view, it seems appropriate that the final large section of the volume is made up of his translations. It seems as if Merton's varied choice of format—lyrics, translations, prose—reflects a realization that if he is to write "in a season of fury" he must use various methods.

These poems sometimes employ the informal manner of the shorter lyrical poems which appeared in *The Strange Islands;* yet there is an element of anger in this volume altogether new. One of Merton's primary concerns seems to be to find ways to express his horror that modern man has become so destructive. A fundamental theme in the new book is man's apparent willingness to surrender to technology, coupled with a mad desire to hold possessions and manipulate others—the very things which hold him back. The gentle "An Elegy for Five Old Ladies," reprinted from *Selected Poems* and mentioned above, develops these themes. It is one of a group of poems which stresses man's loss of self because of his inadvertent embrace of things which he cannot control. A recognition of such a destructive situation is the basis of concern in several of these poems about a world where technology runs man, and not the reverse. "Why Some Look Up to Planets" also exemplifies the theme;

it is about man's race into space, and correspondingly his race away from himself. Man simply accepts what is given to him, yet he hardly knows what this means. He seems willing to consent to anything:

> What next device will fill the air with burning dollars
> Or else lay out the low down number of some Day
> What Day? May we consent?
> Consent to what? Nobody knows.
> Yet the computers are convinced
> Fed full of numbers by the True Believers. [13]

"Gloss on the Sin of Ixion" is a poem which develops the related theme of man's fascination with machinery. Similarly, the even-more frightening "Chant to Be Used in Processions Around a Site with Furnaces" makes us rethink the holocaust as it raises fundamental questions about how men accommodate themselves to the most appalling circumstances.

It is no accident that within this volume of "emblems" Merton included numerous elegies. The world he portrays was fast changing because of man's violence. "And the Children of Birmingham" is perhaps the most startling of these poems which deal with death. The horror of a fairy tale has become real: "the children of Birmingham / Walked into the story / Of Grandma's pointed teeth . . ." (*E,* 33). Other elegies are included—"for Ernest Hemingway" and "for James Thurber"—and complement poems which are about technology and man's brutalization of his fellowmen. Merton does not like what he sees; but he reports greater and greater struggles for money and power. He says as much in the prose meditation "A Letter to Pablo Antonia Cuadra Concerning Giants," also part of *Emblems,* and discussed below.

Emblems includes many poems that suggest a concern about the corruption of human innocence. "Grace's House," about a child's drawing, and "A Picture of Lee Ying" stress the natural goodness of people uncorrupted by human society. The poem called "Grace's House" celebrates a child's vision where everything is in order. [14] The poem about Lee Ying was occasioned by a news photograph of a nineteen-year-old refugee being returned to her native China from Hong Kong. It is a meditation on the fact that men have learned so easily to ignore real human problems. The poem is constructed to suggest a series of barely connected thoughts; Merton chooses to use no punctuation, as if we do not want to have a complete thought on such a subject:

Refugees from China have caused alarm

When the authorities are alarmed what can you do

You can return to China

Their alarm is worse than your sorrow

Please do not look only at the dark side in private life these are kind men

They are only obeying orders. . . .

(E, 21)

The implication is that such unfortunate things are constantly done by those who will not think through the implications of their own involvement; people not only surrender to technology—they surrender their wills to others; they live in false worlds because of their own fears. This idea can be connected with the beautiful poetic parable, also in this volume, about a girl supposedly changed by magic into a pony.

"Macarius and the Pony" gently tells us that *we* must be extremely careful in making judgments about others; the legendary townspeople of this poem learn that their daughter had not been changed at all:

> Your own eyes
> (Said Marcarius)
> Are your enemies.
> Your own crooked thoughts. . . .
>
> (*E*, 16)

This poem, based on Rufinus's *Historia Monachorum*, chapter 28, is characteristic of the most important single group in the collection. Here the anchorite, Marcarius, whose thoughts are not "crooked," speaks the truth, a truth like that which the child Grace senses, and for which Lee Ying clearly hopes. Through such poems Merton wants man to realize that truth has been clouded by frantic activities, by man's submission to technology, by the wishes of others, and by his own selfish desires. In another and contrasting group of poems Merton stresses man's need for an appreciation of what is essential. In the contrasting group he amplifies themes about solitude, simplicity, truth, and quiet. "Song for Nobody" and "Love Winter when the Plant says Nothing" remind us, as Merton does in so much of his prose of this period, that the first step toward unity is through self. To be quiet is to begin to be whole. Such poems are clearly central to this volume—especially since they contrast with the overt fury reflected in the title, as well as with the ironical poems already discussed. Observe "Night-flowering Cactus": the poet would have us know that truth and the true self are difficult to see; the metaphor of the hidden flower speaks:

> Though I show my true self only in the dark and to no man
> (For I appear by day as serpent)
> I belong neither to night nor day.
> Sun and city never see my deep white bell. . . .
>
> (*E*, 49–50)

"The Fall" functions in a similar manner: "He who has an address is lost. . . . Yet, to tell the truth, only the nameless are at home" (*E*, 53).

This kind of poem prepares us for the real centerpiece of this volume, a prose-poem entitled "Hagia Sophia." In it Merton meditates, as he does in *New Seeds of Contemplation, Thoughts in Solitude, The New Man,* and many other poems, on the mystery of God's presence in the universe. Man, however, is so busy with his personal thoughts and activities that he often fails to experience God's wisdom. In this meditation the poet stresses the fact that the Wisdom of God is present and in its silence even "cries out to all who will hear" (*E*, 62). It is a mystery, and we must trust to find it.

This prose-poem is arranged in four sections: "Dawn. The Hour of Lauds"; "Early Morning. The Hour of Praise"; "High Morning. The Hour of Tierce"; and "Sunset. The Hour of Compline." In the opening Merton imagines a man who is awakened in early morning and who is then suddenly "standing in clarity, in Paradise." The image is a quiet particular one: this man is someone who has been asleep in a hospital. He is someone who has "defended," "fought," "planned," "guarded," "loved himself alone," "watched over his own life all night"—but suddenly, the voice of the nurse and her cool hand makes him realize that he could never be self-sufficient; the poet then announces, "This is what it means to recognize Hagia Sophia" (E, 63).

In the second section Merton meditates on the fact that men cannot "hear mercy, or yielding love, or non-resistance, or non-reprisal," yet all these things are the expression of God's simplicity. In sleep we abandon ourselves, and in the same kind of abandonment we should awake. If we could give up ourselves, we could awaken to pure simplicity, and thus partake of the eternal.

In the next section the poet meditates about how the "Face of God" is diffused by Hagia Sophia. This part of the poem is a celebration of the inexhaustible feminine principle as manifested in the world. The care of life is not, as Western men might like to insist, through aggressiveness and control, but through tenderness and mercy.

In the final section, the poet meditates about Mary as mother, and "the one created being who enacts and shows forth in her life all that is hidden in Sophia." Here Merton reminds us that God is crowned, not with the glorious, but with "the one thing greater than glory . . . weakness, nothingness, poverty." Throughout the poem Merton reminds us that God himself is sent forth a poor and helpless, "a homeless God, lost in the night, without papers, without identification," but nevertheless present for any who would be still. The implication throughout the various parts of *Emblems* is that most of modern society is drifting away from such stillness.

The long essay which is printed immediately following "Hagia Sophia" is, in subject matter, a direct contrast to the prose-poem. That essay, a "Letter to Pablo Antonio Cuadra," is a twenty-page statement about contemporary society. Merton writes about two predominant forces and

the truth . . . that there is a little of [both] even in the best of us. (E, 71)

Gog . . . lover of power, Magog . . . absorbed in the cult of money: their idols differ, and indeed their faces seem to be dead set against one another, but their madness is the same: they are two faces of Janus looking inward, and dividing with critical fury the polluted sanctuary of dehumanized man. (E, 73)

In this sober reflection Merton assesses the fact of a dehumanized world in which few care who you *are*. What seems to be important is what labels can be affixed. Such themes became the core of many of the essays, reviews, journal entries, and poems which poured from his pen during his final years as he became surer of his contemplative vocation and ever-more actively concerned about the confusion of contemporary civilization.

Chapter Six
Movement
Closer toward the World

> *Sophia is the mercy of God in us. She is the*
> *tenderness with which the infinitely*
> *mysterious power of pardon turns the darkness*
> *of our sins into the light of grace.*
> *Hagia Sophia*

Some Disputed Questions

As Merton developed a surer sense of his responsibility as contemplative, he relaxed in that role, and was able to turn his mind more toward questions about contemporary society. So much of what seemed wrong with contemporary life was, in his opinion, the result of man not being at peace with himself, and this became, perhaps, the strongest single theme in his writings about society during the late 1950s and early 1960s. Peace in the world can only exist, Merton continued to emphasize, if man recognizes the core of his own being. It was certainly with such ideas in mind that he assembled essays for *Disputed Questions* (1964). While such ideas about man's need for harmony appear in less developed form in many other places, it is finally in this collection that the mature Christian humanist steps forth to examine his contemporary world. Subsequent books, considered in this chapter, represent further advances of this ever-more compassionate writer as he makes connections between his contemplative life and the needs of all men for an awareness of a contemplative spirit informing the active life.

The early Merton, as writer, possessed a great desire to be successful and, as we have already observed, produced an enormous range of materials; yet we can now also appreciate that, during his middle years at Gethsemani, he underwent a severe crisis of doubt about what he should write and publish. Once he began to resolve those questions which had seemed so significant during this middle period, he became freer to range over wider territory.[1] As he did so, he perfected a talent for producing essays and meditations which were a combination of analysis of man's condition and a compassion for man who had to live beyond the world of the monastery. As Merton examined particular issues (especially with regard to government, race, and the peace movement) he came under severe attack from critics who felt he had gone beyond his appointed role as a contemplative and Cistercian priest. He was even forbidden to write about the Vietnam war.[2] We now understand that, with increasing urgency in the 1960s, he realized he had to speak; this does not mean that he suddenly changed his interests. In fact, while so much of his writing was introspective, a basic concern throughout the body of all that writing had always been mankind's unconcern for truth and for others.

As a contemplative but also a writer concerned with problems of how to live within a society which pays little attention to truth, or to persons as persons, Merton increasingly sought artistic ways to remind contemporary men of how they are affected by misuses of language. Such misuses can, he warned, even appear to result in short-term gains, but in the long run disrespect for persons, language, and the truth can only cause problems. He therefore sought to remind men of their need for harmony and order, which can only begin with an honest recognition of reality and each separate person's dignity. If at any point the individual is forgotten, or forgets other persons, abuse of language quickly follows. In Merton's view man's short-sightedness as the pace of modern culture accelerated seemed to be rapidly making him less than human; often with good intentions man ends up distorting fundamental truth. To put it succinctly, his view of the modern world was one where many men seemed to be losing any ability to distinguish the true: appreciation of truth was apparently being lost because of increasingly greedy, cruel, and lustful pressures common to a society which encourages man to ignore the truth and to be primarily concerned with fitting in, or with his own satisfaction.[3]

Even before he decided to enter the monastery of Gethsemani in 1941, the aspiring writer had expressed his concerns about man's abuse of language. In his *The Secular Journal,* that record of the two years preceding his entrance, Merton frequently meditates on men's lack of concern with the truth: who needs truth when it is possible to get by with opinion? In 1940 he had written:

Instead of having faith, which is a virtue, and therefore nourishes the soul and gives it a healthy life, people merely have a lot of opinions. . . .

An opinion isn't one thing or the other: it is neither science nor faith, but a little bit of either one. It is a rationalism bolstered up by some orthodoxy.[4]

Related ideas are developed in the 1941 novel *My Argument with the Gestapo,* the book about a war in which few of the characters seemed to know why war was being fought. Nevertheless they chose to fight. Merton's novel is fantasy, yet it is a successful indictment of modern society precisely because he made clear he was (simultaneously) amused and horrified that so many people in France, in England, and in Germany could be so little concerned with the truth. As Merton's narrator writes this journal account, there is overwhelming evidence that few people want to confront the truth because it seems (at least on the surface of things) easier to live with half-truths and delusions. Little changed in the two decades which followed. Merton's two final books of poetry, *Cables to the Ace* and *The Geography of Lograire,* are therefore also significant as studies which investigate how Western man has abused language by twisting it for his own selfish purposes. Both of those book-length poems incorporate many related themes, and basic to their poetic development is Merton's assertion that Western man often no longer honors others. This is so much the case (whether we are talking about the language of advertising, police, administrators, missionaries, or explorers) that in many cases man seems to have lost his ability to recognize that distortions have become commonplace.

To call a group of essays *Disputed Questions* suggests how Merton's mind was moving in relation to questions about the world. The contents of this book reflect the seemingly paradoxical development of his writing. More concern about solitude and silence led Merton to an awareness of his fundamental responsibility to suggest links between his insight as monk and his understanding of questions that people in the world faced. Prompted by the conviction that "the world has moved a very long way towards conformism and passivity" during the past twenty years, Merton wrote the essays of *Disputed Questions.*[5] In his opinion the great delusion of our time is the delusion of a "humanism" within a society in which man has been alienated from himself by economic individualism and lost in a mass society where each person is hardly distinguishable from others. What he wants his readers to realize is that the vocation of any person "is to construct his own solitude as a *conditio sine qua non* for a valid encounter with other persons," and only from such solitude can one build toward cooperation and communion.

The first part of *Disputed Questions* opens with an important consideration of the art of Boris Pasternak, revelatory of Merton's own convictions, since it perceives the value of Pasternak's writing precisely in that author's presentation of life as mystery. Merton's view of the strength of Pasternak lies in the combination of literary ability and moral courage. Here, once more, there are ties between this essay and Merton's own work both in years preceding and to come. He explained that he was excited about Pasternak because there were many connections between what the Russian artist accomplished and the tradition of "natural contemplation" which had been important to the Greek Fathers after Origen. In Merton's view Pasternak apparently beheld the spiritual world working itself out in the mystery of the universe. His strength "lies then not only in his own literary genius and in his superb moral courage, but in the depth and genuineness of his spirituality as well" (*DQ*, 32).

In *Disputed Questions* Merton is concerned above all with "the relation of the *person* to the *social organization.*" The questions which he poses take many different forms; he considers, for example, issues of a philosophical nature about solitude versus community as well as specific concrete questions. His aim is to raise questions about how each person within a modern mass society must develop his vocation as person. In his preface Merton insists that he does not mean by this being an individual: "The individual, in fact, is nothing but a negation: he is not 'someone else.' He is not everybody, he is not the other individual. He is a unit divided off from the other units." A fundamental point made by the book is that too often modern man has come to rely upon conceptions of mankind as units who form aggregates. This is in Merton's view one of the great errors and weaknesses of our time, "the delusion of a culture where man has first been completely alienated from himself by economic individualism, and then precipitated into the morass of mass-technological society." In all the essays of *Disputed Questions* Merton seeks to demonstrate that man has become separated from himself because he has put too much faith in things beyond himself. Man can never find himself if he insists on looking elsewhere than in the self. Therefore, in Merton's words: "In order to find our own souls we have to enter into our own solitude and learn to live with ourselves" (*DQ*, xi). Similarly, he recognizes that many of Pasternak's insights into modern society are like the pessimistic recognition of Sartre. Both recognize the blind alley of *Huis Clos*—"no exit"— yet the Communists try to maintain that such a blank wall does not exist, while

Pasternak sees the blind alley and sees the wall, but knows that the way out is not through the wall, and not back out by the way we came in. The exit is into an entirely new dimension—finding ourselves in others, discovering the inward sources of freedom and love which God has put in our nature. . . . (*DQ, 48*)

So much of what Merton praises in Pasternak derives from his recognition that the individual is much more important than any collectivity. Directly related to this consideration of Pasternak is the immediately following essay about Mount Athos, one of the most significant monastic centers of all Christendom. Following this is an article about St. John Climacus, a consideration of a new translation of *The Ladder to Divine Ascent.* All three essays are closely related in their consideration of the importance of individual spirituality.

The second part of *Disputed Questions* consists of two long studies: "Christianity and Totalitarianism" and a study of love as creative force. The essay "The Power and Meaning of Love" is a careful analysis of Christian love, wherein Merton insists that obedience without love produces only dead works, "external conformity, not interior communion" (*DQ,* 117). He draws many insights together through metaphor and examples which speak to modern society. The early parts of the essay outline the corrupt varieties of love which he believes are so common in modern man. Man cannot exist without love, and if genuine love is absent then man will find a substitute.

Many other essays in the volume treat particular aspects of man's need to love, and to manifest that love. Essays on sacred art and sacred decoration examine specific questions about the degradation and impoverishment of Christian symbolism. Essays on particular figures who are models, such as the solitary Blessed Paul Giustiniani or St. John of the Cross, and an essay about "The Primitive Carmelite Ideal," stress man's need to seek the positive joys of solitary contemplation.

"Notes for a Philosophy of Solitude" outlines a theoretical justification for the solitary life. Merton does not mean religious withdrawal; he therefore mentions Thoreau and Emily Dickinson at the beginning of the essay. The hermit withdraws from other men *not* because he rejects them, but so that he can be closer to the heart of the church. Withdrawal, Merton demonstrates, is a form of love for other men. "It should never be a rejection of man or of his society" (*DQ*, 192). Any true solitary is someone who has gone beyond the individualism of a shallow "I"; true solitude cannot be selfish. Merton therefore rightly says that "without solitude of some sort there is and can be no maturity" (*DQ*, 206).

Seeds of Destruction

Precisely because of an awareness that the contemplative life is not negation, or a withdrawal, Father Louis wrote essays about the immature and selfish actions which he observed in the contemporary world. A growing awareness of his own need to examine issues which had earlier seemed to be beyond monasticism led him to think about problems of selfishness, separation, race, and fascism in our culture. He beheld selfishness as an almost inevitable step toward a disintegration of bonds between people which could under other circumstances lead to unity. The title of another book, *Seeds of Destruction,* an echo of the earlier *Seeds of Contemplation,* announces his concern. In the "Philosophy of Solitude" he noted that "unless one becomes empty and alone, he cannot give himself in love"; in *Seeds of Destruction* he stresses the fact that the monk possesses freedom, but not "from" time, rather "in" time, and that therefore he also has an obligation to speak, "to identify [himself] with the cause of people who are denied their rights."[6]

A group of essays about "Black Revolution" and racism begins with "Letters to a white liberal" and confronts the fact that if a situation is such that "*minds are full of hatred and where imaginations dwell on cruelty, torment, punishment, revenge and death,* then inevitably *there will be violence and death*" (*SD*, 7). Merton speaks boldly, and asserts that the black American "has come to realize that the white man is less interested in the rights of the Negro than in the white man's own spiritual and material comfort." He then warns his liberal readers that black people have had enough of rhetoric. The black man is now telling man something about the need for a vital and Christian relationship. All are at a moment of crisis, a critical hour. Merton reminds us that this "can be the hour of vocation . . . we can respond to that inscrutable will in a faith that faces the need of reform and creative change" (*SD*, 65). But much of what he does in *Seeds of Destruction* is to point out the need to act in good faith.

Merton's admiration for William Melvin Kelley's novel, *A Different Drummer,* is expressed in the second essay of this book; Kelley's novel evokes a moment of *kairos*, the mysterious moment when grace effects action. The title of the novel derives from Thoreau's essay on "Civil Disobedience"; the theme of Kelley's story about change coming without warning was of interest to Merton because it seemed to be prophetic. Kelley's mythical setting shares characteristics with all the deep Southern states and provides a fictional place for Negroes to act within a moment crucial in the development of a modern American consciousness. The entire black population simply decides to leave the state and this mystery is not planned or organized. It simply happens, but it occurs because the time is ripe and some of the characters in the novel shed their guilt. A related theme is echoed in poems, *Conjectures of a Guilty Bystander*, and other essays produced throughout the final decade of Merton's life. He saw the dilemma of civil rights as a concrete chance for contemporary man to act if he can somehow bring himself to do so.

The many different essays of *Seeds of Destruction* demonstrate that hate, destruction, and separation from others can only lead to isolation of individuals. Two of these essays are about the role of the Christian in today's world: one is a series of reflections on John XXIII's *Pacem in Terris;* another is entitled "The Christian in the Diaspora." Both are reflections about Christian responsibility in a difficult time. Following these essays is a piece called "A tribute to Gandhi." The connections are clear; Merton's admiration for the spiritual force of Gandhi is related directly to his realization that in large part modern society has become one in which systematic use of deception and untruth to continue to take advantage of others remains at the heart of many actions. For Merton, what was so significant about Gandhi, and what set him apart from others, "even the most sincere and honest of them," is manifested by the fact that "Gandhi is chiefly concerned with truth and with service, *svadharma,* rather than the possible success of his tactics upon other people, while paradoxically it was his religious conviction that made Gandhi a great politician rather than a mere tactician or operator" (*SD,* 229–30). This comment is especially appropriate to a collection of meditations about racism, alienation, and hate. The rationalizing of those who have little respect for the truth is altogether different from Gandhi's *satyagraha,* the vow to die rather than say what he does not mean. The significance of *satyagraha* for Merton becomes apparent when he reflects that it is much more than just a matter of conforming words to inner thoughts. Aims, plans, actions, outlooks, attitudes, habitual response all speak of our inner being and all "reveal our fidelity or infidelity to ourselves" (*SD*, 230).[7]

The essays in *Seeds of Destruction* treat the problem of how to live in the modern world. The concluding "Letters in a Time of Crisis" are thirty-four specific approaches to contemporary problems. Letters to priests, writers, seminarians, the mayor of Hiroshima, a publisher, a Quaker, a new convert, close friends, and the famous—all attack the range of the problems which Merton addresses. Each letter is a minor work of art; each is addressed to a specific person. In them we see a writer who has decided that he can no longer remain silent.[8] The foundation of this kind of thinking is already present in earlier writing. One book, published some three years earlier, is especially interesting because it is a kind of bridge between the ideas treated in *Seeds of Destruction* and earlier writings. That book included a "Letter to an Innocent Bystander." Merton's concern seems to be that in reality there are few innocent bystanders.

Titans and Contemporary Wisdom

An earlier book—and a link between the outspokenness of *Seeds of Destruction* and earlier writing—is *The Behavior of Titans* (1961), a collection of investigations about Western history and Promethean man. This poetic book provides the groundwork for later experimental prose; thematically it is related closely to all the materials examined within this chapter. There are three tightly related divisions in *Titans;* the first provides the title for the book. In his opening section Merton provides meditations about the two Prometheus myths which derive from Hesiod and from Aeschylus. He sees these different versions of the Prometheus myth, one negative, the other positive, as two ways of thinking about man's relationship to God and as something directly related to the crisis of the present moment. For Merton, the Prometheus of Hesiod is identified with Cain while the Prometheus of Aeschylus is to be identified with Christ on the cross. In the one, "Guilty, frustrated, rebellious, fear-ridden, Prometheus seeks to assert himself and fails. His mysticism enables him to glory in defeat."[9] In the other myth, the god suffers, yet is compassionate; toward this Aeschylean version Merton is sympathetic. In the same way he is sympathetic toward Atlas, who patiently waits and holds up the entire world. This Atlas, who wishes well for mankind, is at peace with himself and with the world. Not so the angry rebellious Prometheus, and it is this Promethean man which the modern world resembles, the victim, the martyr, the one who will go down "in a luxury of despair" (*BT*, 18).

The second part of this book includes a "Letter to an Innocent Bystander," a statement which makes it clear that Merton now realizes that it is no longer possible not to speak up. As has been suggested, this letter is groundwork for the explosion of letters which appear in *Seeds of Destruction;* it is also fuel for the musings of the later volume *Conjectures of a Guilty Bystander.* Merton's "Letter to an Innocent Bystander" makes it clear that it is not possible to remain "innocent," especially if man continues to say nothing while Promethean man attempts to be God. Merton insists that we dare not forget that since man "has decided to occupy the place of God he has shown himself to be by far the blindest, and cruelest, and pettiest and most ridiculous of all the false gods. We can call ourselves innocent only if we refuse to forget this, and if we also do everything we can to make others realize it" (*BT*, 63). This letter is followed by another document somewhat wryly called "A Signed Confession of Crimes Against the State," a whimsical piece in which the writer declares he is guilty of enjoying himself in the quiet of his woods on a pleasant afternoon. Obviously, Merton's point is to imply that while it might be suspect to be caught simply enjoying oneself on a peaceful day—without trying to manipulate and organize or control—it is precisely such acceptance which modern man has forgotten. Man desperately needs to cultivate such a contemplative attitude as a balance against constant manipulation and selfishness.

The third part of *The Behavior of Titans* includes a study of Herakleitos and a compilation of the "Fragments" of Herakleitos. These parts of the book can be related to Merton's appreciation of figures as diverse as Aeschylus and Pasternak. He admired Herakleitos as a prophetic spirit who saw beyond the limits of his Ionian world. For that ancient philosopher too much analysis and judgment can cause man to become immersed in illusion; then men "can no longer see the deep, underlying connection of opposites, because they are obsessed with their superficial separateness." For Herakleitos true wisdom does not consist in the willful, or arbitrary selection of many conflicting principles. Instead wisdom seizes "upon the very moment itself, and penetrates to the logos of thought within that dynamic harmony." The enigmatic sayings of Herakleitos suggested the Zen *mondo* to Merton.

Herakleitos remains of special value today because he keeps reminding man of the artificial divisive fictions which civilization constructs. The heart of Merton's attraction to Herakleitos seems to be summed up in these words: "Herakleitos, wielding the sharp weapon of paradox without mercy, seeks to awaken the mind of his disciple to a reality that is right before his eyes but that he is incapable of seeing. He wants to liberate him from the cult of 'vanity' and to draw him forth from the sleep of formalism and subjective prejudices" (*BT*, 83). Herakleitos is of importance for modern man because his parables speak of a spiritual order close to that of the Gospel. Important parallels exist between the thought of Herakleitos and Christ: "The aristocracy in which Herakleitos believed was then not an aristocracy of class, of power, of learning (all these are illusory). It is an aristocracy of the spirit, of wisdom: one might almost say of mysticism and of sanctity" (*BT*, 93).

When we stand back from books such as *Disputed Questions, Seeds of Destruction,* and *The Behavior of Titans,* we see Merton as writer looking for effective ways to confront man's destructive fascination with illusion. In his essay about Herakleitos Merton looks back to the earlier thinker to try to isolate what seems most essential in life. Interestingly, during this same period Father Louis was continuing to keep a careful day-by-day account of his own daily reflections and, no doubt, there are links between Merton's speculations about Herakleitos, his *"Letter to an Innocent Bystander,"* and the spirit and tone of his numerous journal entries which were eventually crafted into the contrapuntally titled *Conjectures of a Guilty Bystander.*

Conjectures of a Guilty Bystander

To contrast this series of meditations with either of the preceding journals published by Merton is rewarding. *Conjectures* gives the appearance of being the least organized of any book which Merton had published, yet it is in fact very carefully organized and is a crucial key to his ongoing development as contemplative and artist. In *Conjectures* Merton is making connections between his world as a solitary and the active world for which he exhibits compassion. Further, as a carefully controlled work of art, the journal shows that this writer had learned to organize private conjectures in a way that would draw author and reader together. So while *Conjectures* may give the appearance of being loosely organized, each of its five basic parts is definitely planned to achieve a particular end as Merton meditates on the need to live well.

Merton's paragraphs are often much more than just "conjectures"; they are speculations built on the foundation of earlier reading, thinking, and meditating. In the five parts of the book he guides his reader through a series of observations and meditations which reveal him as no longer willing to be a bystander. So much of what he includes emphasizes this fundamental realization; at one point (toward the end of the book) he jokingly says, "I think I will have to become a Christian."[10] *Being* is the focus of that final division of the journal. In parts 1 through 4 Merton meditates on (among other things) dreams, deceptions, the paradise of the present, and the necessity of choice.

Conjectures is the product of a writer now at ease with himself, but of one no longer at ease with choosing not to speak. Paradoxically, however, speaking out might demonstrate the necessity of being silent. As a record of someone who has found that often it is best to remain silent, Merton's text functions ironically; he is drawn into the world, yet he still values the silence of the cloister. What he has learned in that silence cannot easily be passed on to others. *Conjectures* is thus a book which comes out of silence, but which leads the reader (as has been the case for Merton himself) directly back to the world and then back again to quiet.

Conjectures is Merton's personal record and a meditation about contemporary needs. It is, as well, the raw material which will be fashioned into more essays and poems. Note, for instance, these words within the section "The Night Spirit and the Dawn Air":

At every moment we are sent north, south, east, and west by the angels of business and art, poetry and politics, science and war to the four corners of the universe to decide something, to sign something, to buy and sell. We fly in all directions to sell ourselves, thus justifying the absolute nothingness of our lives. (*C,* 196)

This is a capsule version of the long poem *The Geography of Lograire.*

It should be emphasized that as Merton became more interested in the intricacy of the world, as is demonstrated by all the books considered in this chapter, he simultaneously became less interested in castigation. His report of a moment he experienced in downtown Louisville is characteristic of changes in attitude: "I was suddenly overwhelmed with the realization that I loved all these people, that they were mine and I theirs, that we could not be alien to one another even thought we were total strangers. It was like waking from a dream of separateness . . ." (*C,* 156).

It is commonplace to assert that Merton became more compassionate as he matured in his role as contemplative and writer. The value of a book like *Conjectures* is that it demonstrates how he was learning to make the best of embracing the world while remaining aloof from aspects of it. He writes: "To leave things alone at the right time: this is the right way to 'stop' and the right way to 'go on.' " He recognized that, in his task as writer, he would speak for many "even when I seem to be speaking out only for myself." He now saw his role of monk-writer as part of a chain of events that was begun with his first decision to come to Kentucky. Each day which followed was a link in the chain, part of the whole. He also realized that through an intense attentiveness to the particularities of each day it was becoming possible for him to be less concerned about the succession of historical or political events; the pattern of a particular day then becomes "more and more woven into the great pattern of the whole experience of man, and even something quite beyond all experience. I am less and less aware of myself simply as this individual who is a monk and a writer, and who, as monk and writer, sees this, or writes that" (*C,* 245). Which is to say he was learning more effective ways to lead readers to an awareness of how they might find their true selves through forgetting of self. His late essay "The Day of a Stranger" beautifully illustrates this point.

In *Conjectures,* Merton stresses that all man's acts are implicit commitments, but he also notes there is a genuine crisis in today's world because of the near-bewildering complexity of "almost infinite contradictory propositions and claims to meaning uttered by millions of acts, movements, charges, decisions, attitudes, gestures, events, going on all around us." This crisis will not be solved if men are willing to go along with distortions which ignore the truth of the whole for the purpose of attaining a short-term goal. We must find ways to see the whole. Yet much of the Western world has lost a vision of the whole because it is content to swallow various kinds of propaganda. Perhaps, Merton asserts, the most serious kind of propaganda is that which informs man that he should "adjust."

Merton asks: "Adjust to what? To the general fiction. . . . 'Trying
to adjust' involves a whole galaxy of illusions. First of all you take
yourself very seriously as an individual, autonomous self, a little
isolated world of reality . . ." (C, 264). Merton stresses that too
much concern with self can result in a distortion of the truth, but
too little concern with self is also dangerous. The development that
he and his writing underwent during his literary career might be
described as a systematic inquiry into how he might communicate
his attempt to get at the truth of his being—and what it means to
be a person: *not* to adjust; *not* to accept without questions; *not* to
assume that the general fiction is preferable to the truth is, therefore,
the thrust of all his writing, as becomes especially clear in *Conjectures*.
His questions about what it means to be in solitude, and what it
means to exist without manipulation of facts, are important because
those considerations allow readers to see that if they, too, are to live
as separate persons, no false individualism which grows out of a
distortion of the truth can have a place in their lives.

In *Conjectures*, Merton accordingly observes that so much of man's
living is the result of various kinds of propaganda. He notes that
the violence of propaganda is that "by means of apparent truth and
apparent reason, it induces us to surrender our freedom and self-
possession to institutions. Propaganda predetermines us to certain
conclusions and does so in such a way that we imagine that we are
fully free in reaching them by our judgment" (C, 237–38). In other
words, bad propaganda succeeds because men want it to do so. It
brings a kind of satisfaction for which they long: "If war propaganda
succeeds it is because people want war, and only need a few good
reasons to justify their own desire." In *Conjectures*, Merton is also
concerned with just how such procedures were followed by Germany's
Third Reich. Surely we can see, he urges, that devotion to obedience
during that regime has parallels with contemporary American history.
(It is not surprising, therefore, that he became an important
spokesman against the Vietnam War.) He wants readers to begin
to understand that their society is one which encourages a mind-
lessness dependent upon hardly thinking at all, rather actual
nonthinking.

In a related essay called "Events and Pseudo Events" Merton
outlined how easily mankind sees the errors of others, but, he insists,
that is not enough: "We cannot begin to face our real problems
until we admit that these evils are universal." We have been trained,

he believes, to think that we are "objective," but that objectivity is "In fact an image of ourselves as 'objective' [and] we soon take our objectivity for granted. . . ."[11] Such is the way Western man arranges his life and language. If Communist dogmatism is more blatant, or rigid, or bureaucratically dense, our refusal to see our own nonobjectivity is just as devastating. Such a refusal to examine the basis of our action is a kind of "superstitious worship." "The fact that the image is not made of stone or metal, but of ideas, slogans and pseudo-events only makes it all the more dangerous" (*FAV,* 154–55).

Raids on the Unspeakable

Raids, one of Merton's favorites, like *The Behavior of Titans* and *Conjectures,* fits no easy category. It is poetry, meditation, abstract art, elegy, literary criticism, celebration, essay, autobiography, and more. In it we see Merton at the height of his artistic powers, yet no longer worried about producing "art," and paradoxically doing so with great success. We should remember the collection, *The Behavior of Titans,* which appeared three years earlier and which stands as a model for this book. The many parts of *Raids on the Unspeakable* had been developing during a three-year period. The book is yet another series of meditations; in it the writer attacks the void which so many in the modern world seem to accept as normal. Each of these raids focuses on one particular absurdity of modern life, some myth which man has come to accept as normal. (A few of these pieces are reprinted from the earlier *Titans;* "Atlas and the Footman," "Martin's Predicament," and *Prometheus: A Meditation.*)

Merton's speculations in *Raids* center on the fact that so many persons seem to desire reconciliation with the world at almost any price. He meditates, therefore, on Man who is always in a rush and who will not take time. This is the very man who has lost all sense of identity precisely because he spends so much energy trying to adjust to what the world requires of him. The goal of Merton's book is confrontation of the void and emptiness of modern life. One of the most effective meditations in the book is entitled "The Time of the End Is the Time of No Room." It is a meditation about massed-man and the mentality of crowds: already there was no room at the inn for Christ:

His being born outside that crowd is even more of a sign. That there
is no room for Him is a sign of the end.

   . . . the tidings of great joy [are not] announced in the crowded inn.
In the massed crowd there are always new tidings of joy and disaster. . . .

Hence The Great Joy is announced, after all, in silence, loneliness and
darkness, to shepherds "living in the fields" or "living in the countryside"
and apparently unmoved by the rumors or massed crowds. These are the
remnants of the desert-dwellers, the nomads, the true Israel.[12]

If man would find room for Christ he must find an open space.

Another theme fundamental to *Raids* is man's selfishness and
emptiness in contrast to the need to be open to the strength and
goodness of God. Merton meditates, therefore, on the craziness of
a world where man insists on running with the herd in "Rain and
the Rhinoceros," a consideration of the plays of Ionesco; he sings
of Flannery O'Connor's prose and its honest depiction of "man's fall
and his dishonor" (*R,* 42). He also provides an extensive meditation
on Adolf Eichmann; and he goes back to Ibn Abbad, a Muslem of
the fourteenth century (who may have had indirect influence on St.
John of the Cross), to provide readings. Merton concludes the book
with two meditations about art and poetry and the modern world.
Each of these essays might be analyzed at length; they are more
than just essays, rather manifestos wherein Merton stresses his belief
in the power of art to help man. *Raids* is a collection of pieces which
stress man's need to empty himself of the superficial and to make
room for the essential. Merton wants to make sure that the void is
not filled with only more conformism and dishonesty.

Violence and War

During the 1960s, as Merton meditated about the drift of American culture, he frequently found it necessary to write about a common
mentality which accepted a climate of war and violence as inevitable.
A collection of essays published under the title *Faith and Violence* is
an overview of his most important considerations on these subjects.
That book, subtitled "Christian Teaching and Christian Practice,"
collects essays on pacifism, war, racism, and unbelief. Such essays
reflect Merton's growing suspicion that much of modern Christianity
had little effect on the actions of mankind. There is no single essay
in this collection about Adolf Eichmann, but Eichmann's name turns
up in many separate essays, as well as in other related essays and

books, for example, in *Conjectures of a Guilty Bystander*. Merton's interest in Eichmann exemplifies his continuing concern about a drifting society which could so easily twist meaning beyond sense. He saw Eichmann not as a madman, but as a reflection of a violent society which had given birth to a new kind of criminal:

> The Eichmann story shows the breakdown of forensic concepts of morality and demands an existential respect for the human reality of each situation. Without this respect, principles will never regain their meaning in concrete life. Meanwhile there is no legal machinery to deal with such moral disasters. What judgment could *add anything* to the judgment already implied in the fact that a man who was by certain accepted standards quite honest, respectable, sane, and efficient could do the things he did without feeling that he was wrong? The judgment falls not on Eichmann alone, but on our whole society. (*C*, 288)

Violence, Merton insisted, is done in all manner of bureaucratic ways. During these same years Merton wrote a poem about Eichmann which he called "Epitaph for a Public Servant"; an ironic inquiry into related questions. Merton imagines Eichmann speaking; the words, contorted to suggest how this "public servant" had come so easily to distort reality, both make little sense *and* reflect horrible facts:

> Yet I was saddened at the order
> I lost all joy in my
> Work
>
> To regain my joy
> Without any reason
> I joined the Party
> I was swallowed by the
> Party. . . .[13]

In books such as *Disputed Questions* and *Faith and Violence* Merton asks how man can resist such patterns, such a willingness to conform, such complacency. In *Disputed Questions,* he had already indicated some models that contemporary man might emulate. His essays on Pasternak and Christian love, already discussed, give some guidance. Connections can also be observed between that volume (and other essays discussed in this chapter) and the basic themes of *Conjectures*

and *Faith and Violence;* Merton admired Pasternak's strength because
it combined literary ability with moral courage: "He is a defender
of everything that can be called a spiritual value" (*DQ*, 32). For
Pasternak, language could not be "material" which a poet uses; in
fact, in Merton's opinion, "this is the sin of the Soviet ideologist
for whom language is simply a mine of terms and formulas which
can be pragmatically exploited" (*DQ*, 20). And, Merton implies,
so it is with much of institutionalized language and conformism.
In contrast to such ideological formulations, the "inspiration [of a]
poet's creative intelligence is married with the inborn wisdom of
human language . . . then in the very flow of new and individual
intuitions, the poet utters the voice of that wonderful and mysterious
world of God [and] manhood—it is transfigured, spiritualized and
divinized cosmos that speaks through him" (*DQ*, 20–21). More
than anything, what Merton admired about Pasternak was that poet's
vision of a fluid, ever moving, developing cosmos. He qualified,
"It is a vision appropriate to a contemporary of Einstein and Bergson:
but let us not forget that it is also akin to the vision of St. Gregory
of Nyssa" (*DQ*, 21). Throughout *Faith and Violence* Merton also
stressed man's fundamental need to avoid strict analysis by concepts
and formulas. To do so guarantees loss of contact with basic intuitions. Genius and concern for individuals will not fit ready-made
classification. In a related essay in *Disputed Questions* entitled "Sacred
Art and the Spiritual," Merton examined questions about the confusion and extremes of modern civilization where, on the one hand,
we live in a mass culture that combines totalitarian with passive
conformities, while on the other, we see all around us "futile gestures
of individualistic rebellion, and exhibitionism" (*DQ*, 151). His point
is the fundamental one that man needs to see what is already here:
"We are a generation of men who have eyes and see not, ears and
hear not, because we have let ourselves be so completely and abjectly
conditioned by words, slogans and official pronouncements" (*DQ*,
153). There are certain basic facts which have to be acknowledged.
Man has to learn (again) to steer a middle course between conformism
and futile rebellion.

Many writers and thinkers Merton admired were Christian prophets
whose resistance during World War II seemed to anticipate the
needs of thinking men today, and several of the essays in *Faith and
Violence* stress this. Dietrich Bonhoeffer is an example, as is the
Austrian peasant, Franz Jägerstätter, who refused to fight in what

he believed was an unjust war. His simple statement, "I cannot turn the responsibility for my actions over to the Führer" was not easily understood by his fellow countrymen during the war; yet his witness (and the meditations and commentaries he wrote) stand in striking contrast to the evasions of a man like Eichmann.

Merton emphasized that Man must not let institutions do his thinking for him; to do so is to guarantee the loss of the individual's soul. In lives such as Bonhoeffer's, or Jägerstätter's, or in Simone Weil's, Merton recognized an independence of thought that articulated his own deepest concerns and the concerns of thinking Western European man during this century. He noted that Simone Weil had a gift for analyzing the nature of modern society and its oppression. Of course, she was not alone in realizing that war in 1938 (still so close to World War I) was absurd and meaningless; and she was able to go further to suggest what could cause such a war. In Merton's words she understood that "behind the empty symbols and objectiveless motivation of force . . . [was] a real force, the grimmest of all the social realities of our time: collective power" (*FAV,* 82). Merton felt Simone Weil raised one of the most crucial questions for contemporary men:

"How will the soul be saved," she asked her philosophy students in the Lyceé "after the great beast has acquired an opinion about everything?"
    The void underlying the symbols and the myths of nationalism, of capitalism, communism, fascism, racism, totalism is in fact filled entirely by the presence of the beast—the urge to collective power. We might say, developing her image that the void thus becomes an insatiable demand for power: it sucks all life and all being into itself. (*FAV,* 82–83)

As long as real, individual, human values are plunged into nothingness in order that collectivity may attain to some ideal, the soul is in danger of being lost. This is what happens with all blind acceptance of institutions. Weil questions, "why must one be able to make war? This no one knows any more than the Trojans knew why they had to keep Helen" (*FAV,* 83). Merton again and again stresses that it is a matter of each individual needing to assume responsibility for all his actions. (Here we could, of course, draw parallels between Merton's thought and other recent Christian writers who have meditated upon the dilemma of the individual in a mass society—Caroline Gordon, James Agee, Flannery O'Connor, and

Walker Percy.) Within the essays of *Faith and Violence,* Merton raises issues which he felt were significant for men who find themselves in a world which increasingly seeks to function collectively, without accepting individual responsibility. In the spirit of his earlier letters in *Seeds of Destruction,* as part of *Faith and Violence,* he writes a "Letter to a Southern Churchman," in which he urges that too much of "declarations and pronouncements" tends not to clarify, but to do just the opposite:

While silence can constitute guilt and complicity, once one has taken a stand he is not necessarily obliged to come out with a new answer and a new solution to insoluble problems every third day.

   After all, was it not Bonhoeffer himself who said it was an "Anglo-Saxon failing" to imagine that the Church was supposed to have a ready answer to every social problem?

   When one has too many answers, and when one joins a chorus of others chanting the same slogans, there is, it seems to me, a danger that one is trying to evade the loneliness of conscience that realizes itself to be in an inescapably evil situation. *(FAV,* 145)

   Still another valuable way of appreciating Merton's concerns about our fragmented modern culture is the book edited by Gordon Zahn, *Thomas Merton on Peace* (republished as *The Non-violent Alternative*), which gathers additional speculation on these basic questions. Merton's concern about man's destructive tendencies is the core of this important collection. Zahn reprints several pieces from *Faith and Violence,* while the overall arrangement of his book is more inclusive; essays and poems are taken from many different books and publications to provide an overview. Some of the questions examined in this chapter are treated in detail in Merton's own essay "War and the Crisis of Language," included as part of *Thomas Merton on Peace.* Merton's reflections are an attempt to examine what he calls the malaise of antilanguage—contemporary "denatured language."[14] His fundamental point is clear, and should be related to all of the material discussed in this chapter; Merton's view is that the faith in materials and the breakdown of language are inevitably intertwined: "The incoherence of language that cannot be trusted and the coherence of weapons that are infallible, or thought to be: this is the dialectic of politics and war, the prose of the twentieth century" *(OP,* 235).

A posthumous gathering of essays which have been published under the title *Ishi Means Man* provides another approach to Merton's concerns about language and an appropriate conclusion for this section. This book raises questions about how Americans have twisted their views of, and language about, native American Indians in order to justify their own prejudiced thinking. Suffice it to point out that the essay "Ishi Means Man" as the title for the book stresses Merton's conviction that labels are insufficient for getting at the essence of individuals. Merton was especially intrigued by the story of the last remaining member of a small tribe of California Indians who had been forced to live in seclusion from white men; one of these Indians was "discovered" at the turn of this century, and his language was a curiosity for anthropologists, as he himself was a kind of living exhibit. Yet while some of that unique language was shared with the white man, the last living member of a lost tribe died never having revealed his name to others. The loss of this group of Yana Indians, and knowledge of its culture was, for Merton, a symbol of the carelessness white men have exhibited toward countless numbers of people assumed to be "savage." What Merton realized was that this small band of primitive Indians, driven further and further back into the foothills as their traditional hunting grounds were infringed upon, led a life quite in contrast to the aggressive "Forty-niners" who had driven them into seclusion.

As a parable the story has meaning. The white man's assumption had been that these "savage" Indians were to be eliminated. Yet we can now perceive that in such a primitive culture there was a strength and goodness altogether absent in their conquerors. It is quite significant that this "wild man," this last member of an "inferior race," "never told anyone his real name. These California Indians never uttered their own names, and were careful about how they spoke the names of others. Ishi would never refer to the dead by name either."[15] The last "wild man" and his tribe were driven into seclusion because of infringements by white men who had come looking for gold, and thus to develop "civilization," but those who came into the Indians' territory never really tried to appreciate the people who were there. The parable is clear. Respect for each man as person, and respect for the language of others, go hand in hand.

What Merton wants his readers to realize, throughout his career and especially during these final years, is that no person can afford to let someone else, and certainly not a group, do his thinking and speaking—or indeed, his praying—for him. Still another recent collection, published as *Love and Living,* amplifies many of these ideas—and those essays, too, might be examined as proof of Merton's continuing concerns about how men use language within a society where the individual is so frequently forgotten. All of the books examined in this inquiry into how this author's literary interest brought him closer to the world also reflect an abiding concern about a society deeply in need of the contemplative awareness which as a monk he had come to value so highly. *The Literary Essays of Thomas Merton,* which include a wide range of essays, brings still more evidence to bear about this concern. Much of Merton's concern as just described, however, tends toward the analytical; and while he realized the value of such analysis, on another and a more personal level he was experiencing still other changes in perspective which allowed him to concentrate on a different plane of awareness, something which could never be fully analyzed or explained. Such changes were in process partly because of Father Louis's continuing interests in Eastern ideas, religions, and modes of being; those interests in the East led him to still more ways of writing. These developing interests, especially with Eastern ideas, contributed to a productive tension in a writer who was becoming more and more aware of the need for simplification, but who through such insight, would find many new and unusual ways to communicate simplicity.

Chapter Seven
East as Support for the West

The sage is quiet because he is not moved,
Not because he wills to be quiet.
                    Action and Non-Action

Gandhi

Merton's appreciation of Gandhi can be interpreted as a symbol of his own spiritual convictions and of changes within his writing, for in Gandhi Merton saw the fruits of someone who through the focus of a foreign culture had been able to appreciate his own culture more deeply. Gandhi's philosophy spoke to Merton because it was a specific approach from the East which he realized should be of use in contemporary America. Gandhi, who had learned from Thoreau's essay on "Civil Disobedience," was a man for whom truth always remained fundamental. *Gandhi on Non-Violence,* a collection of Gandhi's writings edited by Merton, reflects these realizations, and is also a clear indicator of this writer's developing use of a wide range of materials to expand intellectual, moral, artistic, and spiritual horizons. Merton's introduction to this collection shares characteristics with some of the prose-poems found in *Behavior of Titans* and *Raids on the Unspeakable.* He noted: "We enter the postmodern (perhaps the post-historical) era in total disunity and confusion."[1] Called "Gandhi and the One-Eyed Giant," this essay might be read as a preface to the final phase of Merton's career as monk and writer. He emphasizes that the spiritual life is *not,* as sometimes conceived in the West, a private affair. On the contrary, an individual's spiritual life is "simply the life of all manifesting itself in him," and as any person's interior life deepens, Merton insists, that person becomes engaged in the crucial struggles of all people. Thus follows the paradox that the only way to liberate oneself is through seeking "true liberty for all."

Merton's concern with the East could be examined at great length. Individual studies which focus on his interest in various religions and philosophies, as well as his use of classic Eastern thought and poetry in his own creative writing or his organization of his Asian journals (compiled after his death), would all be significant areas of study.

113

In drawing together the stories of *The Seven Storey Mountain* Merton acknowledged his awareness of non-Western traditions, but this played a minimal role in those early years. It could even be maintained that at that time Merton relished how he had found the peace and solitude basic to his experience as a contemplative within an atmosphere he assumed to be largely Western. Merton's mature concern with the East constitutes a considerable change from the younger writer, who—although impressed by Bramachari while still at Columbia, and having read translations of Eastern sages before he ever became a monk—had been by his own admission relatively ignorant of how he might integrate such knowledge into life and action. The early Merton seemed convinced that it was possible to live, pray, and write while supported by traditions formulated almost wholly within the Christian heritage.[2] During the subsequent career we see him gradually modifying that stand, for as he wrote and studied he was drawn into a fuller awareness of non-Western traditions which helped him to develop his life and artistry. Moreover, as such interests in early Christian monasticism developed, he grew increasingly aware of the history of monasticism in the West as a movement which paralleled important Eastern traditions, whose assimilation would prove valuable for Western man.

Interestingly, as the writer Merton became more intrigued by non-Western traditions, his interest in producing conventional formal poetry declined. Much of his early poetry, symbolized by a title like *Figures for an Apocalypse,* clearly emerged from a love of biblical, liturgical, and monastic traditions within the Roman church, along with an abhorrence of the apparent drift of the modern world; and a principal strength of that earlier work was his apparent lack of need to look beyond the bulwark of Western religious traditions. Such confidence changed, especially during the late 1950s and the ferment of the 1960s, and new ways of thinking and writing developed. While it may seem surprising, Merton actually strengthened his Christianity and his skills as writer by opening himself to these new ways of thinking and being.

Through various writers within Eastern traditions, from Gandhi to Chuang Tzu, Merton grew more convinced that society is not a fixed and finished fact, but rather something which is constantly "becoming." He saw that much of Western man's mistakes derived from a belief that evil was irreversible, while the concept, for example, of nonviolence, as practiced by Gandhi, assumed a dynamic and "non-final state of all relationships among men." For much of the West, "evil" is to be eliminated (Hitler is Merton's example); but for Gandhi sin is simply recognized as an everyday fact and "The only real liberation is that which *liberates both the oppressor and the oppressed*" (*G,* 14). Thus in the practice of nonviolence one can no longer rest assured by oversimplifications that seem so clear-cut.

Comparisons should be made between Merton's fascination with Gandhi's writings and his own incorporation of ideas from non-Western culture into his essays and experimental writings. As Merton thought about the fragmentation of contemporary society, Gandhi seemed important because of his refusal to oversimplify while remaining sure of his belief. At one point within *Conjectures* Merton quotes Gandhi's *My Non-violence:* " 'The business of every God-fearing man . . . is to disassociate himself from evil in *total disregard of the consequences.*' " Merton states the God-fearing man "must have faith in a good deed producing only a good result. . . ," and *Conjectures* is his compendium of evidence supporting this view; modern man has "sacrificed the power to apprehend and respect [what he is and] what truth is . . . and has replaced this with a vague confusion of pragmatic notions about what can be done . . . what is permissible, what is feasible, how things can be used, irrespective of any definite meaning or finality contained in their very nature."[3] Concerned with such practicality, Western man is concerned more and more with consequences, yet this is achieved at the expense of forfeiting any ability to see things whole. In Merton's view, Western mass-man often finds himself choosing "lesser evils" for the sake of "some imaginary or desperately hoped for good consequences" (*C,* 118), yet such imagined good is frequently formulated by institutions, not by persons. When he reflects about Gandhi, or when he writes this journal, Merton reminds modern man that he must not trust society to think for him precisely because everything remains so confused. What modern man must somehow learn to do is to "recover his inner faith not only in God but in the good, in reality, and in the power of the good to take care of itself and us as well, if only we attend to it" (*C,* 119).

Each of Merton's selections from Gandhi's writings is meant to have practical application, but there is always a looking beyond the immediate moment: thus "Non-violence is not a garment to be put on and off at will. Its seat is in the heart, and it must be an inseparable part of our very being" (*G,* 24). Merton's gathering of

Gandhi's sayings serves as a handbook for those who would practice nonviolence, as a tribute to Gandhi, and as a record of the editor's widening interest in subjects which go far beyond what one might expect of a Christian monk. Much of what Father Louis learned from his own contemplation, reading, and the writing of poetry must have seemed to be encapsulated in the concise words of Gandhi:

> If we remain non-violent,
> hatred will die as
> everything does from disuse.
>   (G, 21)

A *satyagrahi* cannot wait or delay action till perfect conditions are forthcoming. He will act with whatever material is at hand, purge it of dross and convert it into pure gold. (G, 14)

These often enigmatic sayings of Gandhi must have appealed to Merton because of their poetic quality. The cryptic insights often function like poems as they reverberate outward: "Our non-violence is as yet a mixed affair. It limps. Nevertheless, it is there and it continues to work like a leaven in a silent and invisible way, least understood by most. It is the only way" (G, 74). We can see how Merton, as a monk and as a social commentator, must have appreciated the compression of such wisdom; the fact that he chose such material for his selections indicates his approval. For Merton, Gandhi's wisdom developed because of a life of denial and sacrifice, not a life lived out of selfishness, but one lived for others. Surely that life must have reminded Merton of monastic ideals. So often throughout Father Louis's final years his own concern about language and living shared similar characteristics. Merton saw, from Gandhi's example, that he, too, had to go back into the marketplace.

The Wisdom of the Desert

There is no doubt that as Merton's religious and artistic interests kept expanding his faith in his way of life as a monk was strengthened. There is no better evidence of this than his translation of some of the sayings of the Desert Fathers, a book which reveals, even more than his tributes to Gandhi, his poetic hand shaping material from the *Verba Seniorum*. This interest in the Desert Fathers grows out of the same concerns which brought Father Louis to write essays such as those of *Disputed Questions* or *Faith and Violence,* an interest in man's need for love and solitude, but here his method is much more obviously the method of poet. Each of the tales which he includes in his "personal collection" is "a free and informal reduction,"[4] and, whereas there is a strong sense of urgency implicit in the essays just mentioned and in the collection of writings by Gandhi, with this book of sayings of the Desert Fathers the focus seems to be most fundamentally on enjoyment. Merton pointed out that it was for such reasons that collections such as this one had originally come into existence, and he saw no reason why he should not also have the pleasure of making such a collection for himself and his friends.

The Wisdom of the Desert, Merton's collection of writings by the monks who were the earliest Christian hermits, can be studied along with his essays published in *Mystics and Zen Masters.* Both collections explore common ground shared by East and West and demonstrate that Merton was interested in the possibility of support between various religious traditions. Above all, *The Wisdom of the Desert* reflects his awareness of the responsibilities of Christians who feel called to seek God in solitude far away from society. Thus he was attracted to the writings of these hermits who were drawn to the deserts of Egypt, Arabia, and Persia during the fourth century, men who "abandoned the cities of the pagan world to live in solitude because they regarded society itself as a shipwreck from which each single individual . . . had to swim for his life." Those holy men had refused to allow themselves to drift with society; and Merton recognized them as prophets, representatives of what modern social philosophers "call the emergence of 'axial man,' the forerunner of the modern personalist man."

Merton's main interest in these early contemplatives—and this is clear from the translations he provides—derives from the practical wisdom embodied in their writings. Such stories could make available to modern man basic sources of energy long blocked "by the accumulated mental and spiritual refuse of our technological barbarism." Simplicity, concreteness, and a direct appeal to the experience of man were the qualities which Merton admired in the proverbs and tales of these early hermits. He notes that in the *Verba Seniorum* there is a repeated insistence on the primacy of love—love which takes one's neighbor as one's other self and loves him with "humility and discretion and reserve and reverence." Once these Desert Fathers got a foothold on such solid ground, they realized their "obligation to pull the whole world to safety after them." One short tale reflects the flavor of Merton's selections, and the wisdom he so admired: "There was a certain elder who, if anyone maligned him, would go in person to offer him presents, if he lived nearby. And if he lived at a distance the elder would send presents by the hand of another" (*WD*, 61). This is the complete narrative, yet it implies much about the powers modern men lack. Such simplicity suggests a "new" consciousness which, of course, is not new, but something which had been largely forgotten in the modern world.

Merton's inclusion of a variety of stories about the simplicity of those early hermits reflects his own interests and priorities. He includes many tales that stress humility and the giving of one's self to others. In addition, many of the stories emphasize the use of what one has, rather than the wish to gain something else: "One of the elders said: It is not because evil thoughts came to us that we are condemned, but only because we make use of evil thoughts. It can happen that from these thoughts we suffer shipwreck, but it can also happen that because of them we may be crowned" (*WD*, 45). Paradox, and an emphasis upon what might not usually even be recognized as valuable, are important devices in many of these stories. Each of these tales functions like poetry, and through the focus upon particulars Merton indirectly guides his readers to see the importance of what they may have ignored. The beauty of such insights and method stresses simplicity—such a method allows Merton to make points in a positive way which he had earlier made in a negative or merely expository manner. Castigation of the world, frequent in earlier poetry, and elaborate analysis has no place here: on the contrary, the focus is upon the fact of sin within each person, and the need for each individual to do everything possible to perfect himself. The method is one of good example.

A "Zen" Consciousness

It is not surprising that Merton was also studying and writing about many different varieties of mysticism during the final decade of his life. His *Mystics and Zen Masters* (1967) includes diverse approaches to these and related subjects. Perhaps the most notable feature of this late collection of essays lies in the affirmation of subjects as far-ranging as "Classic Chinese Thought" and "The English

Mystics," "Protestant Monasticism" and "Zen Buddhist Monasticism." In these essays he demonstrates the similarity between and among various traditions. Each of them probes some unlikely place to delineate common assumptions and beliefs.

Merton sets out to show readers that there is a "wealth of experience" which has accumulated in various approaches to mysticism and that it would be a mistake to ignore this treasure, as has, of course, been the case in much of Western civilization, especially since the Renaissance. Merton's concerns here are related to those in his introduction to Gandhi's writings, but his avenue of investigation has been considerably widened. Importantly, he stresses the similar patterns in a wide range of mystical traditions as something quite relevant to "the crises of modern society."[5] Western thought is largely cluttered by reliance on practicality, efficiency, and selfishness. Merton's job is to find ways to remind his readers that there are other valid ways of living.

In his consideration of "Classic Chinese Thought," Merton emphasizes the fact that it is only because of a loss of a sense of unity that man has become reliant upon rationalization. Modern society is so extremely ordered and organized that the primitive, self-forgetful man is no longer easily found. Nevertheless, the ideals as outlined by a thinker like Lao Tzu, can still remind us of our need for wholeness. Merton quotes the poet: "It was when the Great Tao declined / That there appeared humanity and righteousness" (*MZM,* 49). The point is clear, yet Merton insists if we choose to ignore such wisdom we make it more difficult to move back toward the unity which is.

Similarly, Merton saw a value for Westerners in Zen Buddhism, and he believed that Western society and individual Christians could profit from the concrete practice of Zen. Such meditation could help man attain enlightenment, above all, to "see with his own nature, yet this does not mean man's rational nature, the seat of our empirical consciousness." It is rather a need for enlightenment through what the mystics called the " 'ground' of our soul or of our being." Zen insight, then, consists in the direct grasp of "one's 'original face,' " yet man arrives at this mind by having no mind. To put it differently, Merton insists that Westerners are "plagued with the heritage of . . . Cartesian self-awareness, which assumed that the empirical ego is the starting point of an infallible intellectual progress to truth and spirit, more and more refined, abstract and immaterial." He realized that something crucial had been left out of much Western consciousness.

In essays on Zen Buddhism Merton sought to make man aware of this serious sin of omission. He also stressed that, in a paradoxical way, Western man's sin of omission was also a sin of commission because he insists on doing too much, while in Zen Merton saw the aim was

the creation of an entirely new consciousness which is free to deal with life barehanded and without pretenses. Piercing the illusions in ourselves which divide us from others, it must enable man to attain unity and solidarity with his brother through openness and compassion, endowed with secret resources of creativity. (*MZM*, 287)

He qualified that, for instance, the Zen of Hui Neng is not a "mystique of passivity and of withdrawal. It is not a resting in one's own interiority but a complete release from bondage to the limited and subjective self" (*MZM*, 41). It should be noted that within these essays Merton is not, in any way, giving up his Catholicism; rather he sees that Christian belief is strengthened by a focus achieved through a new way of being (not thinking).

Merton's interest in Zen Buddhism and in other methods of becoming attuned to the universe can be profitably approached in relation to much of his own creative writing. His attraction to the Eastern wisdom of mystics is not unrelated to his admiration of many of the Western mystics, and his essays (for example, in *Disputed Questions*), the translations in *The Wisdom of the Desert*, and the poems written in the late 1950s all suggest that Merton was finding many ways to focus on what seemed essential. All of this prepared him to read and absorb additional non-Western materials. In addition, Merton's admiration for D. T. Suzuki, correspondence with him, and eventually meeting with him in 1964, allowed Father Louis to extend such concerns and to sharpen his observations of parallels between Christianity and Zen. Another collection of Merton's essays—published under the title *Zen and the Birds of Appetite*—represents additional concerted thinking about the complementarity of Western Christianity and Zen. This collection includes a dialogue entitled "Wisdom in Emptiness," written with D. T. Suzuki, and the entire book is another reflection of Merton's developing artistic strength, which increased as he became more attuned to non-Western modes of expression.[6]

Just as the Desert Father elder who would send gifts to any person who maligned him, Merton was coming to stress a freedom which expressed an awareness of others and minimized personal self-awareness and subjectivity. The essays of *Zen and the Birds of Appetite* emphasize repeatedly that modern man remains in desperate need of being so liberated "from his inordinate self-consciousness . . . his obsession with self-affirmation, so that he may enjoy the freedom from concern that goes with being simply what he is and accepting things as they are in order to work with them as he can" (*ZBA*, 31). Merton acknowledged that to fulfill such needs modern man might simply return to the lessons of the Gospel. But he suggested that we would also do well "to turn to Asian religion," and thereby come to a more accurate understanding of "unworldliness." Through such non-Christian traditions it is possible "to come to grips with reality without the mediation of logical verbalizing." It was not a matter of turning away from Christianity (he saw parallels of Zen in Christian experience in Meister Eckhart) but a matter of man's need for a radical "new consciousness."

Clearly what occurred during those final years of Merton's career was a developing awareness of what Western man might achieve through an inclusion of impulses from non-Western thought and practice. And as this began happening Merton's artistic interests also shifted to some degree. One is reminded of the simple Zen garden which as novice master he constructed near the noviate, a demonstration that through a careful rearrangement of basic elements man is able to see more clearly. Merton's experiments with photography are another example of changes which took place in his own sensibility during these years. In fact, three distinct creative areas within Merton's final years demonstrate his absorption of non-Western practices and a utilization of such approaches. In translations within the extensive entries of his journals, and in formal essays and poetry, we see this artist growing increasingly familiar with ways to adapt Eastern approaches to his own creative ends. Perhaps best of all Merton realized that through Zen man can "see directly." This is a clue to much of his own continuing reevaluation of Western culture.

Chuang Tzu

Merton's interests in many varieties of Western thought as material for poetry and other art shows his conscious attempt to avoid a stereotyped approach to modern civilization's problems. Related to this was his continuing interest in South American poets, who, in his opinion, had roots close to the native people. Merton translated and encouraged such poets. His closeness to Ernesto Cardenal is a beautiful example of this. His attraction to the classic Chinese poet Chuang Tzu reflects a similar interest. He saw that in Chuang Tzu one might learn to avoid the manipulation of facts and get to the essentials of living. His free translations of texts from Chuang Tzu became one of his favorite projects, a very personal rendering of the classic poet who, he said, was "my own kind of person."

When he sent this collection of translations of the classic poet Chuang Tzu to the press he called his "readings" of Chuang Tzu "ventures in personal and spiritual interpretation."[7] He insisted that not all of these "renderings" can even qualify as poetry. One of the most obvious things about them as poems, however, is Merton's obvious enjoyment of the "spontaneity" reflected in them. They are successful as poetry because they provide fresh, clean, insightful looks at the nature of man.

The key to the thought of Chuang Tzu, and a key to appreciating Merton's own artistic development, is the fact that all beings are in a constant state of flux, and all life is a continual development. What may seem impossible from one perspective seems therefore to make sense from another. Thus the poem "Three in the Morning" provides a solution for monkeys who refused three measures of food in the morning, and four in the afternoon—simply by reversing the number of measures given in afternoon and morning.

To learn to see the present in terms of the "complementarity of opposites" is central to Chuang Tzu's view of the world. Merton renders the conclusion of "Great and Small" in this way:

> He who moves with the stream of events
> Is called a wise statesman.
>
> Kui, the one-legged dragon,
> Is jealous of the centipede.
> The centipede is jealous of the snake.
> The snake is jealous of the wind.
> The wind is jealous of the eye.
> The eye is jealous of the mind.
> Kui said to the centipede:

> "I manage my one leg with difficulty:
> How can you manage a hundred?"
> The centipede replied:
> "I do not manage them."
>
> (*WCT*, 88–89)

Through such wisdom he sought to reassess aspects of his own life, and this reassessment had a definite effect on his writing. As we have seen, *Conjectures of a Guilty Bystander* provides glimpses of how that reassessment took place. Merton was learning that true *contemptus mundi* is "a compassion for the transient world and a humility which refuses . . . to set up the church as an 'eternal' institution in the world." And, he qualified, we cannot "despise the transient world of secularism in terms which suggest an ecclesiastical *world* that is not itself transient."[8] *All* things of the world are transitory, yet of course some things do not change.

When Merton chooses texts from Chuang Tzu his emphasis is upon the changing and substantial. He seeks to render these poems into translations which will speak to today's reader who needs to be reminded of the essential as compared to the transitory:

> Great knowledge sees all in one.
> Small knowledge breaks down into the many.
> [or]
> The true men of old
> Slept without dreams,
> Woke without worries.
> Their food was plain.
> They breathed deep.
> True men breathe from their heels.
> Others breathe with their gullets,
> Half-strangled.
>
> (*WCZ*, 40, 60)

Merton's fondness for such poems also reflects his distancing of himself from the role of poet, yet joined, paradoxically, with enjoyment of that role too. His style in these "renderings" of Chuang Tzu is clipped, terse, like the best "Zen-mystical" poems of *Emblems*.[9] He must have felt that some of his previously published poems, such as "Song for Nobody," were complemented by these poems of Chuang Tzu which he clearly enjoyed rephrasing into English:

Where is Tao?

Master Tunk Kwo asked Chuang:
"Show me where the Tao is found."
Chuang Tzu replied:
"There is nowhere it is not to be found."
                                    (*WCZ*, 123)

In all of the writings which draw upon a knowledge of the East, Merton seems to be saying that, like Gandhi, men must honor the world, not abstractions; they must learn to see life as a whole; they *"must do good irrespective of the consequences."* We have seen that Father Louis believed that the Western mind is blinded by expedience; Westerners quite literally bound up in explanations and excuses are "no longer able to *see* directly what is in front of [them]." Progress at the technological level "has in fact been a progress in servility," and thus we have "made ourselves incapable of . . . happiness which transcends servility and simply rejoices in being for its own sake."

Through writings which emphasize Eastern themes Merton sought to reintroduce into Western consciousness a liberality of approach. In his view such a unified existence had been lost because Western man continued to impose expedient choices on ever wider areas of his existence. Through Chinese poetry, the Desert Fathers, through an awareness of Zen and non-Western myths, Merton sought to show modern man how he might begin to reform. In an essay about the Zen Koan, Merton demonstrated Rilke's empathy with Buddhism because it forced man to stop trying to be "objective." But he also admitted that Western man refuses "healing because we insist on preserving our status as spectators."[10] Merton's study of the Zen Koan emphasizes an awareness of the desirability of a "state of pure consciousness which is no longer 'consciousness of.' "

All the concerns outlined in this chapter led naturally into the last phase of Father Louis's contemplative and artistic journey, and to the final literary works he produced which culminated in the *Asian Journal,* a record of, in his words, "being at last on my true way after years of waiting and wondering and fooling around."[11]

Chapter Eight
Experimental Poetry

Slowly slowly
Comes Christ through the garden....
                    "80," Cables to the Ace

New Ways of Seeing

In much of the poetry written during Merton's final years we see a poet who could demonstrate the virtues of silence, but also the liabilities of too much noise. As a hermit Father Louis experienced the quiet he and others needed, while at the same time being allowed imaginatively to see, hear, and imagine the frenetic excitement of a world becoming ever-more noisy than that of the 1930s he had left. His editor, James Laughlin, once commented that Merton used to request that copies of the *New Yorker* be sent to him, and Laughlin added that he thought one of the reasons Merton enjoyed that magazine was its lavish advertisements.[1] In those sophisticated and glamorous ads Merton saw reflected the delusions and myths common to his contemporary materialistic society. The point remains, however, that he did enjoy the magazine; and there is a crucial difference between the mature Merton's compassionate awareness of the illusions of the world, as reflected in this later period, and earlier writing which was almost arrogant and disdainful of the world. So one of the most important facts about *Cables to the Ace* and *The Geography of Lograire* is a definite compassion for contemporary mankind—even if for a mankind often lost in its own technology and in a mass-culture mentality. Man is so busy that he can no longer be; he becomes instead what others wish him to be.

A basic fact about Merton's later group of poems (collections despite what some might wish to maintain) is his concern for others, coupled with his spontaneity and enthusiasm. At the same time, in this final phase of poetic production, Merton appears to be less concerned with these poems as finished works. Some years earlier his thinking about the nature of poetry had shifted. He had come to see poetry neither as just providing precise information, nor expressing how the poet felt. It was more. Approached in this way poetry is information and feeling, but it is also a reflection of making things out as one lives and writes. The poet's concern must not be merely the production of finished objects, works to be crafted and exhibited, like something preserved in a museum. In his "message to poets," published in 1964, Merton had announced: "We who are poets know that the reason for a poem is not discovered until the poem itself exists. The reason for a living art is realized only in the art itself." And in the same essay he warned against a poet losing such innocence for the poet cannot pretend to be an expert with all the answers.

He also acknowledged that the Western world had seldom shown respect for poets; already in Plato's *Republic* there was no place for poets or musicians; and today, he noted, "the technological Platos who think they now run the world we live in . . . imagine they can tempt us with banalities and abstractions. But we can elude them merely by stepping into the Heraklitean river which is never crossed twice."[2] He also insisted that "no one can enter the river (of poetry) wearing the garments of public and collective ideas." Poetic immediacy springs from a mind divested of banal abstractions. Just such steps toward a poetry of immediacy were taken by Father Louis the artist. The fact that he was finally able to live as a hermit in seclusion from other members of the Abbey of Gethsemani is a symbol for the general development of his art during his final three years.

The concern in this chapter is with the development of the mature poetic abilities; when doing so, we must remember that, paradoxical as it may seem, while the poetry (and other types of writing) became more experimental, Merton's desire to be recognized as a successful poet was considerably modified. During these final years he became much more relaxed in a new role, and as he phrased it in the prologue to *Cables to the Ace*, subtitled "Familiar Liturgies of Misunderstanding," "the old poet . . . changed his address and his poetics are on vacation. / He is not roaring in the old tunnel."[3] He implied that he needed a change from the predictability of what had been produced earlier, and he admits that it might be difficult for old readers to follow his new ways.

Difficulties for readers stem from the fact that much of what they had come to expect from this sometimes pious, reverent, orthodox "religious" poet was no longer so visible in the persona of *Cables*. Father Louis of the Cistercians was no longer the same. He had become much more playful. This "new" writer, with a new address, had absorbed so much from other traditions that his writing, and especially the newest poetry, would even seem shocking to those familiar only with an old liturgy. But Merton's artistic growth, attested by his journals, correspondence, and essays, had been a gradual development; thus with the proper perspective there is nothing dismaying about the changes in his poetry too.

Merton's journey toward an embrace of the immediate could also be discussed in terms of his developing interest in calligraphy and photography; it could be examined in terms of his personal development as reflected in correspondence and journals. My recent article on the journals as a step toward contemplation provides systematic evidence of changes in Merton's way of approaching the world, himself, and his writing, through the refinement of his journals. Above all, it should be noted that Merton's sometimes ironic and inquisitive approach to the responsibilities of contemplative and writer resulted in art that built upon an increasing assimilation of techniques characterized by spontaneity and living, enthusiasm and loving. The collection *Cables to the Ace* best demonstrates this side of Merton—a poetic skill which revealed that while he could not provide the answers, he would continue to raise some questions. He chose to raise such questions by having fun with poems which are difficult, usually indirect, and often ironic.

Cables to the Ace

Cables to the Ace is a collection of poems which exhibit Merton moving toward new ways of expressing his experience of silence and the contemplative existence, and also reflecting his concern for the contemporary milieu. The ninety poems, lyrics, and prose-poems function as a collage and challenge the reader not to look for direct messages or old techniques. The cables remain indirect because it is only through the oblique that this poet can make us begin to sense what he knows (not understands!).

Various commentators have explained how the book is structured and how its diverse contents bring about its effects. Luke Flaherty, for instance, maintains that an imaginative union of East and West is a central factor of the poem; yet such an ordered reading of the book probably assigns more unity than Merton himself sought.[4] It seems best to think of the collection as a series of beginnings. Merton's own comments about the book are illuminating in this regard because we see that his attitude was complex and included a desire to produce poetry that had characteristics of formal art, but also retained the pull of ironic, informal, and antipoetic characteristics. For these reasons Merton was not particularly concerned that the book might be judged by accepted standards. He knew that his reader would be wondering: "Why not more pictures? Why not more rhythms, melody, etc.? All suitable questions to be answered some other time." As poet he indicates that if he is going to get at the truth he will have to do so in a way different than has been formerly expected. One is reminded of Flannery O'Connor's remarks about her aesthetic which stresses that extraordinary means are necessitated when one is confronted by an audience which is no longer in the habit of observing.[5] O'Connor said that for those who are blind, or almost so, you have to write with large figures; for those who are deaf, you must shout. An awareness similar to this underlies Merton's approach in *Cables;* he realized that we live in a world where language has become so contorted that it is extremely difficult to honor the truth. No one listens; instead they hear what they want to hear, or are content with noise, never with listening.

The prologue for *Cables,* dated May 1967, makes it clear that this group of poems will differ from those that preceded it. The poet knows that his readers will be surprised. He indicates that his ironies will be "no less usual than the bright pages of your favorite magazine," a way of implying that the world is so full of noise and meaningless symbols that perhaps the only way to handle such a fact is to play a similar game and, therefore, inundate the reader with words and images. Perhaps after man has been blitzed by such chaos, he may again be able to recognize true, honorable, and clean uses of language. As Merton indicates, man needs "massive lessons of irony and refusal." Being surrounded as he is by noises, noises which "are never values," it is almost as if he has forgotten proper ways to use language. It was with such ideas in mind that Merton wrote the concluding sentence of the second poem in *Cables:* "The sayings of the saints are put away in air-conditioned archives"; and a similar idea is developed in many of the poems which follow. Contemporary man has forgotten how to look, listen, read, even to speak.

This poet informs us that we must come to these cables with care, especially so when language is no longer used carefully:

> Come shyly to the main question
> There is dishonor in these wires
> You will first hesitate then repeat
> Then sing louder
> To the drivers
> Of ironic mechanisms
> As they map your political void.
> (*Ca,* "#5," 4)

Merton's speaker seems to be convinced that the only way we can get at essential questions is to strip away the accretions and the evil of a world full of misused, misnamed, misinterpreted, mistaken language. Yet strength will develop as man learns to "sing louder."

Gail Ramshaw Schmidt, who first studied the manuscript and notebooks for *Cables,* has indicated that these poems fall into three basic sections or movements which function like concentric circles or spirals, as the poet moves closer to an expression of what is wrong (and right) about man's apprehension of the truth.[6] She focuses on poems "#7," "#45," and "#80" as stages in this movement. Each of these lyric-prayers is a significant step in a kind of spiral staircase which allows the speaker to move the reader toward an awareness that methods to pray, to meditate, to appreciate silence and wholeness still remain. Yet most men seem to have lost contact with such basic facts.

Poem "#7," entitled "Original Sin," has the subtitle "A Memorial Anthem for Father's Day"; in this lyric Merton reminds us of man "walking and talking" but out of contact with the facts of history, and even the fact of sin. Therefore, he needs to be reminded to "Weep, weep . . . For the Father of the lame. . . ." While the three-part description of *Cables* by Schmidt is perhaps more rigid than necessary, such a spiral pattern is important. Finally, there are more cycles within the book than three, yet there is little doubt that all of the parts which Schmidt has focused upon as crucial moments in the overall pattern are extremely significant. Each of the three poems culminates a movement; all are prayers; and all reflect a speaker who makes progress toward the spiritual and away from the noise(s) of the world. In each instance the poet suggests that we can begin again.

There are several other places in the collection, in addition to these three poems, where Merton speculates about how to begin again; his speaker makes one new start in the following way:

> I think poetry must
> I think it must
> Stay open all night
> In beautiful cellars. . . .
> (*Ca*, "#53")

This is one short, evocative example of another new beginning. In fact, these lines sum up a general pattern in the book. The poet says that man must recognize the need to be independent; to make such poetry (to live a real life) means that he should not be dependent upon others, and especially not dependent upon worn-out language which someone else, or a committee, has formed. But one must descend into the darkness of self if true poetry and life are to be found.

Manuscript study shows that the earliest section to be written for this book is the part called "Imperatives." These ironic commands suggest much about what Merton achieves in the entire book as he laments man's unwillingness to descend into darkness. Written first, and an underlying pattern in the composition of the poem as a whole, these short ironic comments are the imperatives for which Merton has no respect:

> 1) Move that system.
> 2) Eat more chunks and get young.
> 3) Own a doll that glows.
> 4) Swallow cash.
> 5) Advance and have words with Barbecue.
> 6) Make noise in bed.
> (*Ca*, "#69,")

His job as poet (or antipoet) is to make his readers aware of the absurdity of such commands, while at the same time making them aware that their very lives are influenced in all kinds of subtle, and not so subtle, ways by such uses of language.

In *Cables* it becomes necessary for Merton to write poetry that suggests man's loss of respect for life itself; he does this to point up the loss of respect which apparently has become flagrant in society as a whole. Poems "#60," "#61," and "#62" illustrate Merton's method—a technique already apparent in the 1941 novel, *My Argument with the Gestapo,* namely, the technique of a collage reflecting a world full of distractions, a world which promises everything to those who accept it, yet which makes little sense.

The first part provides crazy words of encouragement:

> Oh, said the discontented check, you will indeed win like
> it says in the papers, but first you have to pay.
> The bridges burn their builders behind them.

There is an ominousness buried here; the promisory note seems to be speaking words of encouragement, but then the following lines— about black people, the blues, and not winning—cancel the initial words of false hope with the surprise: "The colored weepers try their luck with strings." We realize little good can follow.

Poem "#61" entertains the contradictions of a popular advertisement for cigarettes. Here the worlds of dream, fantasy, reality, and Madison Avenue clichés, run together:

> I will get up and go to Marble country
> Where deadly smokes grow out of moderate heat
> And all the cowboys look for fortunate slogans
> Among horses' asses.

These lines begin with the speaker's resolve that he must act decisively—yet he seems to realize that his mind is mostly a mix of wish and confusion. Marlboro becomes Marble and the ads (and their promises) are fused with the deeper realization that such ads are silly; the fake cowboys look glamorous, and while they are looking for something which makes sense, they are already lost.

Almost as if a message had been sent from another sphere, poem "#62" begins with a long quotation from Dōgen: "Abandon your body and soul into the abundance of light sent from above and give no thought to enlightenment or illusion. Only sit like a great void of fire. . . . Think of what you cannot think. In other words, think Nothing." Good advice, but difficult to abide by when one is full of a mixture of interest in the world, and an awareness of the need to turn away from it. One's wall of separation is not sufficient; the speaker replies: "All very fine, but his wall is full of cracks. The winds blow through in every direction. He claims his light is out and secretly turns it on again to read novels. . . ." Merton is clearly making fun of himself, and the last line goes even a step further: "He builds a big fire to keep beginners warm: give him credit for his kindness." The poet implies that his own writings have provided material to get others started in the spiritual life, but he himself remains at a distance from any ideal such as that recommended by Dōgen. To think of what you cannot think requires a lot of sifting away of the unessential; especially is this the case when noises continue to fill up our lives.

Merton's task in this long collection of interrelated poems is not unlike that of Whitman in *Leaves of Grass,* or Hart Crane in *The Bridge;* he seeks a way to acknowledge the real world of everyday reality; but through that everyday fact and physical reality he also suggests the spiritual. Thus as Walter Sutton has suggested, *Cables* participates both in the epic tradition of American poetry and in experiments in American free verse.[7] Merton's poems are both private exercises and conscious reflection on larger patterns in society as a whole. This is apparently why these poems can be simultaneously funny and serious. American society continues to seek the spiritual, but it has gotten so far off track that it has become amusing. Laughter, then, might be a valid way to get back to what is most important.

Much of *Cables* is meant to entertain. The poet is simply enjoying himself and that is fundamental. Unfortunately, some commentators do not understand this. They feel that a proper synthesis has not been made and wonder if one can both smile and remain serious. For them, Merton seems to be writing too many different kinds of poems at once. Yet the collection does work together, and much of the fun is provided through very complex poetry compressing a great deal of meaning. Poems "#20a" and "#20b" might be singled out for attention. Both are microcosmic views of Western man's (sad or amusing) history, and both are packed with literary allusions. In "#20b," "To daughters: to study history" Merton alludes to Joyce and Shakespeare, to Mark Twain and Augustine, as he reminds daughters not to make the same mistakes as men. In these few short lines he is saying that women should be careful about getting caught in the web of words and history, but at the same time they must get caught if they are not going to repeat the tragic history of man once again.

Certain sections of *Cables* stand out. Poem "#80," "Slowly, slowly. . . ." for instance, possibly the culmination of the entire book and the final and crucial moment in the cyclical movement outlined by Schmidt, reassures the reader that even amid the noise of the contemporary world Christ will come to find the lost disciple. There is a definite link between this poem and "#20b," discussed above. The speaker announces:

> The disciple will awaken
> When he knows history
> But slowly slowly
> The lord of History
> Weeps into the fire.

The hymn, "Slowly, slowly" occurs within a context of many other poems which stress frenzied activity. It is a culminating prayer, preceded by other specific prayers. It is also a reminder that, although we are surrounded by noise, if we stop to praise God, he will come. In the notebook containing the first drafts of this poem, Merton labeled it "Slowly hymn." It functions as one more beginning and, of course, it is just the opposite of all the "imperatives" which man so easily heeds.

> Slowly slowly
> Comes Christ through the ruins
> Seeking the lost disciple
> A timid one
> Too literate
> To believe words
> So he hides. . . .

The fact that Merton added the French phrase "*(Pourrait être continué)*" at the end of this book is significant. *Cables* is both a finished product, and a collection which could be continued indefinitely. Merton's point is that man will continue to be surrounded by noise and chaos, but even with that fact new beginnings, new poems, new appreciations of reality come, if man will stop to find ways to praise God.

Both of the long experimental poems, *Cables* and *The Geography of Lograire*, might be described as Merton's exploration of ideas (sometimes contradictory) which aim at a synthesis that is impossible without a blending of Eastern and Western ideas. Basic to *Cables,* and also the source of much of its fun, is its contradiction. A complete explication of this complex poem has not been attempted; but it is helpful to remember that the method employed is an allusiveness which draws upon Merton's reading of major poets such as T. S. Eliot and Shakespeare, and of mystics from both Eastern and Western traditions. In the mosaic of the poems as a whole, Merton builds a bridge between Eastern and Western myths while the quiet each person needs is at the center. Scattered throughout *Cables* are references to Zen and mysticism and hence the enigmatic nature of many of the poems; through them the speaker makes it clear that he is moving toward transcendence.

Dōgen, the Zen master, says within *Cables:* "Concern yourself with nothing. . . ." Yet, as we have seen, the very next lines suggest the difficulty for anyone as inquisitive as Merton in trying to follow such advice, because "He [the speaker?] claims his light is out while he secretly turns it on again to read novels." The beauty is that his speaker does (at least somewhat) care about nothing; and the paradox is that everything then takes on brilliance and value: "Once you become aware of yourself as seeker, you are lost. But if you are content to be lost you will be found without knowing it, precisely because you are lost, for you are, at last, nowhere" (*Ca,* "#84"). *Cables to the Ace* reflects Merton's wide reading and indicates that he was increasingly aware of the need to find oneself precisely by disassociating oneself from the conventionally accepted. We should note that just like his speaker who claims the light is out while he reads novels by night, Father Louis continued an extremely wide variety of investigations. Still more of his reading and thinking is reflected within the final long poem, a work described as a "purely tentative first draft," one he hoped might become a much longer poem. Here again, in technique, Merton moves beyond conventions.

Lograire

As we have seen, Father Louis became increasingly interested in the relationships of the sacred and the secular during the latter part of his career. His interest in Eastern religion and philosophy, the poetry of Chuang Tzu, Gandhi, all indicate how he was seeking to find answers to questions about the world. His awareness of too much concern with doing, too much concern with understanding, too much concern for one's own specific good rather than the good of all, characteristic of much of modern Western society, led him to raise still broader questions about the drift of society. Such is his basic concern in the long experimental poem, *The Geography of Lograire*. He wrote in his "author's note" that the book stood as the beginning of a project, a draft of a longer work in progress, in which there are necessarily many gaps.[8] It is a poetic overview of Merton's thinking about a civilization that had grown fat, often at the expense of other cultures, absorbed, abused, and ignored.

This poem is an inner cartograph, a search for understanding by Merton, and an investigation of certain aspects of mind important for the poet's own understanding which also illuminate the general experience of European civilization during the past several centuries. At times *The Geography of Lograire* reads like a journal; at other times it reads like notes for an anthropological or sociological study. At still other times the text functions like the record of a nightmare or the lyric presentation of a vision only partially remembered. Together, its many parts provide an investigation of several themes that Merton felt Western man did not wish to confront. Thus, the poem is about how European man in his self-righteousness has been unable to accept the structures of other cultures, but instead projects his own wishes and desires upon the cultures which he seeks to dominate.

Although Merton's method can be very private, his construction of this sometimes travelogue illuminates the experiences of all men. The method results in a poem that, while occasionally seeming to be notes for a projected work, explores various Western connections to African, Central American, Arab, Melanesian, and American Indian cultural and literary patterns. The author's note emphasizes that

This is only a beginning of patterns, the first opening up of a dream. A poet spends his life in repeated projects, over and over again attempting to build or to dream the world in which he lives. But more and more he realizes that this world is at once his and everybody's. It cannot be purely private any more than it can be purely public. It cannot be fully communicated. It grows out of a common participation which is nevertheless recorded in authentically personal images. (*GL,* 1)

Lograire is on one level a catalog of Merton's reading, because the poem is so absolutely and unabashedly straightforward in its use of sources which are not "assimilated" in the manner of T. S. Eliot or Ezra Pound. Yet we might do well to remember that in a fundamental sense Merton was trying to avoid such assimilation. Similarly, we can think of this draft-book as a combination of effects deriving from a knowledge of poets like Eliot, and Eliot's influence in relation to the "Tradition," but also effects deriving from William Carlos Williams, whose methods are often just the opposite of Eliot's. Just as in Williams's *In the American Grain,* Merton sought to develop a method which sometimes mirrored his sources.

The poem is far more, however, than a reading list. Merton always thought as a poet—even during the years when he did not produce a large amount of formal poetry. What seems to have happened during these final years when he lived as a hermit is that he was able to achieve a synthesis (or at least a beginning toward one) which drew together a life's work of reading, writing, and meditating. The result is an ambitious draft that begins with Father Louis's reading, moves to the poet's own life and its mythic patterns, and then moves beyond to imply parallels between such patterns and all Western dreamers. The fact that Merton was corresponding with Louis Zukofsky as he wrote *Lograire* might also be noted. Merton's attitude toward Zukofsky can be observed in their correspondence and in a review he published on Zukofsky's poetry.[9] Merton admired the precision of his method celebrating the most minute aspects of language and reality. Zukofsky knew that each word must be honored, and it was with this same reverence that Merton composed *Lograire. The Geography of Lograire* is an ambitious poem that draws upon an awareness of innovations made by many poets including Pound, Eliot, and Williams; it is also an extension of concerns earlier elaborated in *Cables to the Ace.* Like *Cables,* it is about the alienation of the self, but it focuses ultimately upon the alienation of all in the Western world who have lost contact with the essence of being human. *Lograire* is an elaborate, sometimes personal myth, that seeks to get at the false assumptions of the Western world.[10] The poet expresses his awareness of the value of other cultures through an expression of Western man's unawareness. From the viewpoint of his imagined outsiders who analyze and attack Western myth Merton's speaker lets his readers see their own false assumptions.

The most fundamental accomplishment in *Lograire* is to imagine the coming of the white man to other cultures by describing that arrival in terms of other people. Thus the Spanish conquest is seen in an altogether different light, and we are made to understand that the Western myth (of superiority and progress) denies the myth-dream of other cultures. Merton's procedure always remains quite specific. His investigation includes an account of the Kane Relief Expedition to the North Pole used to suggest how Western man flees from himself and from self-knowledge. Then a contrasting view of medieval Moslem life follows where the emphasis of the culture is clearly upon the numinous rather than on material concerns. In still other parts of the poem Merton investigates the Cargo cults (based on the arrival of military ships loaded with goods) that grew up with the arrival of Americans in Melanesia and New Guinea during World War II. He was convinced that such cults developed because of the extreme emphasis placed on material goals in Western society. He wrote to his editor: "If [these people] want Cargo it is not only because they need material things but because Cargo will establish them as equal to the white man and give them an identity as respectable as his . . . if they believe in Cargo it is because they believe in their own fundamental human worth and believe it can be shown in this way" (*GL*, 149).

The poem's wide variety of sources, along with the poet's meditations, together stress how the peculiarities of cults formed by primitive people provide insight into our own distorted values. It is the trust of such simple people, combined with a desire to have what they see others possess, which causes confusion. The poet imagines: "Jesus Christ is now in Sydney waiting to deliver Cargo to natives without the intervention of white men. He has a steamer and it is all loaded. But he does not yet have the proper clothing. Jesus Christ is waiting in a hotel room for someone to bring him a suit" (*GL*, 104). Merton utilizes many such seemingly odd ideas derived from a wide range of non-Western sources within the section "East" of *The Geography of Lograire*.[11] The opening lines are based on *Travels in Asia and Africa 1325–1354*, a book by the Muslim, Ibn Battuta (1304–69). The following poem picks up on Bronislaw Malinowski's journal about his travels in the South Seas, *A Diary in the Strict Sense of the Term*. However, the work incorporates extensive rephrasing, condensation, and rearrangement. In other sections of "East," where there are numerous references to Cargo cults, the account is based primarily on Merton's reading of three books, and again basic facts are rearranged to strengthen the poetic presentation. With such a specific method, Merton was able to emphasize that such myths are significant reflections of basic problems within (or generated by) Western culture. In many of the examples Merton chooses to incorporate into *Lograire,* his underlying preoccupation seems to be that Western man has too often assumed superiority and in that process forgotten to look at the complexity of the other cultures which he encounters.

Structure of a Dream

The basic structure of *The Geography of Lograire* is four part. Labeled South, North, East, and West, four cantos provide glimpses and fragments of Merton's poetic world that reflect the four corners of the globe, yet more often than not glimpses of a world suppressed or forgotten by others. The poem is, then, a record of Merton's personal geography—his own meditations and readings recorded. Sometimes there is "literal and accurate quotation with slight editing and with . . . much personal arrangement" (*GL,* 140).

Merton wanted to remind readers of how in so many different cultural situations there remains a common pattern of living and dead (persons and myths) which go together to build the culture. It is implied that Western man is frequently concerned only with control, with doing, with manipulation, and, therefore, forgets that his life is a continuum with many other individuals and cultures. Merton seeks to map out a geography which includes details hitherto uncharted. His purpose is to demonstrate how the public and private worlds of man merge, and to demonstrate that there are many more common world-wide patterns than we choose to remember. Anyone's life (physical, mental, spiritual) is acted upon by a myriad of influences. Thus in his "Prologue: The Endless Inscription" Merton recalls his own Welsh ancestors; he also alludes to Dylan Thomas's poetry; and he echoes Joyce and the Catholic liturgy. He suggests thereby some of the complexity which will follow. The poet's main task is to reveal the complexity and interrelationships of diverse cultures, a complexity which apparently has often been ignored. As the poet reveals the complexity of his own "myth-dream" he implies the complexity of others, dreams of others who have not even sought to articulate what they feel in the presence of a dominant, aggressive, and materialistic European-centered culture.

A complete explication of *The Geography of Lograire* would involve an investigation of all of the separate poems in the volume.[12] For instance, the long section "I: Queen's Tunnel" in the North canto is probably the most difficult single section of the poem because it relies heavily upon details from Merton's biography. No exhaustive attempt is made here to illuminate all of that eighteen-page section. The analysis of the book which follows is primarily concerned with demonstrating Merton's use of historical, anthropological, and travel documents to build important sections. Some sources upon which he relied still remain to be identified, but with all the materials which editors have identified it is possible to see how Merton crafted this poetry from many sources.

The first canto, "South," deals with changing myths about race, both in the American South and in Central America. Toward the end of this canto the focus of the poem moves to the destruction of the native central American Indian cultures by the Spanish early in the history of the new world. Just as William Carlos Williams charted the destruction of Cortez in *In the American Grain,* Merton here provides a new view of the Mayan people and their beliefs so little understood by Spanish chroniclers. Merton may have made his own fresh translation from the Spanish of Fray Bernadino de Sahagun's (1499–1590) *Historia general de las cosas de Nueva España,* for some of the lines are directly dependent upon that work.

In section 8, "Ce Xochitl: The Sign of Flowers (Mexico)," details about a festival of flowers in honor of the god Xochilhuitl are related; then Bishop Diego de Landa (1524–79) is quoted: "Such were the services which their demons commanded them" (*GL,* 26). Landa, we might note, has the distinction of having burned as many of the Mayan books as he could find. Merton's obvious point is that Western man destroyed much of the Mayan culture before he could understand it. The section of the poem which follows includes a discussion of early Mexican art. Section 10, "Chilam Balam (Yucatan)," is based on *The Book of the Jaguar Priest: A Translation of the Book of Chilam Balam of Tizimin.* Here again Merton's technique is to quote from a primary source, then to arrange the quotations in a way which emphasizes the losses sustained when the Yucatan culture was supplanted by other civilizations.

The manner in which Merton developed some of the *Lograire* poems from source, to prose translation, to paraphrase, and then to poetry has been carefully traced by Gail Schmidt.[13] Merton's arrangement of this poetry implies that a similar kind of destruction of culture continues to take place today. Thus in section 11, "Dzules

(Yucatan)," he alternates between specifics documenting the destruction of Yucatan culture four hundred years ago and the supposed need to keep inferior people in place today. The overall effect of the South canto is to create the impression that Western (Christian) man thoughtlessly destroys other cultures that he encounters, without providing a replacement; killing for no reason: "Geography is in trouble all over Lograire" (*GL,* 60).

In "North" Merton traces various kinds of escapes symbolic of Western man's inability to confront reality. In "Queen's Tunnel" various flights are charted, examples of man's attempts to get away from the realities of his guilt. Here Merton's dream becomes nightmare.

Religious persecution is the subject of North, section 3, "The Ranters and Their Pleads." The bulk of this section is quoted directly or excerpted from a study of millenialism in seventeenth-century England. Merton's interests in this poem are based on the psychological phenomenon of what happens if an idea or belief is suppressed and how it may then manifest itself in some other way. Preceding this particular poem Merton included another about perverted uses of sex within the modern world. All of this seems to be preparation for section 4, "Kane Relief Expedition," a part of the poem heavily reliant upon Dr. James Laws's journal of that expedition in 1855.

The poetic expedition, within the structure of Merton's poem, is symbolic of Western man's attempts to conquer nature, to redo the natural world which he finds. The actual 1855 expedition was a search in the bays west of Greenland for a lost Arctic expedition. This section documents the white man's attempt at supremacy over the native Eskimo's land. Yet just as we realize at the conclusion of "South" that perhaps more harm than good has been done during Western man's exploration of the new world, in this section we see that the pride of Western man can be crushed. The natural setting described is a threatening one: "Two thousand feet / Into the rain / Not a spot of green" (*GL,* 71) and finally the iceberg forces the expedition to turn around. Through a juxtaposition of specific details Merton makes it clear that the members of the expedition had little respect for the country they were entering. Finally the iceberg proves too much of a foe and the Europeans, bent upon planting their flag in still one more place, are forced to retreat. One of the underlying meanings of this canto (relating back to the prologue, moving through the various modes of escape charted in "Queen's Tunnel," and through the craziness of religious hysteria in the seventeenth century) is that the European culture which Merton evokes is literally on the run from itself. The icebergs, however, are "like churches / Slow sailing gifts" (*GL*, 69), and finally they work to force man to realize that he must recognize his place within the world.

In the "East" canto the basic point emphasized is the inability of Westerners to understand the East. Both the introduction to this section and "East with Ibn Battuta" are reliant directly upon Ibn Battuta's journals about travels during the years 1325–54. This canto emphasizes the contrast between Eastern and Western customs, a contrast so great that words can only begin to suggest the amazement that a Westerner would have felt in the presence of such a completely different culture—one where a slave would behead himself for love of his master; or large sums of money would be spent hiring singers "To chant the Koran / Day and night." The emphasis is upon a way of life where the physical is clearly important, but the spiritual is even more so.

In sections which follow Merton writes about the Cargo cults, movements, he notes, in primitive societies which "are means by which primitive and underprivileged people believe they can obtain manufactured goods by an appeal to supernatural powers." Cargo theology, he wrote, follows "a certain constant type of pattern" which includes:

(a) a complete rejection and destruction of the old culture with its goods and values.

(b) adoption of a new attitude and hope of immediate Cargo, as a result of and reward for the rejection of the old. This always centers around some prophetic personage who brings the word, tells what is to be done, and organizes the movement. (*GL*, 148)

Merton is interested in such cults for a variety of reasons. They stand as an example, once again, of the rise and fall of mythic systems. In addition, they emphasize problems of verbal communication. His method is again to paraphrase and quote his sources. He begins with "East with Malinowsky." This poem derives from Bronislaw Malinowski's South Sea Island journal about trips in 1914–15 and 1917–18. In Merton's rearrangement, Malinowski's journal stands not just as a record of what he observed, but also as an inadvertent self-condemnation of the observer. East, section 3, "Cargo

Songs," is cast in the framework of a dialogue: Sir William MacGregor, a British provincial governor, natives, anthropologists, and missionaries. While the governor may express some gestures of respect toward the natives, it is clear from his arrogance ("No one shall sit higher in Trobriand than I") that he has little genuine respect for the natives. Expression of fears that maybe the natives will rebel are interspersed with comments which strike chords with other parts of *Lograire* as a whole. Thus:

13. *Ein undankbares, schweres Missionsfeld* said the father on his return.

19. "I gave them portions of tobacco and they all walked away without posing long enough for a time exposure. My feelings toward them: exterminate the brutes" (Malinowski). (*GL*, 94–95)

The section which follows "Place Names" provides glimpses of Christian Western explorers who changed the names of places they visited.

In section 5, "Tibud Maclay," a character introduced in an earlier poem becomes the hero. Written from the point of view of the natives, Merton's object is to reflect the enthusiasm and respect which non-Westerners exhibited for the white man. "Sewende (Seven Day)" and "Cargo Catechism" (sections 6–7) relate specifics of various myths associated with cargo cults in Australia and New Guinea, for example, "John the Volcano" about a specific cult in the New Hebrides. These parts of the poem are based upon historical material, but in each instance Merton's method is to build up a poetic montage from the real incidents.

East, section 9, "Dialog with Mister Clapcott," also has its basis in fact. In 1923 in the New Hebrides a British planter was actually murdered in anticipation of the arrival of cargo. The final section of East, section 10, "And a Few More Cargo Songs," reintroduces many of the motifs used earlier. In these poems the native is willing to ignore what he knows of the past to obtain what he hopes the cargo cult will bring. By going to sources provided by travelers, missionaries, and still other documents Merton constructs a poem with roots in reality. By then emphasizing certain points, he demonstrates how myths supersede one another, and especially how this has been the case in the West's confrontation with other cultures, South, North, and East.

When Merton turns westward in his final canto his myth-dream does not improve. The opening poem, "Day Six O'Hare Telephane," is a satire of American activity—always going—but seldom knowing to what that activity leads. Merton's image of O'Hare airport becomes near-surrealistic. The planes resemble weird insects. In between such flashes he provides quotations from an Eastern sage who advocates nonaction, and we are reminded of essays on mysticism and Eastern thought.

The final two sections of "West" consider the treatment of the American Indians who were overwhelmed by the white man. Merton was intrigued by the idea that throughout American Indian culture during the latter part of the nineteenth century rumors developed about the restoration of Indian lands, the death of the white man, and the return of the dead. Week-long festivals were held to signal the return of the dead. These ceremonies, like the cargo cults elsewhere, were a way for the weaker culture to react to the impact of the expansion and greed of European culture. Merton's use of Ghost Dance materials stresses that the Indians sought their self-determination. But these were idle wishes and he had to conclude: "After a while the dreaming stopped and the Dream Dance turned into a Feather Dance. It was just a fun dance. It was mostly a white man's show" (*GL,* 137).

In *The Geography of Lograire* Merton is also interested in the fact that all myths are transient and, therefore, subject to rapid change, especially when pressure is brought to bear against them. Sometimes he appears to be more editor than poet, but his long poem provides both an intriguing cultural study and a valuable way of defining man's relationship to other men, a relationship which the poet insists is extremely fragile. Perhaps his most important contribution in *Lograire* is to warn his affluent, comfortable readers that there must be many ways of thinking about one's relationships to God and to others, and that it is arrogant to assume that one answer alone is *the* answer. Through the journey which he imagines in this poem and by relying upon travel records and historical documents about earlier specific journeys, he is able to build a work which, while private, is also a poem which stands as a parable of Western man's inability to appreciate the myth-dream of other cultures. This is a very private side of Merton who no longer feels he has all the answers, but who can, through poetry, keep on raising questions.

Merton's accomplishment is to demonstrate how "primitive" cultures have been fundamentally disrupted by Western man during the past several centuries. The result of such a view of history is a poem which allows us, as Western readers, to see that much damage has been done; but it also allows us to see that we can still learn, even make quite successful poetry, from facts about the cultures with which we have collided. Merton's career was one, as we have seen, wherein he was moving closer and closer to a celebration of other cultures. His Asian trip (which led to his untimely death) is the culmination of that interest; and *The Asian Journal,* which is full of references to those he was meeting and to books he was reading (often Eastern classics), is a final example of Father Louis's developing realization of how those with religious interests within the West could strengthen faith by being open to realities other than conventional Western ones. It is interesting to observe that in the composite *Asian Journal*—with its diverse facts, observations, reading materials, notes—Merton continued to write poetry. He always remained very much the poet, one concerned with how to make sense of a world so complicated, so unobserved, yet so awe-inspiring.

Chapter Nine
Monastic Journey

Geography comes to an end,
Compass has lost all earthly north.
Sacred Heart 2

All of Thomas Merton's writing can be described as sketches and outlines of his life's journey, a journey completed only at his death. The enormous number of books and essays reveal a man who with his pen made numerous beginnings as he became paradoxically both more *and* less self-reliant. One is reminded of Emerson's phrase about the true voyage never being a direct line, but a continual tacking back and forth, a continual readjustment.[1] It is somewhat the same with the contemplative. Already in *Thoughts in Solitude* Merton stresses that contemplation is not a thing so much to be sustained as an activity to be striven toward. With Emerson's image in mind, it is possible to evaluate many of Merton's posthumously published writings such as *The Asian Journal.* This significant volume, not a finished book, was compiled from three different journals kept during the final months of Merton's life. Private notes, travel records, and notes on reading were combined by editors to make this book. It is an unusual testament—the working notes of the writer-contemplative. It is as well an inadvertent summation of Merton's accomplishment both as monk and as writer.

Perhaps better than any book of his last years, this composite Asian journal demonstrates that Father Louis remained fundamentally a writer. Here is manifested evidence of the same man who wrote a *Secular Journal* almost thirty years earlier, yet this last journal is quite different in tone. Clearly, more than anything else we see (as in the last two books of poetry) that Merton had finally learned to relax. He was now, in his words, "at last on my true way after years of waiting and wondering and fooling around."[2]

The Asian Journal, while a valuable record of day-to-day activities, is also much more; it is a record of a writer working things out as he encounters them. We see evidence of Merton amassing evidence of all the things which fascinate him as he moves from city to city in a routine completely different from monastery or hermitage. At one point he lists the people and places he must see; then he notes that

The way in which I have been suddenly brought here constantly surprises me. The few days so far in Dharamsala have all been extremely fruitful in every way: the beauty and quiet of the mountains, my own reading and meditation, encounters with lamas, everything.

In a way it is wonderful to be without letters. . . . (*AJ*, 103)

He was certainly enjoying this chance to absorb new experiences, and more than likely this trip would have led to much additional writing had Merton lived. Even in its unfinished state, the journal exhibits poetry in the making. Thus "Song of Experience: India: One, Poem and Prayer to Golden Expensive Mother Oberoi," a satire about an elegant hotel with "immaculate carpets" and "all the am / bassadors from General Electric," and lines jotted on the "Kandy Express" train are poetic notes about the meeting of West and East. Merton seems to be looking about him for items to note, to comment upon, to make connections with, and so forth. As a traveler who was suddenly allowed to go to the places which before he could only imagine, he had to verbalize what he saw; the hermit-author of *The Geography of Lograire* was now able to participate in what before he could only dream. His intense weeks in Asia were in some ways like a capsule of all he had earlier imagined:

> We rush blindly
> In a runaway train
> Through the great estates
> Headlong to the sea.
>   (*AJ*, 227)

Throughout this *Journal* we see Merton (priest-intellectual-poet-tourist) asking himself questions; revising opinions; and putting various pieces of information together. Fascination with people; places; comic strips; houses of worship—all are given attention. Sometimes the trip seems almost crazy; at other times it makes very good sense. He writes:

I saw the other side of Colombo going out to the Katunayake airport. There were many screwy Catholic statues exhibited in public but sometimes under glass, so that the Catholic saints came a little closer to Ganesha and Hindu camp after all. Suddenly there is a point where religion becomes laughable. Then you decide that you are nevertheless religious. . . . (*AJ*, 238)

In his *Asian Journal* Merton observes that there is a religious element in all life and in all culture. In these final months of his life he continued to develop his facility for joining into "The General Dance" which he had so well described in the concluding pages of *New Seeds of Contemplation.*

Contemplation and Love for Others

Merton demonstrated in both his life and his writings that it was possible to lead a contemplative existence in today's world; in addition, he was able to demonstrate that such a life was of great significance for people outside a monastery. This idea became more important toward the end of his life, and one of the posthumous collections of essays, *Contemplation in a World of Action,* suggests again that connections between action and contemplation are essential whether one is a monk or lives in the world. Basic to this awareness is Merton's emphasis that no contemplative exists in stasis, for even in the cloister it is always a matter of balance between quiet and action, never a matter of one or the other, but both blended.

In other essays in *Contemplation in a World of Action* which examine the difficulty of pursuing the contemplative life, Merton writes that there is no way for the true monk to be unaware of the major questions and problems, fears, and anxieties of modern man. Within this group of essays he examines man's need to establish harmony within himself and with God, even when the world definitely remains a problem. The final essay of the book provides an overview of the monk's need for affirmation, and there, as in other essays, the value derives from Merton's consciousness about monasticism as a two-way consciousness. In this essay, made of notes from a taped conference, Merton admits it may be that

"contemplative" is a bad word. When we talk about ourselves, monks, as contemplatives, we come face to face with the problem that we are not more than contemplatives. We are not prophets. We are failing in the prophetic aspect of our vocation. Why? Perhaps because we belong to a Christianity so deeply implicated in a society which has outlived its spiritual vitality and yet is groping for a new expression of life in crisis.[3]

All of the essays in *Contemplation in a World of Action* express the writer's conviction that there are ways for the traditional discipline of the monastic life to lead toward fruitful activity. His assurance is that such insights will be of help for all men if the monk can serve as prophet.

The same optimism can be observed within another posthumous collection edited by Naomi Burton Stone and Brother Patrick Hart, *Love and Living.* In these essays Merton again confronts the fact that it is all too easy for monks to blame the world for a loss of love; however, he emphasizes throughout this group of essays and meditations that all men are implicated. For example, he reminds his readers:

The desecration of symbols cannot be blamed . . . on the forces of secularism and atheism. On the contrary, it unfortunately began in religious circles themselves. When a tradition loses its contemplative vitality and wisdom, its symbolism gradually loses its meaning and ceases to be a point of contact with "the center." . . . When the symbol degenerates into a mere means of communication and ceases to be a sign of communion, it becomes an idol. . . .[4]

When a man bows down before idols communion is lost; this can happen both inside and outside a religious community. These essays raise significant questions, not just for a monastic audience, but for all in the contemporary world. Merton writes about man's need to be open and concerned. Significant is the fact that these meditations cover a wide range of thought and reveal his own extensive interests. He asks what constitutes a university; a street; the meaning of Christian humanism? He provides meditations on fundamental concepts and words often misunderstood—Love, Divinity, Purity, Death. It is these fundamental facts that modern man tends to ignore. Within *Love and Living* Merton also analyzes the thought of Teilhard de Chardin in connection with Christian humanism.

The emphasis in much of Merton's writing, but especially toward the end of his career, is upon mankind's most fundamental needs. He knew that developing contemplative habits, for example, was not an easy matter, but he also insisted that it was worth whatever effort was necessary to form such habits, for it was through contemplative experience that one really begins to confront the essentials of living. His reflections in *Contemplative Prayer,* the last book completed before his death, are especially valuable because they reflect his mature thought about what it means to confront one's nothingness so one can develop a relationship to God. In that book he states that the "monk who is truly a man of prayer and who seriously faces the challenge of his vocation in all its depth is by that very fact exposed to existential dread."[5] In *Contemplative Prayer* he also makes connections between his reading of contemporary writers, such as Camus and Sartre, and what he recognized as man's most fundamental needs. In the recently published *The Literary Essays* Merton's fascination with Albert Camus, who honestly sought to evaluate a time of rebellion without God, is made clear. (Merton wrote seven essays about Camus and apparently was planning a book about the French writer.)

Of course Merton would not choose the despair of the existentialists. On the contrary, *Contemplative Prayer* is his mature expression of the conviction that man must strip away the inessential so that he can recognize his relationship to the essential. In this, the final book, we have a return to themes treated in books such as *The New Man* and in poems like "Elias," but what seems to be especially worth observing is the fact that here Merton wants his reader to see that contemplative prayer is hardly something esoteric; it can constitute the very essence of living well in the day-to-day modern world. In an unpublished manuscript entitled "The Inner Experience," he examines related subjects. Raymond Bailey sees this treatise as a matrix for all of Merton's thought on mysticism. In it Merton asserts the real experience for which man strives is "inner experience." It should be noted that within this "inner experience" manuscript Merton stresses connections with the realities of a modern world.[6] He is not writing about abstractions, but about what it means to be and to pray. In this manuscript and in *Contemplative Prayer* we see reflected a writer less and less concerned about himself.

Still another way Merton treated contemplative themes is in the occasional poetry written during the final years of his career. It is not surprising that while he was able to carry out the radical experiments of *Cables* and *Geography* he continued to write still other lyric poems which remained rather more conventional. We see such poems, along with other experiments, added to his oeuvre in the *Collected Poems* which was published in 1977.

"Sensation Time" and Uncollected Poems

The manuscript for an additional volume of poems was complete at Merton's death, but that gathering was not published as a separate volume; it became part of the *Collected Poems,* a thousand-page volume. These new poems do not exhibit startling changes in technique, yet there are several points to be noted; interesting is the fact that Merton continued to experiment with various techniques. Thus, while many of his final shorter poems are conventional, others, especially the prose-poems, are unusual. Two characteristics stand out about the lyrics in this final collection. Merton includes many personal pieces in which he seems almost horrified at what he sees reflected about contemporary man, who remains unaware of his need for contemplation; but Merton is also able to attain distance, and even to laugh. This is so because he sees many connections between his life and others, while he also seems to realize that his poetry means much more to him than it ever can for others. Both "The Originators" and "With the World in My Bloodstream" bring this point home (these are the first two poems in the collection). There is a kind of lightness in many of these poems, even though Merton's view of the contemporary world (and history) is sometimes almost frightening. His title poem "A Song: Sensation Time at the Home" also exemplifies this. This poet certainly realizes that poetry will have little immediate effect—especially upon readers who are caught up *only* in their own sensations. This is the world of *Cables* where

> Experts control
> Spasms
> Fight ennui
> While giant smiles and minds
> Relax limits
> Save $$$$$.

> > > > (*CP,* 630)

It is a world which seems to be in large part lost, yet more important it is one about which the poet speaks kindly, with wit and irony, even though man seems to have given up by giving in. "A Tune for Festive Dances in the Nineteen Sixties," about man's loss of identity, is a related poem. "Man the Master" amplifies the same themes, but again in a humorous way. Man seems so busy that he has forgotten about himself, *as self:*

> Here he comes
> Bursting with individuals

> All his beliefs fat and clean. . . .
> With innumerable wits and plans
> Nations and names problems and resolutions.
> *(CP,* 637)

In some of these poems there exists a consistent note close to disgust. Poems such as "Picture of a Black Child with a White Doll" and "Man the Master" illustrate this. Yet it is important to realize that while there is such a somber quality, even close to bitterness, there is as well a lightness to balance it. Thus, on the one hand, Merton can provide a gaiety, yet on the other he will not bring himself to stop thinking about the distortions of contemporary man. The poet smiles, but he cannot forget his "First Lessons About Man" which are that

> Man begins in zoology
> He is the saddest animal
> He drives a big red car
> Called anxiety. . . .
> *(CP,* 624–25)

Somewhat the same must be observed about the three prose-poems which close this collection. All treat man's misuse of language, the twisting of language to his selfish benefit, not for the benefit of others, yet all of these prose-poems are also presented with distance and humor which makes it possible for Merton's compassion to shine through. These three prose-poems which conclude "Sensation Time" are further indications of the writer's interests toward the very end of his career. "Plessy vs Ferguson: Theme and Variations" might be compared to the noise of *Cables* since in both language seems often to be used to obscure rather than to clarify. This is a study, above all, in the abuse of language. "Rites for the Extrusion of a Leper" implies that the Church itself can be guilty of language abuse. Merton's point is that civil government and the church continue to find ways to arrange meaning for their own benefit.

The last prose-poem, "Ben's Last Fight" apparently means many things. It seems to be an autobiographical poem, and it also is a statement by Merton about poetic technique. Father Louis is saying that he has learned that he can now relax. Fights with rules, with language, with the changing concerns of the world of man, are interesting, but ultimately of little lasting import; yet words can help man to remember such facts, too.

Merton—Seeker as Model

As Merton the monk matured he felt he had fewer definite answers, but simultaneously he became surer about his life and vocation. One of the things about which he was confident was that he would continue writing. This was his gift, and this was the way he might lead others to wholeness. In all of the many books which constitute the final phase of Merton's career, and especially in poems and studies which examine his encounter with the East, he sought ways to remind himself and others of the truth, the true way, the essential, the unchanging. Such also is his concern in *Contemplative Prayer,* a book as harsh and unyielding as Henry Adams's *Education* or Eliot's *Four Quartets,* yet if it is harsh, it is also full of love. In each of the final collections there is reflected, above all, an enthusiasm and concern for others who must also search.

Merton's gift was one which allowed him to use words to lead others into the same kind of journey which he had made, a journey, we should remember, only hinted at by words. Words allowed Merton to sort out the good from the bad, the confusing from the clear, the debilitating from the invigorating. Words were ultimately the way he traveled. Words were the way he made connections between the contemplative life and the lives of others, between what he came to know and his responsibility to keep building bridges toward other people in need of such experience. Yet through words he also indicated his suspicion of words.

We cannot minimize Merton's accomplishments in prose—as letter writer, as essayist, as journal writer. As a commentator about social action, prayer, literature, mysticism, problems of identity, race, war, and urban problems, he provided many avenues of thought and meditation for an enormous audience. All such essays are significant facets in his overall career, yet it was always through analysis of self, and in metaphor, that he best communicated his awareness of what it means to find one's true self. Yet through words of analysis about himself he reminded his readers of the need to forget the self. Metaphor remains the core, yet the very fact that both Merton's poetry and prose is so diverse is the key: he developed many ways of writing to reach many different audiences. Ultimately it will be through an appreciation of his diverse production, as shaped by poetic abilities, that all of the career will be appreciated. He was convinced that as a contemplative it was important to give his life— while as monk he also learned to give that life *as* a writer—and while all of this is true, his writing, in a curious way, was often more for Merton than for an audience.

Audience often seemed almost an afterthought. Merton—as writer—worked it out for himself and for God. It is not surprising, therefore, that the center of his accomplishment remained his most personal work as poet or autobiographer. In the journals we see him recording his journey. In the poetry we find the compression of his craft. In both his genuine love of language, well used, is always apparent. Through language he developed his contemplative awareness.

Still to be Done

Essays to be collected; other biographies to be published; more letters to be edited; poetry to be studied; unpublished manuscripts to be assimilated; journals to be edited; relationships to be drawn; notebooks to be studied; photographs to be printed; drawings to be seen; fellow monks and literary friends to be interviewed; sealed correspondences to be unsealed—such are the items waiting to be done. We will be a long time waiting for all of this.

Merton would be amused if he could see the army of scholars at work on his literary production. Yet he would also be pleased that so many readers can gather so much, learn, *be*—because of what he has given us. Above all, Thomas Merton's writing is a gift, and through that gift given to him, others can make a similar journey.

Chapter Ten

An Afterword:
Scholarship and Thomas Merton

> *Man's home-made image is his enemy. This*
> *must be destroyed*
> *With straight words and paradox.*
>
> The Moment of Truth

The Continuing Interest in Merton

Much has been written about Thomas Merton/Father Louis, but little about the productive tension which existed because he was both monk and almost compulsive writer. This book has been concerned with that productive combination and with how this writer-monk integrated his two roles. To understand Merton's accomplishment fully we would need to assimilate all of his diverse writings as well as the growing scholarship about him. A reading of all his posthumously-published writings as well as recent studies about him indicates that while the writing has merited substantial attention, the creative use Merton made of his paradoxical need to affirm silence through language remains a subject in need of more systematic investigation. This afterword provides a guide through the most recently available of Merton's writings, not investigated systematically in the book, as well as a study of how scholars are approaching him, his works, and the interrelationship between them. As an overview of Merton's writing which continues to appear, and as a study of trends in Merton scholarship, this afterword surveys patterns basic to an understanding of Merton who during all his years as a religious was *both* monk and artist, thus a writer whose interior life is reflected in his writing.

Merton chose to be a cloistered contemplative within one of the most austere monastic orders in the Church. Paradoxically, while his affirmation of that enclosed way of life was an affirmation of silence, his life as a contemplative led him to be one of the most prolific writers in the modern world. His decision in 1941 to be a cistercian monk was made with the knowledge that he might have to renounce being a published writer. That did not happen, and as Merton grew in his love of the contemplative life he matured as a writer who gave voice to silence. Solitude allowed him to treasure community and silence allowed him to honor words. His very way of life led him to feel the necessity of speaking out about a world which seemed out of touch with the insights of the contemplative.

Father Louis wrote scores of books and hundreds of articles during his twenty-seven years at the Abbey of Gethsemani and we are now beginning to realize the complexity of what this man of silence produced. He died while in the prime of life, yet his writings keep appearing year after year and no doubt this will continue for decades. During the past twenty years several collections of Merton essays have appeared as well as the meticulously edited *Asian Journal of Thomas Merton* and three shorter journals.[1] Some of the books by him published after his death have been examined in the preceding chapters.

The day may come when there will be more books by Merton published after his death than the fifty he saw through the press. This will hardly be surprising, for it was through the printed word that he confirmed his monastic vocation. He wrote volumes of poetry, essays, autobiography, scores of essays and numerous reviews. He also wrote enormous numbers of letters, and there are detailed journals for each phase of his life. The recent Mott biography, as well as material published by the late John Howard Griffin, incorporate such primary documents. Four book length bibliographies have been published about his work.[2]

Since his death, books by Father Louis have flowed from presses at a steady rate. Several of these were in process at the end of his life and others have been subsequently edited. Since 1968 Merton books on prayer, various collections of poetry, a novel, collections of essays, letters, journals, introductions to foreign editions, photographs, as well as the composite *Asian Journal* have appeared.[3] And we know that there will be several additional volumes of essays, letters, and journals. The correspondence is now being edited. Some of Merton's monastic orientation notes, accumulated during the years he was Master of Scholastics and Novice Master, will also be published by Cistercian Publications. These lecture notes run to a dozen volumes. As an example of the prolific industry of this contemplative, one can note that the correspondence files alone at the Thomas Merton Studies Center of Bellarmine College include approximately 1826 separate files, and that in some singular cases there are scores of letters spanning decades. Letters to Jacques Maritain, Jean Leclercq, Daniel Berrigan, and Ernesto Cardenal would each constitute a minimum of four books if both sides of the correspondence were printed. Correspondence with literary friends and editors, such as Robert Giroux, Naomi Burton Stone, James Laughlin, Sister Thérèse Lentfoehr, and Robert Lax, would constitute additional books. Letters to fellow monks would make more volumes. Such material promises to add to the Merton corpus in decades to come. [4]

Then there is the growing secondary material. Most of it can now be called "second generation" Merton scholarship, for a considerable amount of valuable critical writing was accomplished while he was still alive, and appeared shortly after his death. Much of the "first generation" material is especially valuable because it was written by persons close to him—friends, fellow-monks, literary associates. But now a new body of scholarship is developing, generated not so much out of close acquaintanceship with Merton, the person, but from close attention to his published works. The large number of graduate theses on Merton, completed and in progress, provides still another indication of his continuing importance in American culture. His books remain in print, and his writings are frequently discussed. Those examined in this survey demonstrate his continuing value as poet and writer and suggest his promise for many future readers.

Some awareness of the critical studies which appeared immediately after his death and which provide the background for this bibliographical survey is necessary to appreciate the variety of work which scholars are producing. The first collection of essays about Merton was appropriately called *Thomas Merton, Monk*. These close-up portraits, edited by Brother Patrick Hart, O.C.S.O., are written mostly by persons who were acquainted with Merton. [5] Frequently cast in the form of a remembrance, the essays provide valuable glimpses of Merton's multi-faceted personality. A further evaluation of some of Merton's relationships with society, *Thomas Merton, Prophet in the Belly of a Paradox* (1978), is more analytical. It shows that a distancing had begun to occur in the decade after Merton's death. Still a third significant step has been taken in another recent collection, *The Message of Thomas Merton* (1981), which traces the complexity of Merton's thought, and suggests how his message will be studied in the future. The new *The Legacy of Thomas Merton* (1986), demonstrates other aspects of Merton's accomplishment because it connects his writing with larger patterns within monasticism and the church.

In these collections we see scholars gradually distancing themselves from a writer who was foremost a monk, but who always remained aware of his world. He was a contemplative who realized his obligations in (and to) the world; thus he must be appreciated both as a contemplative and as a social critic. Like Emerson and Thoreau, he knew that the contemplative and active modes of existence reinforce each other. The human person needs both. Considerable discipline is essential if humanity is to find its proper relationship with God and with other persons. This conviction was already made clear in the first scholarly books about Merton. Now, with more primary material available and many more studies completed, we can see even better that language and the creative tension of being both comtemplative and writer were always at the core of Merton's activity. When Dennis McInerny, John J. Higgins, James Baker, Frederic Kelly, and Raymond Bailey published their books, *The Collected Poems of Thomas Merton* and the first volume of letters had not yet appeared. Consequently, none of these five scholars devoted mush energy either to the poetry and correspondence or to questions on how the life informed the writing. They did valuable groundwork, but in retrospect their books seem in need of revision, in part because they are so closely tied to theological or social questions. We can now perceive more definitely that there were never two Mertons. As monk and writer, and as man of God seeking God's mercy, he lived his life as a whole — and while he did so he formed reflections of it, for himself and others, through his concern for language.

Higgins' 1971 study *Merton's Theology of Prayer,* (published in paper as *Thomas Merton on Prayer*) offers "a synthesis of Merton's understanding of prayer, showing its centrality within the thought of his spirituality."[6] Higgins, a Jesuit, informs us that Merton's concern with prayer involved no radical changes but was a gradual unfolding, as he became more aware of the mystery of God. If what Higgins stresses is true (and I think it is), then the emphasis on social criticism in James T. Baker's book, *Thomas Merton — Social Critic* (1971), published the same year, needs qualification. Yet Higgins' book does not always distinguish between the early and later Merton as carefully as it might. Baker's book is, in fact, a kind of companion volume to Higgins'. Baker provides an overview of Merton's social outlook and explains how in the course of his life Father Louis seemed to become increasingly aware of obligations to the world.[7] Merton's social criticism developed slowly over a period of decades and flowered within the monastic environment. This relationship becomes clearer in a book by Frederic Joseph Kelly which followed three years later and is in some fundamental ways a synthesis of the types of work done by Higgins and Baker.

Frederic Joseph Kelly Jr's *Man Before God: Thomas Merton on Social Responsibility,* appeared in 1974 from Doubleday.[8] Kelly examines writing on social topics, and in his study the social dimensions which grow out of man's love of God are stressed. Responsible social actions, Kelly points out, must grow from a proper relationship to God. And clearly such growth is what Merton's life and writings are about. Thomas Merton, as Father Louis, became knowledgeable about mysticism precisely because he would not forget the world.

Thomas Merton on Mysticism by Raymond Bailey (Doubleday, 1975) traces the steps in Merton's journey inward.[9] In this study we see how Merton's appreciation of the mystical life changed; his attitude was simplified as he became more aware of the radical simplicity of life itself. Bailey's book is an excellent guide to the interrelationship of Merton's life and writings as he read more about various mystical traditions. William Shannon's *Thomas Merton's Dark Path*, (1981), commented upon later in this afterword, provides more detailed information about Merton's interest in mysticism to show that he kept refining his appreciation of mysticism through formal writing while at the same time his spiritual life was being refined.

Throughout his dual vocation as monk dedicated to prayer and man committed to words Merton remained fascinated by the relationship between silence and the word, between the contemplative state and the need to articulate an awareness about the contemplative. The first books to appear after Merton's death investigated questions which grew out of his concern with prayer, theology, mysticism, social concern and responsibility, and are basic steps necessary towards understanding his complexity. We are now witnessing many additional steps in Merton scholarship and a greater awareness of the relationship between his aesthetics and artistic skill which strengthened his approach to both God and man.

Posthumous Books by Merton

Poetry reveals the unity of Merton's vision more consistently than anything else, for in it Father Louis comes closest to articulating what can never be verbalized. It is in the poetry that the intensity of contemplative need and an awareness of the problems of articulation manifest themselves. This is true of Merton's early formal modernist poetry as well as the later poetry which was anything but traditional. Merton himself sometimes called his last poems "anti-poetry." *The Collected Poems of Thomas Merton,* now available as a paperback, is a prodigious opus, hardly what he would have planned had he lived to see such a volume through the press.[10] Containing more than one thousand pages, it includes most of the poems as they first appeared, together with a very large number of uncollected, manuscript, and fragment poems. This volume will prove of great value in understanding an ambitious, enigmatic poet. Merton believed that his writing clarified things for him, and many of the poems are a working out of questions. Not surprisingly, he wrote quite different kinds of poetry at different stages within his life. Merton lived as a cloistered monk, but his art, the voluminous correspondence, his wide-ranging abilities as a questioner of his culture and as a spokesman for modern man's contemplative need made him a major force in religious thought. When all his poems are studied systematically they will prove to reveal many things on many levels.

Often successful as technical exercises, Merton's poems also chart spiritual development. More importantly, they reflect American culture in the nineteen-forties, fifties, and sixties, that thirty year period when Merton was active as a writer and during which, ironically, he became ever surer of his identity as Father Louis, monk. Beyond that they also provide specific poetic consideration of the spiritual life and its ingredients—solitude and silence. To study all of Merton's poetry will take a long time, and scholars must remember that as his own sense of vocation developed he himself raised many questions about how best to write poetry. The early lyrics of *Thirty Poems* (and *Early Poems*) are technically tight and intellectually challenging, yet sometimes too predictable in their patterns. As we have been shown earlier, the later poems are open, experimental, alive, questioning. Some readers have not yet accustomed themselves to the apparently radical change in Merton's poetic manner. In fact there was no radical change; he simply became more willing to admit that he did not have all the answers, and he allowed the wisdom of others (other traditions, styles, philosophies) to help him to approach the infinite wisdom of God. The volume of collected poetry does have an uneven quality, but this would be true of anyone who wrote so much while living such a full life. And had he lived, Merton himself would have certainly collected far less for such a volume.

It is fortunate that New Directions has made *The Collected Poems* available in a paperback edition. (The cloth edition priced at $37.50 appeared in 1977 and is out of print.) The paperback edition gathers all the poems published in separate volumes between 1944 and 1969 including a reprinting of the Anvil Press *Early Poems 1940-42* which first appeared in 1971, essentially a selection of poems omitted from the first book (*Thirty Poems,* 1944). In addition, it provides "appendixes" which include poems Merton gathered for an additional volume, "Sensation Time at the Home;" uncollected poems; humorous verse; a French poem; translations of French poems; translations from many other languages; drafts and fragments; and even a selection of concrete poems, almost four hundred pages in all. These appendices alone might constitute the subject of an extended study. Merton's joy in using language prevails throughout.

The Collected Poems documents both the writer's development and many changes in American culture as it moved through World War II, racial discord, and then the Viet Nam war. Merton's earlier volumes reflect a mastery of technique and a revulsion at a contemporary mentality which so easily accepted war. While many of the earliest poems catch a younger poet's delight in having been led to the monastery, successive collections of poems document that the real source of strife for Merton was a struggle not with the world but with the division within himself which he then found reflected in the world. Thus as his poems developed, Merton affirms his knowledge that quiet, peace, solitude, contemplation, inner peace are essential within each person if all persons are to play a significant role in a rapidly changing world. Each poem is therefore part of Merton's journey and, as we can see more clearly, his journey always is linked to contemplation and action.

In time, it will become necessary to collate, verify, date and document variants of these poems. In the meantime *The Collected Poems* provides an enormous fund of information, pleasure, and insight for readers. Better than any other single book available it reflects the energy of Thomas Merton and will help readers trace changes in the poetic career. Many studies will inevitably follow the ready availability of Merton's poetry, but, of course, scholars will have to study the poetry in relation to all the published and unpublished work.

Similarly, the newly published *Eighteen Poems*, released by New Directions, provides insight into the last years of Merton's life and his love for a student nurse, Margie, an episode which has been made common knowledge through the biographical revelations which have appeared in books by both John Howard Griffin and Michael Mott. These poignant lyrics document a moment of crisis in Merton's life, but also demonstrate that even then he remained a writer. Thus the surprising adventure of his falling in love, not at all what a proper hermit should be doing, becomes a reason for lyrics. These should be read by all who might be tempted to gossip about Merton's love for this young woman, for in these sensitive and compelling poems he reveals not just his love, but a wide compassion for humankind in its loves and weaknesses, desires and frustrations.

Merton clearly was able to cultivate diverse fields of interest simultaneously: autobiography, poetry, essays on theology, on contemporary culture, on liturgy, on art. And he did so because his search for God expressed itself in varied modes depending upon the situation in which he found himself. He put all of his energy into whatever project was at hand — in prayer, in conference with a novice, in revision of galleys, writing a letter. As he grew in his contemplative vocation he accepted the use of words as a valuable means of placing himself within a particular moment. Imagine the sheer fun he had writing a letter to his friend Robert Lax, someone with whom he had been close since shared days at Columbia. That exchange of letters in *A Catch of Anti-Letters* reflects their friendship and the *Anti-Letters* are unlike anything we might imagine.[11] While in one sense personal letters, they are also prayers, statements of acceptance by both writers after some twenty-five years of friendship, and they are fine examples of the exuberance characteristic of Merton. These are private documents, but they reveal much about the human spirit and Merton's realization that the greatest satisfaction is found in the simplest things of life. He felt lucky to have Bob Lax as correspondent and the bond of their friendship is everywhere evident in these "anti-letters," celebrations of the immediate. They are about the joy of being oneself, about the joy of pain and sorrow, and the fact that even in the most isolated circumstances one can remain aware of being united with others.

One brief excerpt can suggest the seriousness of Merton's and Lax's play. They were both artists; so while the subject matter of the poem-letters is wide, central is the question of art and its ability to suggest the mystery of life, the sheer fun of being able to stand back from life itself. One Merton letter begins:

How long you think you can hide from the long arm of the postoffice? Where have you been? Have you grown the beard and put on the moppit and entered the sketes and lavras? Where is the long black vestment? Do you know that the sketes and lavras have missed the boat of arrirnamento or perhaps aggornamountain. Let the motto cry out from the captain's bridge as we sail round and round the Agios Horos: "Arriorna-Mount-Athos." This pun will tickle the feet of the Portos. (*Anti-Letters*, p. 147)

These dense letters reveal a good bit about Merton's enthusiasms, interests, his techniques, and most of all his affirmation of life — which of course, also includes death. There are, for example, beautiful letters towards the end of the volume about the death of a mutual artist friend, Ad Reinhardt. Here too careful study might bring still another monograph. Fascinated by Reinhardt's black canvases, Merton sings of his death:

Tomorrow the solemns. The requiems alone in the hermit hatch. Before the ikons the offering. The oblations. The clean oblations all round thunder quiet silence black picture oblations. Make Mass beautiful silence like big black picture speaking requiem. Tears in the shadows of hermit hatch requiems blue black tone. Sorrows for Ad in the oblation quiet peace request rest. Tomorrow is solemns in the hermit hatch of old lutheran reinhardt commie painblack. Tomorrow is the eternal solemns fending off the purge-fire place non catch old skipper reinhardt safely by into the heavens. Tomorrow is the solemns and the barefoots and the ashes and the masses, oldstyle liturgy masses without the colonels and without the sargeants yelling sit down. Just old black quiet requiems in hermit hatch with decent sorrows good bye college chum.

It is all solemns and sads all over beginning to fade out people in process before comes the march of orges and djinns. Well out of the way is safe Reinhardt in his simple black painting the final statement includes all. (*Anti-Letters*, p. 120)

To sing of death in this way is clearly to affirm life.

The first volume of Merton's selected letters, *The Hidden Ground of Love, the Letters of Thomas Merton on Religious and Social Concerns,* which appeared in 1985, is further evidence of Father Louis's love and affirmation of life within and beyond the monastery. These letters, the first of four or five projected volumes of selected correspondence reveal that Merton could be wonderfully attentive to scores of different correspondents.

Some of these letters are formal while many are informal and spontaneous. Together they document Merton's enormous energy and his
ability to focus on different kinds of problems almost simultaneously.
The editor's decision to group the letters alphabetically (and not in a
continuing chronological order) also reveals Merton's skill at being a
friend to many different correspondents. It is almost as if he is able to
assume a different role for each different recipient.

As the evidence mounts it becomes clear that Merton's basic subject
was affirmation, *both* in the life and in the writing. The early Merton,
perhaps smug in the cloister at Gethsemani, tended to emphasize
enclosure. Later broader themes developed. This can be readily observed in the published journals. Barriers between self and others were
broken down as new ways of seeing developed, and new metaphors of
transformation were sought. Elena Malits's book *The Solitary Explorer,*
examined later in this afterword, charts significant stages in Merton's
writing as he witnessed himself changing and thus recognized the need
of new metaphors to suggest that change. The literary record of Merton's personal journey was at first a "secular" diary; then a purgatorio;
still later the mystery of being in a whale; then the paradox of voicing
the silent life; and, ultimately, the irony of the conjectures of an innocent (and finally guilty) bystander. These metaphors constituted ways
to affirm the monk-writer's situation at particular times. Yet he took a
good many words to work his way through many questions to affirmation. Bearing such facts in mind, we read the diverse essays of *Love
and Living* as another of the steps in Merton's journey—one that often
involved his looking again carefully at what we as a people have ceased
to notice carefully.

Love and Living deals with various subjects and is important because
it shows Merton's capacity for reaching out in many different ways.
These essays keep turning back on related ideas: Live well; love now;
celebrate what you are and have; and in that immediate fact of loving,
you will begin to come to an awareness of God. Merton focuses on
essences. Editors have divided this posthumous book into three sections: "Love and Living"; "Seven Words"; and "Christian Humanism."
The first essays treat questions about man's loss of contact with truth,
life, communication. Included here is an essay transcribed from a conference given for novices at Gethsemani on "Cargo Cults of the South
Pacific" which gives valuable insight into the long poem *The Geography of Lograire* (1969).[12] The second section meditates on words
such as "death", "ethics", "war", with which modern man seems to
have lost contact. The final section is a hopeful look to the future. A

minimal scholarly apparatus in *Love and Living* would have proven
helpful. The book was edited from manuscripts which were written
towards the end of Merton's life. "Acknowledgements" state that
almost two thirds of the book had been previously printed, although
often "in considerably different form." This is a minor point, and
scholars will be able to find the variants when the inevitable collected
edition is done. At the core of Merton's concern in these late essays, as
in earlier books such as *New Seeds of Contemplation* and *The New
Man*, is a fascination with the virtues of silence:

There is a silent self within us whose presence is disturbing precisely because it
is so silent: it *can't* be spoken. It has to remain silent. To articulate it, to verbalize it, is to temper with it, and in some ways to destroy it.
    Now let us frankly face the fact that our culture is one which is geared in many
ways to help us evade any need to face this inner, silent self. We live in a state of
constant semi-attention to the sound of voices, music, traffic, or the generalized
noise of what goes on around us all the time. This keeps us immersed in a flood
of racket and words, a diffuse medium in which our consciousness is half diluted:
we are not quite "thinking," not entirely responding, but we are more or less
there. We are not fully *present* and not entirely absent; not fully withdrawn, yet
not completely available. (*Love and Living*, p. 40)

An important fact revealed in these essays is Merton's affirmation of
humankind's proper place in the universe. Yet he reminds us that
peace is paradoxically found by finding one's true self, and by not
allowing issues beyond the true self to infringe.
    For Merton, finding the truth was often an exercise to be ac-
complished through an examination of literature. Increasingly, this was
the case as his career developed, and thus the posthumous collection,
The Literary Essays of Thomas Merton, is valuable as a reflection of
Merton's method. This book demonstrates Merton's concern with the
importance of writing. This first part of the book includes essays rang-
ing from Pasternak to Roland Barthes written late in Merton's career
(1959-68). The second part consists of seven essays devoted to Albert
Camus (1966-68). The third section introduces poets whom Merton
translated (1963-66). The next part, "Related Literary Questions," consists of pieces produced between 1953 and 1968 and raises significant
questions about relationships between art and religious belief. There
are also valuable appendixes which include Merton's master's thesis on
William Blake, early essays and reviews (1939-40), and transcriptions
of two 1967 talks on William Faulkner. The range of Merton's interests

revealed here helps us understand his own writing. These literary essays document that the last years of Merton's life were extremely productive and that both his writing and living were developing because he was often busy studying other writers. Even more important, they provided deeply perceptive insights into many types of literature, from the psalms to modern poetry.

The fact that Merton had studied Blake before he became a monk in 1941 and still sustained that interest late in his career is reflected in an essay about Thomas J. J. Altizer's *The New Apocalypse: The Radical Christian Vision of William Blake*. This is but one example of the connections provided in this volume. Similarly, Merton's appreciation of Joyce (reflected in his early novel *My Argument with the Gestapo*) is clarified by two mature essays about Joyce. Other essays, for example, on the poetry of Edwin Muir or Louis Zukofsky, reflect Merton's developing thought and suggest connections between his art and contemporary writing. Celebrations of J. F. Powers and Flannery O'Connor demonstrate how attuned he was to contemporaries. Still other pieces in the opening section about Faulkner, Simone Weil, William Styron, Rolf Hochhuth, and William Melvin Kelley document a breath of concerns about Christian belief and responsibility. The question raised about Kelley's *A Different Drummer* and Styron's *Nat Turner* reflect a sympathetic concern for what it means to be Black in America. The one hundred and eighty pages of the opening section of this book would make a valuable separate collection.

The second section is in fact a book within a book. Apparently Merton was planning to gather his Camus essays into a single volume, and while we do not know what order he might have chosen, the editor has done well to let the minimal repetition remain. In Camus' thought Merton recognized insights about modern life and the difficulty of being a Christian. One essay, "Prophetic Ambiguities: Milton and Camus," draws parallels between these giants. Merton saw Camus' uneasiness about Western civilization as a challenge to all Christians and Camus' art as a help to believers.

Merton's way of challenging conventional views is one of the fundamental methods of the literary essays. Because he remained open, he could see continuities in others and in what Christian culture needs which others (with more conventional and fixed ideas?) might not see. Thus, his essays on poets not usually read by English speakers, such as Raissa Maritain and Ernesto Cardenal, provide insights into what Merton thought about poets who were beyond the mainstream of culture but who had much to say because of their passionate commitment to belief and art. Similarly, his essays within the third section about literary questions show the development of Merton's thinking about the relationships between poetry and contemplation, and between art and freedom, as well as his realization that to be a successful artist in contemporary society (and to be a Christian) *is* to be alienated from mainstream culture.

The Literary Essays should be read by all concerned with fundamental questions about literature and Christianity, and especially those concerned with the development of Merton's thought. The three appendices provide rather specialized material (early reviews of Ransom, Nabokov, Huxley and others, the two meditations on Faulkner, and the Blake thesis) but always there are original insights. What Merton has to say about Faulkner's *The Sound and the Fury* and *The Wild Palms* could only have resulted from the fortunate conjunction of an intense love of literature and a sure faith in God. The same might be said of this entire book; for example, Merton's extended analysis of Boris Pasternak's writing as literature demonstrates that no successful art can exist which does not reveal that "'individual human life becomes the life story of God'"(p. 80).

Had Merton lived beyond 1968 his literary essays would probably have been gathered into some other arrangement, yet as edited they testify to his interests and faith, and will serve as a challenge to those who seek to understand the contemporary world in the light of the eternal. Through these essays Merton makes it clear that art and literature provide access to the transcendent. The essays of *Love and Living* and *The Literary Essays* reflect the mature Merton reaching out to his world. Another book which adds to Merton primary material, *Thomas Merton on Saint Bernard*, gives a glimpse of a much earlier writer, one who twenty years previously had quietly been building the base for later work as teacher, novice master, and mature thinker.

The essays of *Thomas Merton on Saint Bernard* appeared in disparate places in the early nineteen-fifties; together they show that already early in his career Merton was concerned with the question of how to combine the contemplative with the active life. His systematic inquiries, while sometimes loaded with Latin quotations and occasionally pedantic in tone, are important because they reveal a Merton who was sure of his vocation and becoming convinced that the active and the contemplative must reinforce one another. While early, these studies on Saint Bernard are vintage Merton, full of hints at how he made connections fundamental to his life. Organized into three parts, this book opens with an essay on "Action and Contemplation in Saint Bernard," followed then by "Saint Bernard on Interior Simplicity." The concluding section concerns "Transforming Union in Saint Bernard of Clairvaux and St. John of the Cross." Jean Leclercq's introduction illuminates Merton's approach to Bernard and the timeliness of the subject. Merton saw the need for an emphasis upon a balance between the active and the contemplative, yet, as Leclercq notes, he has assimilated Saint Bernard's theology; thus the essay on Bernard's *The Spirit of Simplicity* is expressed "with precise vocabulary, but also with such breath that what he says is valid not only for the Cistercian Order but for all Christians" (*Thomas Merton on Saint Bernard*, p. 17). This study emphasizes that the active and contemplative are not separate; one feeds the other. Merton, as the scholar, is frankly amazed at his discovery:

It is abundantly clear from all these texts that the contemplative life, as St. Bernard conceives it, is by no means a life of study, still less of research scholarship. However, since mystical understanding is a penetration of the mysteries of our faith and since contemplative wisdom is nourished by the Word himself, it is clear that we prepare ouselves for it by our *lectio divina*. Contemplation is simply the procession, by experience, of what we have read in Scripture. Hence the soul spontaneously seeks God in Scripture, *sciens se ibi absque dubio inventuram quem sitit*. This thirst is not to be satisfied by anything less than the 'kiss of his mouth'—by God himself, giving himself secretly to the soul in mystical experience, casting aside the sensible images and figures in which he came disguised. St. Bernard knew that these hidden meanings of Scripture were revealed more perfectly to the soul meditating in the woods than to the student in the scriptorium. (*Thomas Merton on Saint Bernard*, p. 56)

To look carefully, to enjoy being in the woods, is to be contemplative. Merton's own looking involved many hours in the forest of Gethsemani. We remember Father Louis even once courted the possibility of being the resident forest-ranger, thereby acquiring a ready-made hermitage, but also running the risk of an ivory-tower existence. As he came to love particular trees and places, his appreciation of those particulars deepened. This is recorded in poems and journals, and also through the lens of a camera; for during the final several years of his life Merton proved himself to be an accomplished photographer.

And what better reminder is there of what Merton studied, taught, assimilated, than a series of one hundred of his best photographs? Merton, the contemplative — but always artist by instinct — had a gift with the camera which was strengthened by his association with John Howard Griffin. Some of that story is made clear in Griffin's *A Hidden Wholeness*, a volume which might well be read as preface to a new collection of Merton's photographs fittingly called *Geography of Holiness*.

Deba Patnaik's loving selection and arrangement of some of Merton's best photographs provides yet another important avenue of entry into the world of Thomas Merton. It is fortunate that John Howard Griffin encouraged Merton to use the camera, for he made striking progress in a short time. The photographs of this new collection, beautifully printed and bound, demonstrate that Merton learned to look everywhere for hidden wholeness. Patnaik's collection is the visual expression of what Merton was convinced of intellectually when he examined St. Bernard. In addition, Patnaik's distinguished introductory text provides access to the aesthetics of Merton and shows the reader how closely related those aesthetics were to spiritual insights.

Three portions of Merton's journals which have been lovingly edited into books are also available, and because they combine the written word with photographs they demonstrate how both mediums were important for Merton. *Day of a Stranger* was written in May of 1965 and grew out of a request that Merton generate an essay which would provide an impression of a "typical" day in his life. Since this "journal" was produced early during the hermitage period, it also documents Father Louis's ease in this new way of life. Because it was planned, amplified, and calculated it provides good evidence of how Merton had become so skillful in the use of words to suggest the wordless. The photographs selected as illustrations are chosen by the editor to reflect Merton's word images.

The second journal, *Woods, Shore, Desert* (also with photographs by the author) seems an even better illustration of how Merton learned to meditate with both camera and word image. This journal which was written during May of 1968 is composed of passages taken from a longer journal; placed "onto a dictaphone . . . they were then transcribed by his secretary." As a record of Merton's first extended trip away from Gethsemani this journal is invaluable. A trip to Redwoods Abbey, near the Pacific in northern California, and the small Benedictine monastery of Christ in the Desert provided the reason for the title.

The journal reveals Merton thinking his way into greater contemplative awareness: He wrote, for example:

...I do have a past to break with, an accumulation of inertia, waste, wrong, foolishness, rot, junk, a great need of clarification of mindfulness, or rather of no mind—a return to genuine practice, right effort, need to push on to the great doubt. Need for the Spirit. (p. 48)

The third new journal, *The Alaskan Journal of Thomas Merton,* edited by Robert E. Daggy, derives from the visit Merton made to Alaska enroute to Asia in September 1968. He gave a conference to a group of contemplative nuns at Eagle River, and during the days he was in Alaska Merton also investigated several sites for possible new hermitages where he might relocate. The journal which resulted from Merton's introspection provides a record of his meditations—and many poetic insights, and also stands as a preliminary to the *Asian Journal.* This journal is perfect evidence that Merton combined the roles of monk and artist and that these two roles strengthened each other. This book appears in two editions. The Turkey Press edition includes an Appendix of sixteen letters which Merton wrote from Alaska. The New Directions edition includes the appendix of letters and another appendix of transcriptions of Merton's Alaskan conferences, first published in *Sisters Today* in early 1970s.

Reappraisal

All this new primary material by Merton has set the stage for the writers and scholars (dozens of them) who have published work about him in the last several years. A book which includes some primary material and may contribute to further investigation of the contemplative strain in Merton is the study by William Shannon, *Thomas Merton's Dark Path, The Inner Experience of a Contemplative.* It provides sections from Merton's unpublished manuscript "The Inner Experience", a manuscript which is a reworking of, and addition to, earlier projects.

Shannon's selections from "The Inner Experience" give a glimpse into Merton's thoughts about mysticism and spirituality, but Merton did not want his "Inner Experience" manuscript published as a book, apparently because he had not worked out all of the problems which exist in this composite manuscript. These textual problems have been recognized by Merton scholars, most recently by Brother Patrick Hart who has edited the complete manuscript for installments in *Cistercian Studies.*

Shannon's book discusses the significance of each of Merton's books about contemplation. Secondly, through textual study, Shannon demonstrates how Merton's texts grew. Thus, the chapters on *Seeds of Contemplation* and *New Seeds of Contemplation*, on "The Inner Experience", as well as *Contemplative Prayer*, are deliberate, thoughtful textual investigation of how manuscripts were revised, ordered, rearranged to bring about the books as they were published.

Donald Grayston's *Thomas Merton: The Development of a Spiritual Theologian* is an extremely careful scholarly study of part of the material upon which Shannon touches. Grayston examines the manuscripts and typescripts for *Seeds of Contemplation* (1949), its revision, and the book which evolved out of *Seeds,* called *New Seeds of Contemplation,* which appeared first in early 1962. The conclusion, which conscientious readers of Merton might have inferred, is that Merton developed from a self-conscious, "world-denying and triumphalistic monk" to "a world-affirming, and broadly ecumenical person". Grayston's method is complex and by means of his systematic attention to texts we are able to confirm Merton's radical development as writer and monk.

Shannon's study is an overview of Merton's approaches to contemplation. It analyzes the basic aspects of Merton's development as he moved from his earliest stance, in books such as *What is Contemplation?* and *Seeds of Contemplation*, to final considerations of the same subject in *The Climate of Monastic Prayer.* Shannon, concerned with the evolution of Merton's thought, summarizes its development. Successive chapters trace the evolution of ideas and experience as they develop into complex works. Shannon therefore insists:

It was because Merton was attuned to experience that he was preeminently a theologian—a contemplative rather than a dogmatic theologian. His theology was not an expounding of the truths of revelation in order to offer an intellectual appreciation of them; rather, it was the theology of one who could talk about God because he had first walked with God. For him, God was the burning mystery of Reality. God was the Great Experience beyond all experiences. No one in the twentieth century has articulated that Experience with such clarity of vision as Thomas Merton. (Shannon, p. 233)

This may be an exaggeration, yet it is basically correct. But one could also say that until Grayston's textual work was completed no one had the patience to demonstrate word by word how Merton's thought had evolved. Similar, yet far vaster, are the difficulties of documenting

Merton's life. Contemplation is inexplicable, yet through systematic study we are made aware of fundamental patterns.

Merton's career was an extremely full one, and it will be a long time before we have a complete biography. A valuable intermediary step was provided by Monica Furlong in *Merton, A Biography*. Her book focuses on high points in Merton's life, and the resulting picture is a life full of crises. It is as if Furlong sought a book with a hero — tortured, frustrated, disappointed, but strong — and she found him in Merton. All these qualities are there, no doubt; but we must remember Merton himself often wrote about the other facets of this life; monasticism with all of its problems brought pleasure, satisfaction, and, above all, movement toward union with God and man in a way not readily available outside a monastery. Ed Rice's informal biography *The Man in the Sycamore Tree* (actually a title for one of the novels which Merton wrote in the nineteen-thirties, but destroyed) makes similar mistakes. Rice makes a martyr out of Merton while minimizing the strength of his interior life (the very thing about which Merton wrote so convincingly). Rice's pages about Merton's determination to have a hermitage and how "he was forced to trickery and pressure and evasion to obtain it" give only one version of a story which Furlong qualifies significantly.[13] Her account of the move to that hermitage is apparently close to the truth:

As the 1960s wore on, Merton was moving steadily toward the restructuring of his monastic life. It was as if the fantasy he had woven around his cinder-block building in the woods had come true in the minds of other people as well as himself, and it was becoming less and less a kind of outpost of the monastery, where it was proper to converse with the "separated brethren" (although the Baptist and Episcopalians and Jews continue to come) and more and more the hermitage of Merton's dreams. Merton's sheer persistence in asserting that he needed time alone, coupled with the enormously heavy workload he had carried for years at the monastery and the kind of insouciance in the face of authority with which he had survived the "terrible" years of the 1950s, somehow made it inevitable. (Furlong, p. 270)

As an overview, Furlong's biography of Merton is useful and stimulating, an insightful contribution. Her narrative allows us to see sides of Merton which had been hidden, and it is a dramatic and compelling story. The research and narration of the early years in England is especially good. Yet almost chapter by chapter we are compelled to see yet another crisis develop, and the book moves along slowly toward its inevitable conclusion, the mysterious death in Bangkok.

Furlong's method allows her to build on the crises of Merton's life, but his life must have been more simple *and* more complex than it is presented in this biography. Because Furlong needs to make the book exciting moment by moment, she relies for the first parts of the book rather heavily upon early narratives which Merton wrote. The famous *The Seven Storey Mountain* and the earlier books, *The Secular Journal* and *My Argument With The Gestapo,* provide large amounts of information, but real problems accumulate when these books appear to be used as the main source of information. Especially is this the case with the novel, *My Argument,* an imaginary journey to the England and France which Merton had known from earlier years. Furlong makes it seem as though Merton were writing of actual people he had known in England, yet with only scant novelistic distancing. She also overdoes the terrors of Merton's relationship with his abbot, Dom James Fox, who assumes the role of villain. Merton was clearly sometimes exasperated with the vexations of being under the wing of Dom James, but at the same time his appreciation of his abbot's care and concern can also be traced, maybe even stressed.

A similar deficiency occurs in the chapter when Merton's correspondence with Rosemary Reuther is presented as if he were corresponding with no one else during those months. Such use of correspondence does help tremendously in understanding Merton, and we can be grateful that the Merton Legacy Trust has allowed generous quotation from letters. But while Reuther's exchange with Merton was clearly valuable for him, Furlong makes too much of it:

And now here was a woman and a Catholic, a better theologian than himself, flatly arguing with him and contradicting him, questioning the validity of his vocation and refusing all attempts to charm him out of her cool dismissal of his motives. Merton might, I suppose, have been very angry indeed. In fact, he was fascinated and delighted.

Yes, he said honestly in reply, he was in a crisis and he was much too defensive, and he became frightened of her being so cerebral "probably because I resented my mother's intellectuality." Yes, he did need to get out of the place and move around a bit, only his Abbot wouldn't let him and refused even to discuss it. (Furlong, p. 305)

Furlong has taken certain episodes in the life of Merton and built them into an extremely compelling narrative, but this is hardly the whole picture, and as other biographies are provided they will fill in other parts of the mosaic.

The book published as *Follow the Ecstasy* is also part of that mosaic, but it is hardly more than a rough draft, notes for a biography which John Howard Griffin would perhaps eventually have written if his health had not failed. We can certainly understand the complexities of the job which Michael Mott assumed when he agreed to write the authorized biography first started by Griffin, but started again by Mott, and published in 1984 as *The Seven Mountains of Thomas Merton*. Mott's massive volume will be the basic biographical document for years to come. This sensitive and sensible work is the best biography of Merton. Yet even in it there are problems because of Merton's exuberance and productivity. There is simply no easy way to characterize all of Merton's life.

Often what we find troublesome in others and what we are hasty to criticize about them reveals a fundamental pattern in our own lives. This must have been true of Thomas Merton who often rather strenuously voiced criticism of the industrialization of monastic work at Gethsemani, his abbey. He complained about loud farm implements and of the success of the "chee$e" industry at Gethsemani where he lived as a Cistercian monk for twenty-seven years. As we read Mott's thorough biography, what finally becomes definitely clear is that Merton himself was an industry. Maybe this is the most important fact that remains with a reader after completing this enormous work of documentation. Merton, a man who sincerely sought God through the monastic life, never failed to make a record of this year-by-year, and in many cases day-by-day. Merton is the monk who taught us all silence, but we are (at least to some degree) grateful that 1968, the year he died, came in *before* word processors.

Word processors will be needed to finish the work begun so well by Mott. He provides a very complete record of Merton's life, well-documented and gracefully written. Yet we cannot help but note two things about this biography: 1) Mott himself is a professional writer and he, therefore, is in sympathy with Merton who did so much writing so well; and 2) such sympathy filters what his texts generate. The record ultimately provided is a celebration of successful writing. Thus, "Six very different books by Thomas Merton appeared in 1948" (p. 242), and we are provided with many important details of all these projects. *The Seven Storey Mountain* was "a coup for the publisher" (p. 243); "the reader of *Seeds of Contemplation* (1949) feels compelled to argue with the author in defense of the book" (p. 250), etc.

Of course, we are given all these facts through the lens of Michael Mott: "Only one book of Merton's appeared in 1950, and this had been written five years earlier...." This book, Merton once explained in his preface to *What are these Wounds? The Life of a Cistercian Mystic, Saint Lutgarde of Aywieres,* has been begun as an anonymous pamphlet, and he evaluated it in a 1967 chart as "awful." All of this reminds Mott of Henry James's comment to a newspaper editor, about "this being positively the worst writing he could do" (p. 257). Such detail is interesting, but it reveals insight into Merton *and* insight into the biographer who provides a valuable series of insights into Merton.

Mott's presentation of Merton is often qualified with Mott's remembrance of a phrase, or a poem of some other writer. Another biographer would, perhaps, have chosen other details. With regard to the Lutgarde book, we are informed that Merton thought of calling the book "The Tiger Lily". This is cute, but we also know well that Merton would probably not have given the book so frivolous a title. We may doubt that this would have been a better title even though Mott somewhat ironically tells us so.

Nevertheless this biography is a success. In an era of giant biographies the biographer has to choose between massive documentations such as Joseph Boltner chose for his Faulkner work and a use of details to warp a thesis such as the recent, unfortunate biography of James Agee by Laurence Bergreen. Mott's book is well-proportioned, tailored to stand as a record of facts. Mott provides the facts, though he obviously has to be selective. By means of his access to sealed manuscripts and correspondence Mott is able to put many of the pieces together, and we can see the evolution of Merton the writer. The book has a good bibliography, a fine set of notes, and Mott is scrupulous to document his sources.

This biography is, however, the authorized version of the public Merton, not the private Merton, the Merton who, one of his companion novices reported, would linger longer in the novitiate chapel before the Blessed Sacrament than anyone else. The private Merton is harder to document; also it is a side of Merton of much less interest to readers who enjoy gossip. Not that Mott provides gossip, but Merton-groupies find facts about his being enamoured with this (or that) woman much more interesting reading than details about his being (again) on his knees in the chapel.

Mott's job was to report the significant events in the life. This he does well in a carefully written account. When there are sidetrips, occasioned by a literary thought, such trips are controlled and helpful, yet the total picture remains one of a public Merton. Even the organization of Mott's book *The Seven Mountains,* important geographical spots in Merton's life, becomes (almost) a gimmick for demonstrating the high points in Merton's life. Here we are given that part of Merton which is visible in books, manuscripts, and old journals.

Mott does an excellent job of putting all these pieces together: Thus "his mother's intellectuality" (p. 17); his 1939 detailed written remembrance of 1928 or 1929, quoted at length (pp. 46-47); comparisons of *Seven Storey Mountain* with the *Confessions of St. Augustine* "even before its publication" (p. 76); journal records, and pages torn out from February 1940, to October (p. 157); Merton's stability crisis (p. 273); his private conference with the psychiatrist Gregory Zilboorg (p. 295); problems about censorship (p. 374); Merton's indiscretion with the nurse (whom Mott very gracefully insists on calling only "S"), etc., are all details which cumulatively give us a wonderful portrait of Thomas Merton.

Yet other portraits will also have to be drawn in the future. Two hundred pages of Mott's texts here take us approximately to his discision to enter the monastery in 1941. Another two hundred pages cover the last eight years, or so. The middle part of the book, "Mount Purgatory" really is the central part of Merton's life, the twenty years from entrance to the beginning of the hermitage life, but far fewer pages cover all these years. We need much more information about the years as a monk—formation, decisions, ordination, teaching, work as a novice director. This book is extremely valuable as it stands, but its record will need to be fleshed out by a writer who knows more about what the monastic life demands and gives. My suspicion is that Mott wrote considerably more than is printed here. (Some of the paragraphs lack transitions.) And I hope that he may choose to print elsewhere some of the omitted materials. He stresses in one of his notes that what is interesting about Merton is the fact of his "continuing conversion." This can best be observed by a fellow monk.

Probably Mott realized that he could not provide all the details. Surely he did not want to provide a book of crises as did Monica Furlong. On one occasion Mott stresses that

In much of Merton's writing, early and late, published and private, there is the joy of making noise, and the suffering induced by others making noises, joyfully or not. The bongos are pitted in war against the ocarina, or the "little bastard" who practiced on the trumpet in Perry Street. In time, the scat-singing and another set of bongos gave another answer to the guns at Fort Knox and the very unsilent Trappist tractors (p. 179).

This is beautiful. It is well written. It implies a lot about Merton, as does the entire book. Placed in the proper perspective (an immense chore which must ultimately consider all the primary and secondary material, *and* the details of the life which can be gleaned through interviews), this book is a tremendous addition to knowledge of Merton who lived to make noise best through words. All of this will lead to more. Mott quotes a 7 January, 1967, letter of Merton (p. xxvi) to a thesis writer who wanted to include a biographical section. Merton stressed that he was aware that his life was "not necessarily a history of fidelity to grace", yet he also wrote in the same paragraph that he had tried to give God thanks through his writing and if "I have sometimes helped others to do the same in their own lives, I am glad."

Somewhere, published or unpublished, Michael Mott may already have written an article, a poem, or a novel which probably says something like this. What makes a writer write is a mystery. Mott shows the range of Thomas Merton far better than anyone else. Of course, we know that there was still another range beyond what can be documented. This is all hinted at, especially in the final pages about Asia. Merton writing, like a writing machine, words everywhere, made it possible for a team of editors to put together the posthumous *The Asian Journal*, and made it possible for Mott to provide still more details for this portrait from those same sources. It is truly a continuing story. We have had a good pictorial Merton (James Forest); a sensational Merton (Monica Furlong); and now we have a life by a poet who has great empathy for Merton the writer. What still remains is a life written by a contemplative about a contemplative.

Additional biographical studies will eventually help us to sort out the complexity which is Merton, always monk and always writer. One hopes that some of Merton's literary friends, such as Daniel Berrigan or Bob Lax, might write memoirs. Contributions by his many editors and by fellow monks would also be welcome. James Forest's informal biography about Merton is an example of the value of personal, even biased, views. As did Ed Rice's biography, Forest's informal book provides insights into a side of the man not immediately available elsewhere. (Forest's essay, written for the Twomey collection, *Thomas*

Merton, Prophet in the Belly of Paradox, also provides valuable information about the Merton who was involved in the peace movement.) Forest's *Thomas Merton, A Pictorial Biography* is not a personal remembrance or a memoir, but it serves well as an introduction to the life. The brief text is not documented; Forest realizes he could have provided footnotes, but decided to let the photographs speak for themselves. In seventeen brief sections which support the photographs, Forest provides the outline of Merton's life. The book serves as a tribute to Merton; and even more importantly it may stimulate additional interest in Merton's work among a wider audience. Merton's general appeal could merit extended study.

Furlong and Mott view Merton as a man increasingly sure of his monastic vocation, yet more will likely be done to demonstrate how vocation itself was clarified by the act of writing. Mott acknowledges this fact, and this has been a major theme in my book. Merton's vocation was unusual and should be investigated with this in mind. It is surprising that many of the monks who lived with Father Louis at Gethsemani were only vaguely aware that their Father Louis was a world-famous author. This says much about the monastic life, but it also suggests that Merton himself conspired to keep his literary reputation somewhat hidden within the monastery even though as books appeared year by year he must have found it more difficult to keep the roles of writer and contemplative separate. His published work led to more writing, which had to be done while secluded from other monks and from the world. Decades of separation from others, and especially from other artists, and from most contemporary literature, made Merton a unique writer. During years of seclusion he first (literally) had to raise questions about the nature of his writing, and then, secondly, about his responsibility as a monk and writer. For a period in the late nineteen-forties and early in the nineteen-fifties, he even wondered in print if he should cease writing. Of course he did not, and the value of his questioning is that through questioning Merton worked out an accommodation with the vocation of writing, an activity essential to his contemplative way of life. That vital relationship is the real key to his career. In writing about silence he affirmed his own silent way of life, and also, and even more significantly, in writing about silence he came to a firmer grasp of what those still in the world long for. Like Emily Dickinson or Henry Adams in their self-imposed exiles, Father Louis came to an articulation of a position in relation to universal truths about humankind. His embrace of the mystery of the contemplative

life led him to a surer understanding of what other persons could not
so easily articulate about their needs. He learned to write and then to
let go of writing; thus, paradoxically, over the years his personality as a
writer assumed less importance. This was his way of affirming a unique
way of being, but one clearly needed by others. It was almost inevitable that given his talent and energy he would choose to document
his private journey into silence through poem and diary. What is surprising was how this journey led back to the world.

Merton's poems were at first something which allowed the young
writer to change from being an intellectual and an aspiring novelist to
being a contemplative monk; yet the poems constitute a link with
Merton's earlier experience of the world and were an avenue which
would lead the mature writer back to contact with the world. A similar
pattern informs the journals; detailed records of the moment serve as
meditations which ultimately reveal the impossibility of radical separation from the world. Just as one may be in the world but not of it,
Merton learned that one may well be with the world, but not in it. It
was primarily through his art that he articulated these significant
realizations. Future scholarly research will surely strengthen our
understanding of these crucial relationships. It is not a matter of Merton being hidden away in a monastery in the hills of Kentucky, unable
to be the artist he dreamt, or the hermit he imagined. Rather he slowly
came to the realization that his calling was somehow to combine the
job of writing with the grace of being a contemplative in a particular
place with all its frustrations and satisfactions.

The book *Merton: By Those Who Knew Him Best*, which consists of
transcripts made for Paul Wilkes' television documentary "Merton"
reflects the wide range of persons within and outside monasteries who
testify to Merton's continuing development. Still in process is another
oral history project which promises more detail.[14]

Literary Studies of Merton

Various books about Merton have focused on particular aspects of
his writing, either as man of letters, poet or religious writer. Such approaches are valuable as avenues of approach to Thomas Mer-
ton/Father Louis, always the writer, yet always on his way as a monk.
This allusive writer, however, was never content to think of himself as
a writer who happened to be a monk, or a monk who happened to be
a writer. Instead, as the years passed, the two roles became mutually

supportive. Much recent scholarly writing about Merton allows us to see this, while the same commentary often tries to keep Merton within discrete categories.

Recent literary studies about Merton show how important writing was for him. In different ways the books by Woodcock, Labrie, and Lentfoehr all shed light on the development of Merton's aesthetic. All stress that he was an artist because he was first a man of God. Although isolated from the world of contemporary art, Merton never lost contact with the sources of imagination which feed a good poet. His physical isolation was both a liability and asset. He went his own way, and little by little developed a personal approach to writing, finally his own variety of poetry. He was, however, secretly reading poets such as William Carlos Williams and Louis Zukofsky during the years after he ceased modeling his work on Eliot and Dylan Thomas.[15] He also continued to write to various friends. (There is, for example, another volume of letters waiting to be edited, those between Merton and his teacher Mark Van Doren. This was part of a network of contacts which helped him to progress as artist while simultaneously gaining strength in separation.) When the mature poetry started to flow it resulted from solitude, not from isolation; the quiet which helped to reinforce certain values in his life—solitude, prayer, awareness of others, silence, respect, dignity—provides the boundaries for his career.

Woodcock's study, *Thomas Merton, Monk and Poet,* is the reasoned study of an outsider, not even, Woodcock admits, a practicing Christian. The result is an approach to Merton clear-headed and balanced, objective in fundamental ways. Woodcock reminds us while Merton was separated from the world, his subject matter was more and more the world beyond this world. Woodcock writes and qualifies with Merton's own words:

And if Merton believed that eremitic reclusion was really a necessary extension of monasticism, a pushing of outposts into the farther desert, he also believed that it was quite consistent with his priestly vocation. For to Merton what made the priest different from other men was not his pastoral role, his activities of teaching and advising other men or consoling and praying for them. It was not even that the priest is a man of God, for "The monk is a man of God and he does not have to be a priest." What distinguished the priest is his sacramental role, his role as a "Visible human instrument of the Christ who reigns in Heaven," and this role is carried out when he re-enacts Christ's death and sacrifice in the mystery of the Mass.

This explains at once the beauty and the terror of the priestly vocation. A man, weak as other men, imperfect as they are, perhaps less well endowed than many of those to whom he is sent, perhaps even less inclined to be virtuous than some of them, finds himself caught, without possibility of escape, between the infinite mercy of Christ and the almost infinite dreadfulness of man's sin. (Woodcock, pp. 80–87)

Woodcock's study demonstrates how art and life reinforced each other. Merton truly believed in the "mystical body," but he maintained much of his "existential communion" through writing. Why else all those poems, letters, essays, cables, diaries, translations, prayers, and finally anti-poems, except simultaneously to praise God and to keep reminding persons of what had been forgotten?

Woodcock's analysis of Merton's poetry is frequently helpful as suggestions for future study. He does not try to explicate the poetry in detail, yet he does isolate its predominant features. Thus in a few pages (pp. 34–38) he demonstrates the best of Merton's earliest work even though he may resort merely to labeling a particular poem effective. Woodcock is best when he picks up resonances between the life of the choir and the poems which grew out of the cloister. For example, Woodcock's study of *Bread in the Wilderness*, a book where Merton discusses the psalms as poetry, is well focused. Using this as a key, he demonstrates that Merton wrote "poems of the choir" in which one hears the religious poetry which Merton had theoretically adumbrated in *Bread in the Wilderness*. Yet Woodcock is forced to avoid any extended synthesis and merely gives examples (pp. 55–62). Somewhat the same procedure is used to isolate important poems from other moments in Merton's life. The method picks out what is of value, but only occasionally stops for analysis. One impression created by Woodcock's wise, but often cursory, introduction is that Merton's maturing in monasticism led surely to compassion. If we go the next step and examine Labrie's recent study of Merton's work as art, we are reminded that it was his developing aesthetic sense which allowed Merton to go back toward the world, not to criticize its errors so much as to celebrate unity.

Woodcock's book provides valuable glimpses, samples, and examples, and assumes responsibility for a large body of material. Ross Labrie's *The Art of Thomas Merton* is more carefully focused on questions about art and less concerned with Merton's personality. Woodcock provides a valuable appreciation; Labrie works more as a scholar bringing many pieces of evidence to bear so that he can account for the art which was produced. Labrie's aim is to show Merton's "versatility in mastering various literary forms" (p. xi). Within this framework he has succeded. Labrie demonstrates how the pressures which Merton experienced in producing literary works alternated with a desire for solitude. He also considers problems which Merton experienced within a strict religious order which, for example, required censorship. (The subject of Merton's relationship with his censors would also generate a book length study!)

Labrie asserts that "Merton's problems with writing were the result of his own anxieties about his dual vocation as both contemplative and artist" (p. 7). Merton's artistic drive provides the primary focus, and skillful use of unpublished notes, letters, and various essays is evident throughout this study, especially in the opening chapter in which Labrie outlines Merton's aesthetic. Labrie's examination of concerns about how a modern artist might find ways "to restore the face of nature and the rhythm of natural time as against the abrasive and synthetic pattern of modern life" (p. 17) is good. Yet because Merton produced so much, Labrie's task remains immense and therefore he, too, can only begin to provide the main outlines of what other critics will pursue.

The opening essay of Labrie's book provides a useful overview of Merton as artist. He shows how Merton's approach to art developed, yet also how being artist and contemplative made Merton increasingly aware that he would never put certain types of experience into words. There is a mystery in all life, and especially in that of the contemplative. As Labrie makes clear, it is this mystery which makes it possible for Merton's poetry (and other writing) to continue to open up. The problem of course is that if Merton is suggesting the mystery of the ineffable any critic runs the risk of being overwhelmed.

If there is a deficiency with Merton it is that he tried to do too much in too many ways, and this ambition is precisely what causes problems for any investigator. Forced to categorize the writing into various types — narrative, diary, essay, and poem — the scholar must ignore much so that the investigation's framework can remain intact. Further, and this is even more a problem, an illusion is suggested that Merton somehow kept all of these things in neat boxes. In reality, it was more a matter of one thing feeding another; thus there is little doubt that one type of writing fed others, just as the monastic existence itself contributed to the flow of the writing. Like some of the earlier studies of Merton's thought, Labrie's book provides a valid category for our evaluation of Merton's art. There is nothing wrong with that, but Merton's work was far more unified than critical categories suggest. Above all, as a man of prayer, he wanted to lead others to God through his writing, while paradoxically toward the end of his career he became less interested in "art" as such. This did not mean that he ceased to be an artist or that his art was less effective. Instead it means he had learned to assimilate various techniques into a vision of wholeness. Labrie's label of art, and his classification in broad categories, makes it seem almost as if Merton had several different visions. A deficiency of Labrie's relatively brief study is while he assumes responsibility for enormous categories of writing, he can only provide limited explication. He confesses that the essays gave him most trouble because of their sheer bulk (over one hundred and fifty essays).

Labrie knows Merton was highly conscious of using language effectively. His discussion of the diaries and journals centers around Merton's (or, maybe his superiors') awareness that he might one day turn them into finished works. Labrie demonstrates that part of the charm of the published journals derives from Merton's ability almost to converse with other writers, and maintains further that Merton arranged the journals to give evidence of what he had been reading and thinking while the journals remain, in large part, a conversation with himself. The journals then work on several levels. It is in *Conjectures of a Guilty Bystander* that this is most obvious and this perception of Labrie's could be followed up in greater detail.

Woodcock and Labrie provide us overviews that are selective; this is the case with Sister Thérèse Lentfoehr too in *Words and Silence*. But with Lentfoehr a process of selection had already taken place because of her background as poet, and because of the unusual relationship which she developed with Merton through correspondence over the entire period of his monastic life. Her's is a careful and systematic critique of Merton's poetry, informed by a close relationship which developed with the poet over the years.

Sister Thérèse Lentfoehr's appreciation of Merton's poetry is far more than that of an admiring correspondent. She is a critic who has absorbed his poetry, and can talk about it with wit and sparkle. She knows that it is good. The basic organization of her book reveals a knowledge of many layers in Merton's poetry. It is as if she knows it so well and has been through it so many times that her writing rethreads her way on a journey she has made many times, a journey on which everything seen reflects aspects of the history of the monk-artist who has first made the journey. As a critic, Lentfoehr guides us to the point where we realize that we can trace the journey ourselves.

Sister Thérèse's chapters correspond to stages in Merton's career and basic patterns in his poetry. Dividing her book into three parts, she introduces the early poetry, which is hardly ever static, in her first three chapters. Her middle chapters are called "Zen Mystical Transparencies," "Surrealistic Patternings," and "Recurrent Themes." The chapter on themes shows Merton repeatedly returning to basic themes and images. Her pages about children (pp. 85–89), and the city (pp. 94–96), show how certain threads make up the fabric of these poems. Again, extended studies of all these thematic patterns could be made by others. What I have suggested about Lentfoehr's book does not really indicate its full value. Study of the notes would be a valuable exercise for any neophyte Merton scholar as well as for an advanced student. We have here a poet who knows another poet well and who has access to manuscript material unavailable to others. She has been carefully reading this poetry for years — yet is someone who refuses to idolize Merton. She keeps her distance, yet it is a distance of love and respect.

Merton's isolation from the world of contemporary art was asset and liability. It is in Sister Thérèse's study of the poetry that we can perhaps see such complexity best illustrated. It has been suggested that if Merton had experienced more contact with other artists and with more contemporary poetry in the forties and fifties, his movement away from a predictable "modernist" variety of poetry might have come much more quickly. Yet Lentfoehr's exposition of his poetry demonstrates that strains which were later considered innovative were indeed present early in his career. This is to assert that in some way Merton remained predictable. In other ways, Lentfoehr strengthens an argument for his genius. In *Words and Silence* she traces important patterns in Merton's poetic creations, and as a result we see how each stage grew out of the preceding one. Unfortunately what this means for others is that to understand Merton's affirmation of silence, they have to spend as much time with his writing as his best critics and learn to see his writing career and life as a whole.

Anthony Padovano's ambitious book interprets Merton as a symbol for twentieth century man. His book is a synthesis of Merton's life and work which uses Merton as an emblem. Padovano maintains that the human quest is circular because the successful journey includes acceptance of the essential self: thus it is appropriate that this study of Merton's work is structured in a circle which circumscribes both the biography and the published writing.

Merton's spiritual journey was beneficial for him, and Padovano's exploration and cartography of that journey help us see as Merton did. It helps to guide us through myths which affect our lives. We are shown how Merton reacted to the fragmentation of the contemporary world but how he kept his gaze steadily upon the transcendent. Padovano's point seems to be Merton's journey through the present century was one toward wholeness and a wider acceptance of varying cultures and experiences. Padovano reminds us that it is difficult to read Merton, who (especially in his final creative surges of anti-poetry) was seldom interested in following a straightforward path. Some of the maps provided by Padovano, including those which chart the voracious reading of his subject, are as winding as the Kentucky backroads Merton knew well. *The Human Journey* lets us imagine what Merton must have felt, at least during much of his spiritual journey. It also helps us see the beauty and complexity of much of Merton's writing, which must be seen collectively as his odyssey toward unity. Most importantly, Padovano provides clear exegesis of the final books of poetry, a first-rate but rather surprising feature in a book that often seems an almost psycho-biographical approach to Merton. At other times it seems to be an analysis of aspects of Merton's journey which were most disturbing to him (or to Padovano). Although all these elements have value, the question remains, does it add up to "The Human Journey"? A less pretentious title would have served Merton better.

Padovano has read Merton carefully and gives us a sense of his frustrations, drives, motivations, and longings, mostly by providing insights into the significant writings of the final ten to fifteen years of Merton's life. Naturally, all this does not fall into a neat category, and for Padovano to explain much of Merton's life while demonstrating that the life is a symbol of the century is difficult. When all is said and done Merton "the symbol" remains illusive, and perhaps that very fact should be stressed more. Merton kept looking, yet always within his own rather special monastic circumstances. His monasticism seems to be minimized here, perhaps because information about that is available elsewhere. But the joy Merton found in being an artist seems also to be downplayed. What is central is symbolism represented by a sensitive writer reacting to a frightening century. What we still need is assurance that Merton's vocation was fulfilled. Padovano's book does help, however, in understanding how the man, formed by a lonely childhood and shaped by a love of the world, developed as he did. Of its nature, it is a book written by an outsider, someone who seems to be looking in on a monastic vocation. Not that it could be any other way. Maybe one of Padovano's most valuable points is his reminder that we too need a contemplative (or at least an ascetic) drive. He reminds us that being alone, and making that a virtue, was a major characteristic of Merton's life and writing.

Merton was leery of categories and rightly so. Padovano says, "There would always be something unfinished about Thomas Merton. It is that way with talented people. They are alive as long as they live. But they never fit into final categories." That sums it up. As for Merton's happiness, stability, quiet, joy, simplicity—which were also part of his symbolic journey—we need other books on these subjects.

The Continuing Journey

Merton's accomplishment as artist is fundamental to his life. Even more significant, as recent studies suggest, the life as reflected in the writing became a model for others. Positing writing as a kind of paradigm for others to build upon unifies recent studies of Merton's work. These books might be called theological in approach, although such categorization fails to do justice to these specialized studies of Merton's investigations into man's participation in the pardox of a contemplative journey. As Elena Malits stresses, it was as if through his writings Merton discovered his life. And beyond this is the equally important fact that Merton's significant writing (Sister Elena would perhaps attempt to limit this to the autobiographical writing.) does have a "power that renders it fascinating to others. The stories of his initial and continuing conversion, apparently, have brought some sort of religious conversion in numerous pesons" (*The Solitary Explorer*, p. 153).

It is with the effect of Merton's writing upon other lives and other writers that we must now be concerned. As monk-artist he was preoccupied with finding his own way, yet in that single-minded quest he provided directions for other travellers. As he became surer of his abilities as artist, he ceased being very much concerned with the work of art as a finished object. Writing was recognized more as a reflection of a personal process. It then became more a matter of keeping a record of where he happened to be. Yet that state of being was, of its nature, not to be finished within the temporal world. As Merton himself noted in his *Conjectures of a Guilty Bystander*, "He who arrives is ruined." To keep on the journey knowing that one is but on one's way spiritually was finally one of the most important facts Merton came to live, love, and write about. That fact helps to account both for the nature of his quest and the open-endedness of his writing, especially in the final years. Merton was coming to learn that he would never be done with sketching, jotting, praising, praying. Yet he also was coming to learn that in a sense his earlier vision of life as purgatory was mistaken because if man would but stop to be nowhere, paradise would be at hand.

In the books by Finley, Adams, and Malits, as well as in Padovano's, we see the effect of Merton's systematic quest more clearly than in examinations which focus upon his writing as art. Both types of studies are needed. To combine both approaches (studies of art, and records of quest), as my book has attempted, assists us to see that aspects of writing and living were never separated in Merton's existence. Through art he leads his reader into silence, not just the silence of his own journey, but the silence which all persons embrace if they are to find wholeness. Merton consciously lived his life and he put all his energy into individual moments. Depending upon how readers come to know his work, they may appreciate one aspect over another. Merton played many roles. We might express this another way: both Lentfoehr and James Finley knew Merton, one mostly through reading and extended correspondence, the other through a spiritual friendship at Gethsemani Abbey and then through careful reading and study. This fundamental difference helps to account for the different books which they have produced and also suggests the complexity of the Merton who could be a novice master and friend, poet and enthusiastic correspondent.

James Finley's title, *Merton's Palace of Nowhere*, is derived from Merton's *The Way of Chuang Tzu* and it suggests the mystery of the quest Merton had come to embrace. Finley's volume appeared after a long period of gestation, the result of Merton's influence as novice master, and as friend. (Still another category of studies which could well be included in a survey such as this would be the works written by others under Merton's influence. Here we would have to include books by Ernesto Cardenal, Matthew Kelty, and Henri Nouwen.) Finley's book is scholarly. His primary concern is a human need to be aware of the "true self" within a world where all kinds of activities provide reflections of a "false self." Finley draws upon many of Merton's texts, and Merton's *The New Man* (1961), a book which has not been properly assimilated into the Merton canon, provides a major thrust for his discussion. Finley's explanation of Merton's struggle to say how we realize the true self is a way of understanding both Merton and everyman:

Our struggle does not remove us from our simple, everyday self but confirms its ultimate dimensions. Our prayer does not carry us off into realms unknown for it reveals the unknown depths of each passing hour. Nevertheless the struggle is a real one. The realization of the true self does not fall into our lap like ripe fruit. It is true that in God we live without effort, but it is also true that it calls for a divestiture of self to live without effort. The following text not only refers to the present reality of God's presence but also to the only way for us to realize it.

The desert becomes a paradise when it is accepted as desert. The desert can never be anything but a desert if we are trying to eascpe it. But once we fully accept it in union with the passion of Christ, it becomes a paradise.... This breakthrough into what you already have is only accomplished through the complete acceptance of the cross. (Finley, pp. 114–115)

Still further scholarly studies to come are suggested by Daniel Adams' careful *Thomas Merton's Shared Contemplation: A Protestant Perspective*, published by Cistercian Publications. Adams approaches Merton's vocation as a monastic writer with objectivity. Writing as a Protestant, he examines how Merton's themes relate to the significant traditions of western Christianity. The stress is again on the balance and the combination of contemplation and action. Adams provides an overview of Merton's developing appreciation of contemplation as a subject fundamental to Christianity. Thus, while Shannon's *The Dark Path* provides the base for an examination of Merton's books which deal explicitly with this subject, Adams demonstrates how Merton's consistent interest in the contemplative grows out of ancient traditions. Adams comments not just on what Merton writes, but also on how the writing provides connections for all Christians and those in other traditions. Adams' book places Merton's accomplishment within the mainstream of western culture.

Adams' study of the foundations of Merton's thought—an appraisal of the modern Thomists, St. Augustine, St. Thomas Aquinas, St. Bernard of Clairvaux, Platonic mysticism, The Desert Fathers, St. Gregory of Nyssa, St. Teresa of Avila and St. John of the Cross— suggests both the value of Merton's work and the extent of the scholarly work still to be done. For without a doubt if these nine subjects have provided the organizational outline for just one chapter by Adams, his thoroughness makes it clear that such major building blocks in Merton's spiritual formation should be studied in more detail in the future. For example, Adams makes good use of the articles Merton wrote about Bernard and which first appeared in *Collectanea Ordinis Cisterciensium Reformatorium* in 1953, 1954, and which have subsequently been edited by Brother Patrick Hart under the title *Thomas Merton on Saint Bernard* (already discussed); but clearly more can and must be done in tracing the synthesis which Merton made. The same point might be made when Adams shows the applicability of Merton's thought to today's world.

Thomas Merton's Shared Contemplation provides a systematic investigation of the theoretical base upon which Merton built his world of contemplation and action. All of Adams' chapters are insightful, especially the later ones where he shows that the eremitic life, as Merton lived it, may be the model we all shall have to follow in the future, for few Christians experience the communities we earlier dreamt were possible. Adams points out Merton's definition of *eremus* is "'a certain physical separation from the affairs of the world, but it is intended to indicate our attitude'"(p. 262). Precisely because Merton had learned to accept solitude (and come to terms with himself) he was able to accept humankind, since in solitude one begins to find the image of God in oneself and in others. Adams insists "we must be able to discern the image of God in others." We can easily overlook it if we are not first aware of God's image in ourselves. Merton believed that "'all things carry within them an image of God'" (p. 283).

Looking toward the future, we can posit several important points. Adams builds one of his chapters, "Contemplation in a World of Action" around the idea of the impossibility of an "either/or" choice. Merton came to learn that monks, too, possessed illusions and a monastery was hardly a place to get away from the world. Yet Merton also says that true monasticism serves well as a model in a diaspora situation.

Because it combines approaches, Elena Malits' book, *The Solitary Explorer*, may be the most successful of these "theological" books. Malits traces some of the significant metaphors of Merton's writing. She stresses Merton's growth in solitude and wisdom. In one section, she examines three phrases which recur throughout his career; "to leave the world", "to live in the desert", and "to seek God". These are classic formulations about the monastic experience. Merton's use of these phrases allowed him to clarify his existence and to clarify them into metaphors in such a way that Christians who were not monks might apply his meaning to their lives.

Malits stresses that Merton wrote so readers would identify "with him and his capacity to articulate the deep desires of the human heart" (p. 2). Her opening chapter provides an overview of the changing nature of Merton's "journey" and "his commitment to continuing conversion" (p. 20), a theme which Michael Mott incorporates into his biography. Both Mott and Malits trace the movements of Merton's life which produced the work. Seeing the works and life together prepare the reader for Malits' analysis. Of course this has been the theme of my own book, which argues that Merton could be a successsful man of letters precisely because he was *both* a monk and an artist.

Malits' treatment of Merton's decade-long investigation into the nature of Zen and its relationship to Christianity, and even more importantly its meaning for him, is a good example of the success of her method. Always paying close attention to texts, she is able to demonstrate the gradual refinement in Merton's writing. A similar success attends her judgments about Merton's refinement of understanding about the self. Her chapter "A Mind Awake in the Dark" traces Merton's systematic enunciation of how if we are to become "new men" ""We must withdraw ourselves (in the right and Christian sense) from exterior things, and pass through the center of our soul to find God. . . .'" (from *The New Man*, cited by Malits, p. 125)

Two more specialized studies of particular themes presented in the writings of Merton have also been published. One deals with the theme of solitude and another treats the continuing interest of Merton concerning the East. Even so specialized a study as Richard Cashen's *Solitude in the Writings of Thomas Merton* has broad implications for mankind. Ultimately, says Cashen, Merton's concern about solitude is about "the very nature and destiny of man" (p. 178). Lipski's book, *Thomas Merton and Asia*, while valuable as an introduction to Merton's fascination with Eastern philosophy and religion, only scratches the surface of what remains to be done in this vast subject.

Pieces of the Mosaic

As we survey these various approaches to Merton we find each of the writers seeking ways to find a guidepost to move further along on a journey similar to Merton's. Woodcock, conscious of his separation from the original traveller, is able to perceive the broad outlines of

Merton's dual journey as monk and poet. Labrie, working more as scholar and therefore with a concern for categorization, sees large patterns. This also allows him to look carefully at individual details which suggest how Merton's art functions. Sister Thérèse (who in a sense has had more access than anyone else to Merton's private world as writer) focuses on the poetry; she begins to investigate the intricacies of the poetic world, yet she never forgets it is a guidepost toward a larger world. Padovano interprets Merton's journey as a symbol for all. Elena Malits, coming at Merton from the point of view of a religious studies scholar (but intrigued by his use of metaphor) chooses another aspect for close examination so we can see how his personal journey was a continuing one. Each scholar looks for evidence. Whether general outline, examinations of art, theological background, or investigations of the journey itself, the words crafted by Merton are guideposts for a journey. All these scholars are on similar journeys but because Merton has left behind so much, various routes can be located and followed. In the meantime Merton seems to have taken still more steps forward. My point continues to be that Merton accomplished his work as a writer because he was a monk.

The complexity of Merton as monk and writer, not easily classified and assimilated, is made clearer in the various collections of essays about him and his work. Gerald Twomey's collection is mainly about the social implications of Merton's writing. Just as Merton's photograph was literally posted on the wall of Daniel Berrigan's prison cell, Merton's thought has remained with many during the past several decades. A few lines by Berrigan suggest Merton's impact on those who fought for social justice: as a contemplative Merton stood back from his society, not to criticize it, but to say he had found something else much better.

> In prison remember
> Dame Poverty, her strait uses of man;
> Merton's photo, friend, confident, brother under the skin,
> peering like young Picasso from the wall,
> . . . .
> Merton: that cool brusque cavalier's glance at the
> world: No sale.[16]

Articles by James H. Forest and Gordon Zahn in Twomey's collection provide information about Merton's role as peacemaker and pacifist. Other pieces by John Howard Griffin, and Twomey himself, examine the social implications of writing in relation to questions about race, war, civil rights, and the third world. Still other pieces in the book show Merton's concerns with the East, Church, renewal, and history. Twomey shows how Merton's monastic vocation supported his social vision. Twomey's collection indicates that scholars and friends (sometimes they are both) bring remembrance and systematic investigation to bear. Twomey's book was planned to appear in 1978 on the occasion of the tenth anniversary of Merton's death and it seemed appropriate when that book was planned to focus upon the social themes in Merton's work. Such a collection is a conscious step beyond Brother Patrick Hart's earlier collection, *Thomas Merton, Monk*. It helps us see that the contemplative life easily led toward involvement. In a sense involvement is the critical message in the remaining books to be surveyed here, but as is clear especially from two books edited by Brother Patrick Hart for Cistercian Publications, involvement is much more than just social awareness. In *The Message of Thomas Merton*, edited with a valuable introduction by Brother Patrick, essays by scholars from many disciplines examine aspects of Merton's thought and art. This volume is important for several reasons. The introduction is a masterful summing up of the diverse accomplishments of Merton's work. The essays, twelve of them, each different, seem to have been chosen to provide directions for future study.

Some of the essays in *The Message* such as those by Elena Malits and William H. Shannon, provide extensions to work which these authors have published elsewhere. Other essays are speculative and seem to be designed to provide experimental modes of analysis. Victor A. Kramer's "Merton's Published Journals: The Paradox of writing as a Step Toward Contemplation," John F. Teahan's "Merton's Life and Thought," and George Kilcourse's "'Pieces of the Mosaic Earth': Thomas Merton and the Christ" are valuable as new ways of looking carefully at Merton's writing. Teahan's provocative suggestions about parallels between Merton's awareness of silence, and similar patterns in other twentieth century writers and philosophers promises to be an important area in future study. Still other approaches in *The Message* radiate outward and suggest connections which scholars have still to make. Especially useful are the insights into ecumenism by E. Glenn Hinson, into "Asian Religious Thought" by Deba Patnaik, and into solitude suggested by Chalmers MacCormick. MacCormick investigates some of the implications of Merton's thought for contemporary persons' need for solitude beyond the monastery:

One of the respects in which Merton matured was that in his later writings he showed a greater sensitivity than he had shown earlier to the needs of the married for solitude. Previously he had, to be sure, commended marriage as a particular mode of contemplation and a high vocation, but he had not yet envisaged some kind of union of this vocation with the monastic. In his very important essay on 'Ecumenism and Renewal', however, he reveals a concern, awareness, and germinal wisdom on this theme that might, had he lived longer, have developed into a major statement about solitude and marriage. (This may seem improbable, but it is not unimaginable.) He wrote:

Why could there not be monasteries, with a nucleus of permanently dedicated monks, to which others come temporarily for two or three years, for periods of training or for retreat (as for instance in Zen Buddhist monasticism)? Why could not married people participate temporarily, in some way, in monastic life? (Hart, p. 125–126)

Connections in other essays are made with religious tradition and with secular questions. Both the essays by Lawrence S. Cunningham, "The Life of Thomas Merton as Paradigm: The View of Academe" and Dennis Q. McInerny, "Thomas Merton and the Tradition of American Critical Romanticism," show that Merton's work will not be read in a vacuum.

A recent volume, *The Legacy of Thomas Merton*, reprints essays, most of which first appeared in *Cistercisn Studies*. All of these essays provide evidence of Merton's continuing influence. Essays by important scholars such as Gordon C. Zahn and Jean Leclercq make this book a necessity for a Merton reader who wishes to see how his complex legacy continues. Essays on prayer, the Far East, spirituality, high culture, letters, poetry, solitary life, friendship, spiritual growth, ecclesiological development, peace, and a memoir constitute this volume. Also a revised volume, the new enlarged edition of *Thomas Merton/Monk, A Monastic Tribute*, should be noted because it is a valuable repository of Merton insights and remembrances.[17]

Many different areas will occupy future scholars. There will be more textual studies. There will be many more studies of influence. With the *Thomas Merton on Saint Bernard* volume, for example, it becomes even clearer how dependent Merton was upon classic writers. Also there will be many more consideratons of the implications of Merton's thought for others—and especially for persons outside monastic life. Unpublished Merton manuscripts and additional studies about him promise to continue to appear for decades. Selecting from unfinished materials for publication will take years. Along with reading notes, lectures notes, notebooks, journals and correspondences, there are completed manuscripts also awaiting publication. Merton's voluminous correspondence will take many years to edit and publish. All of this means that our knowledge of him will continue to develop for many years as this man of silence continues to speak.

The most recent and perhaps most essential single addition for scholars of Mertoniana is the new comprehensive bibliography which Marquita E. Breit and Robert E. Daggy have published. This voluminous work updates an earlier book done by Breit and uses bibliographical citations which are reported regularly in *The Merton Seasonal* edited by Daggy. It will be indispensable to all future Merton scholars.

Merton never claimed to be an original scholar, but maybe that was part of his originality. He was a contemplative who experienced flashes into eternity yet he was a man truly concerned about the world. He therefore sought ways of suggesting how we might better think about our world. It is in personal insights both about eternity and the present that we look to find the Merton most hidden. He kept thinking and writing about liturgy, literature, art, history, race, war, politics, society, solitude, poetry, myth, and in relation to all these topics he continues to draw many readers.

Already there are some who unabashedly compare Merton to the Fathers of the Church. In fact, this comparison is not far-fetched. It is simply an expression of the significance of what this compulsive writer from silence had to say, and a statement of his promise for the future. In Merton's journey, as a contemplative and a writer, we have a model for any seeker in a post-modern world, someone fully aware of the need for mystical insight and "existential communion", his working title for *The New Man*. One sees, with Merton, that change is of the essence, but it is through language that communication of any awareness is possible, and it is in communication that steps toward communion are taken. Tracing the steps of this fascinating journey is to see how Merton made virtues of being monk and artist—and how along the way he also produced so large a body of widely read work.

Notes and References

Preface

1. *The Seven Storey Mountain* (New York, 1948), p. 169.
2. *The Secular Journal of Thomas Merton* (New York, 1959), p. 265.
3. *A Thomas Merton Reader,* ed. Thomas P. McDonnell, rev. ed. (New York, 1974), p. 16.
4. *Secular Journal,* p. 270.
5. *Merton Reader,* pp. 16–17.
6. See Brother Patrick Hart's foreword to Merton's *The Monastic Journey* (Kansas City, 1977), especially the opening pages where it is noted that just a few hours before his death Merton had remarked " 'The monk . . . is someone who takes up a critical attitude toward the contemporary world and its structures' " (p. vii).
7. While I will attempt to acknowledge specific debts incurred from the published work of others, I must also thank the innumerable people—friends, monks, and scholars—who will only be the subject of this footnote. Without their encouragement this book could not exist.

Chapter One

1. Facts incorporated in this chapter about Merton's early life are largely derived from *The Seven Storey Mountain,* yet it should be remembered that all of his books, and especially his journals, provide an overview of his continuing journey.
2. Themes concerning the power, use, and abuse of language are present throughout Merton's poetry, in all of the journals, and in many essays on a wide range of subjects. Chapter 6 of this book investigates this important concern of Merton.
3. See especially *A Hidden Wholeness: The Visual World of Thomas Merton,* photographs by Thomas Merton and John Howard Griffin (Boston, 1970), and *The Man in the Sycamore Tree: The Good Times and Hard Life of Thomas Merton* (New York, 1970).
4. Brother Patrick Hart, "A Witness to Life: Thomas Merton on Monastic Renewal," in *Thomas Merton: Prophet in the Belly of a Paradox,* ed. Gerald Twomey (New York, 1978), pp. 173–74.
5. *The Seven Storey Mountain* (New York, 1948), p. 57; hereafter cited as *SSM.*

6. Cf. the poem "The Biography" in *A Man in the Divided Sea,* reprinted in *The Collected Poems of Thomas Merton* and discussed in chapter 3 following.

7. Merton to Mark Van Doren, 9 December 1941, Columbia University Library.

8. Merton to Mark Van Doren headed, St. Lucy's Day, Columbia University Library.

9. *The Collected Poems of Thomas Merton* (New York, 1977), p. 91; hereafter cited as *CP.*

10. "Three Postcards from the Monastery" originally appeared in *Figures for an Apocalypse.*

11. To appreciate the range of Merton's production during these years, see chapters 4 and 6 of this study, as well as his own comments in *A Thomas Merton Reader,* p. 15.

12. Cf. "Letter to an Innocent Bystander," in *The Behavior of Titans* and the journal *Conjectures of a Guilty Bystander.*

13. The recent books by George Woodcock *(Thomas Merton, Monk and Poet)* and Sr. Therésè Lentfoehr *(Words and Silence: On the Poetry of Thomas Merton)* provide valuable perspectives on the poetry.

14. "Prologue," p. 17, by Brother Patrick Hart, and "The Man," p. 19, by Matthew Kelty, in *Thomas Merton/Monk: A Monastic Tribute* (New York, 1974).

15. Copies of these tapes are at the Thomas Merton Studies Center of Bellarmine College, Louisville, Kentucky.

16. Books completed at his death included *The Geography of Lograire,* and *Contemplative Prayer* (originally published under the title *The Climate of Monastic Prayer*), the novel *My Argument With The Gestapo,* and a collection of poetry called "Sensation Time at the Home" which is included in *CP.*

17. See especially "Is the World a Problem?" in *Contemplation in a World of Action,* and the essays on humanism and Teilhard de Chardin in *Love and Living.*

Chapter Two

1. Merton to Mark Van Doren, 28 November 1941, Columbia University Library.

2. Merton to Mark Van Doren, 24 October 1939, Columbia University Library.

3. Merton to Mark Van Doren, 25 August 1940, Columbia University Library.

4. James Laughlin was to become Merton's editor for all of the books of poetry, and many additional volumes. Laughlin's name is mentioned in many of the early letters of Merton to Van Doren.

5. Naomi Burton, "A Note on the Author and this Book," in *My Argument With The Gestapo,* (New York, 1969), pp. 11, 14.

6. This is also the title which Ed Rice chose to use for his biography, cited in chapter 1, note 3.

7. Merton to Mark Van Doren, 18 August 1939, Columbia University Library.

8. *The Secular Journal of Thomas Merton* (New York, 1959), pp. 158–59; hereafter cited as *SJ*.

9. Reviews of *The Secular Journal* indicate parallels with Merton's mature thought. See Phillip M. Stark, in *America* 121 (16 August 1969):102, and J. Leonard, *New York Times,* 10 July 1969, p. 39.

10. Connections might be made between this early analysis and the poetry of *The Geography of Lograire.* See also some of Merton's book reviews produced during the final decade of his life, some of which are reprinted in *Ishi Means Man.*

11. *The Seven Storey Mountain,* p. 368, for Merton's account.

12. *My Argument With The Gestapo* (New York, 1969), "Author's Note," p. 73; hereafter cited as *MA*.

13. Merton's autobiography sold more copies than any other comparable spiritual autobiography, and has continued to be his single most purchased book. It has been published in many editions, as well as in thirteen foreign languages.

14. When the book was reviewed there was enthusiastic response, but that wide recognition caused problems for Merton. In an interview in 1967 he emphasized that it was a "youthful book, too simple, in many ways too crude" (Thomas P. McDonnell, "An Interview with Thomas Merton," *Motive* 38 [October 1967]:31–32).

15. *The Seven Storey Mountain,* pp. 163–64.

16. Robert Giroux to Mark Van Doren, 21 July 1948, Columbia University Library.

17. Cf. "Hagia Sophia," in *Emblems of a Season of Fury.*

18. For other references to John Paul in *SSM* see especially pp. 335–36, 355, 384, 393 ff., and also scattered references about their earliest childhood.

Chapter Three

1. Letters between Van Doren and Merton indicate that Merton left many decisions about which poems to submit for publication to Van Doren. A 22 February 1944 letter relates Merton's specific thanks to Van Doren for making selections and showing the manuscript for *Thirty Poems* to James Laughlin.

2. *A Catch of Anti-Letters,* foreword by Brother Patrick Hart (Kansas City, 1978).

3. Robert Lax to Mark Van Doren, 28 December 1943, Columbia University Library.

4. *A Merton Reader,* pp. 71–75. These reviews originally appeared in the *New York Herald Tribune Books,* May 1938.

5. *Early Poems, 1940–1942* was first circulated as a mimeographed collection and printed in 1971 in a limited edition by the Anvil Press. Citations to *Early Poems* are from *The Collected Poems,* and subsequent references will be noted parenthetically.

6. Sister Thérèse Lentfoehr, in *Words and Silence* (New York, 1979), p. 4, observed that this is Merton's first use of references to enclosures, a pattern which is to continue in much later work.

7. See *The Strange Islands* (New York, 1957), pp. 43–78, and chapter 5 of this study.

8. For a representative review see "Thirty Poems," *Blackfriars* 26 (July 1945):270.

9. Merton's letter to Mark Van Doren indicates that he appreciated Van Doren's editorial work. See note 1, above, and a 26 December 1944 letter (Columbia University Library) that mentions line changes which he felt were improvements.

10. For a spirited attack upon Merton's early poetry as the product of someone "damaged by the tradition of Eliot," see Sr. Susan Margaret Campbell's "The Poetry of Thomas Merton: A Study in Theory, Influences, and Form" (Ph.D. diss., Stanford University, 1954).

11. *Thirty Poems* (New York, 1944). Citations in this chapter are from *Collected Poems,* pp. 27–28.

12. *A Man in the Divided Sea* (New York, 1946), p. 13; quotations from this collection are from *Collected Poems.*

13. Chapter 8 of this study concerns itself with *The Geography of Lograire* and Merton's interests in cargo cults.

14. Reviews of this book were not favorable, and it is important to note that Merton himself was not pleased with the collection. In *Words and Silence* Sister Thérèse Lentfoehr quotes from a manuscript journal: "*Figures for an Apocalypse* came in yesterday. A child's garden of bad verses. I should have pulled out a lot of weeds before I let that get into print. May God have mercy on me. The reviewers won't" (p. 16).

15. His essay "Poetry and the Contemplative Life" was included as an appendix to this volume (pp. 93–111).

16. Merton's epigram is, "And at midnight there was a cry made: Behold the Bridegroom cometh, go ye forth to meet Him" (Matthew 25:6). Quotations from *Figures* are from *Collected Poems.*

Chapter Four

1. *The Waters of Siloe* (New York, 1949), p. 351.

2. *The Sign of Jonas* (New York, 1953), p. 13; hereafter cited as *SiJ*.

3. Just how divided of mind Merton remained is evident from some of the excluded sections of the manuscript written for *Seven Storey Mountain;* for example: "I used to be a writer, but God wants me to die to all that. I shall give up all writing. Nothing more, not even a spiritual journal. Poems I shall renounce forever. . . ." See *Renascence* 2 (Spring 1950):89.

4. Preface to *Exile Ends in Glory* (Milwaukee, 1948), pp. xi–xii.

5. *What Are These Wounds?* (Milwaukee, 1950), p. viii.

6. *Seeds of Contemplation* (1949; reprint ed., New York, 1953), p. 6; hereafter cited as *SC*.

7. "Author's Note," in *New Seeds of Contemplation* (New York, 1962); hereafter cited as *NS*.

8. Extensive comparison of *Seeds* and *New Seeds* has been done by Donald Grayston, "Textual variation and Theological development in Thomas Merton's *Seeds of Contemplation* and *New Seeds of Contemplation*" (M.A. thesis, Trinity College, Toronto, Canada, 1974). Chapters 3–6 of this thesis in revised form were published as "The making of a spiritual classic: Thomas Merton's *Seeds of Contemplation* and *New Seeds of Contemplation*," *Studies in Religion* 3 (1974):339–56.

9. *Bread in the Wilderness* (1953; reprint ed., Collegeville, 1971), p. 87; hereafter cited as *BW*.

10. *No Man Is An Island* (New York, 1955), pp. xvi–xvii; hereafter cited as *NM*.

11. *Thoughts in Solitude* (1958; reprint ed., New York, 1978), p. 13; hereafter cited as *TS*.

12. Merton to Mark Van Doren, 16 October 1954, Columbia University Library.

13. See Flannery O'Connor's letters in *The Habit of Being* (New York, 1979), for example, p. 346.

14. *The Living Bread* (New York, 1956), p. xxx; hereafter cited as *LB*.

15. See chapter 6 of this study for a detailed consideration of *The Behavior of Titans*.

16. *The New Man* (New York, 1962), p. 120.

17. For a careful consideration of some of the more important themes in this book see James Finley's *Merton's Palace of Nowhere* (Notre Dame, 1978).

Chapter Five

1. See *Figures for an Apocalypse,* pp. 93–111. The revised version was published in *Commonweal* 69 (24 October 1958):87–92. Merton also included this essay in the first edition of *Selected Poems of Thomas Merton* (1959).

2. *Commonweal,* p. 92.

3. *The Tears of the Blind Lions* (New York, 1949); hereafter cited as *T.*

4. See George Woodcock, *Thomas Merton, Monk and Poet* (New York, 1978), p. 51.

5. See Sister Thérèse Lentfoehr's discussion in *Words and Silence,* pp. 22–23.

6. Cf. Merton's "War and the Crisis of Language," in *The Critique of War: Contemporary Philosophical Explanations,* ed. Robert Ginsberg (Chicago, 1969), and various passages in *The Geography of Lograire,* especially in the North canto.

7. *The Strange Islands* (New York, 1957), p. 30; hereafter cited as *SI.*

8. Reviews of *The Strange Islands* were not wholly favorable. See, for instance, John Logan in *Commonweal* 66 (5 July 1957):357–58; Donald Justice in *Poetry* 91 (October 1957):41–44; Donald Hall in *Saturday Review,* 6 July 1957, p. 29.

9. Included in *Words and Silence* is an appendix by Merton entitled "The Tower of Babel: An Explanation." This essay was written at the request of those who were preparing a television script of the verse drama, pp. 154–56.

10. In a draft for "The Tower of Babel" which was sent to Mark Van Doren, Merton's drama is arranged as an "Oratorio." The ten-page manuscript is in the Columbia University Library.

11. Cf. passages in St. Benedict's Rule which Merton is obviously satirizing.

12. *Original Child Bomb* (New York, 1962).

13. *Emblems of a Season of Fury* (New York, 1963), pp. 4–5; hereafter cited as *E.*

14. Sister Thérèse Lentfoehr has explained that this poem is based upon a drawing (*Words and Silence,* p. 86).

Chapter Six

1. Various commentators have stressed Merton's development which allowed him to move closer to the world. Two representative articles are John F. Teahan, "Renunciation of self and world: a critical dialectic in Thomas Merton," *Thought* 53, no. 209 (June 1978):133–50; and Gerald

Twomey, "The Doctrine of the Human Person as Image of God in the Writings of Thomas Merton," *Cistercian Studies* 13 (1975):216–23.

2. See James H. Forest's "Thomas Merton's Struggle with Peacemaking," *Thomas Merton: Prophet in the Belly of a Paradox* (New York, 1978), pp. 15–54.

3. My "Thomas Merton's Concern about Institutionalization, Bureaucracy, and the Abuse of Language," *Proceedings of the Southeastern American Studies Association* (Tampa, 1979), pp. 52–58, examines some of these questions.

4. *Secular Journal,* p. 116.

5. *Disputed Questions* (New York, 1960), p. ix; hereafter cited as *DQ.*

6. *Seeds of Destruction* (New York, 1964), p. xvi; hereafter cited as *SD.*

7. See chapter 7 for additional material on Gandhi.

8. While Merton was perfecting the letter as an art form he was corresponding with hundreds of individuals. At the Thomas Merton Studies Center of Bellarmine College there are over 1,700 different correspondence files, and in many cases scores of letters were exchanged.

9. *The Behavior of Titans* (New York, 1961), pp. 17–18; hereafter cited as *BT.*

10. *Conjectures of a Guilty Bystander* (New York, 1968), p. 348; hereafter cited as *C,*

11. *Faith and Violence* (Notre Dame, 1968), p. 154; hereafter cited as *FAV.*

12. *Raids on the Unspeakable* (New York, 1966), pp. 68–69; hereafter cited as *R.*

13. "Epitaph for a Public Servant," in *The Collected Poems of Thomas Merton,* p. 705.

14. *Thomas Merton on Peace,* introduction by Gordon C. Zahn (New York, 1975), pp. 234–47; hereafter cited as *OP.* This essay originally appeared in *The Critique of War: Contemporary Philosophical Explanations,* ed. Robert Ginsberg (Chicago, 1969).

15. *Ishi Means Man* (Greensboro, 1976), p. 32.

Chapter Seven

1. *Gandhi on Non-Violence: A selection from the writings of Mahatma Gandhi,* ed. Thomas Merton (New York, 1965), pp. 1–2; hereafter cited as *G.*

2. Cf. Merton's prefaces to two foreign editions of his books; the Japanese edition of *Seven Storey Mountain* in *Nanae No Yama,* trans. Tadishi Kudo (Tokyo, 1966); and "Preface to Vietnamese edition of *No Man Is An Island,*" in *Thomas Merton on Peace,* pp. 63–66.

3. *Conjectures,* p. 117.

4. *The Wisdom of the Desert: Sayings from the Desert Fathers of the Fourth Century,* trans. Thomas Merton (New York, 1960), p. ix; hereafter cited as *WD.*

5. *Mystics and Zen Masters* (New York, 1967), p. 3; hereafter cited as *MZM.*

6. *Zen and the Birds of Appetite* (New York, 1968). Printed as part 2 of this volume. This dialogue first appeared in *New Directions 17.* It is here cited as *ZBA.*

7. *The Way of Chuang Tzu* (New York, 1965), p. 9; hereafter cited as *WCT.*

8. *Conjectures,* p. 53.

9. Cf. Sister Thérèse Lentfoehr's examination of Merton's "Zen Mystical Transparencies," in *Words and Silence* (New York, 1979), pp. 52–63.

10. *Mystics and Zen Masters,* p. 245. Section 4, pp. 243–47, is devoted to Rilke.

11. *The Asian Journal of Thomas Merton,* ed. Naomi Burton et al. (New York, 1973), p. 117; hereafter cited as *AJ.*

Chapter Eight

1. Interview, New York City, 29 November 1978.

2. *Raids on the Unspeakable,* p. 161.

3. *Cables to the Ace* (New York, 1967), p. 1; hereafter cited as *Ca.*

4. Luke Flaherty, "Thomas Merton's *Cables to the Ace:* A Critical Study," *Renascence* 24 (Fall 1971):3–32.

5. Flannery O'Connor, "On Her Own Work," in *Mystery and Manners* (New York, 1970), p. 113. See also Merton's "Flannery O'Connor: A Prose Elegy," in *Raids,* pp. 37–42.

6. Gail Ramshaw Schmidt, "The Poetry of Thomas Merton" (Ph.D. diss., University of Wisconsin Madison, 1976), pp. 91 ff.

7. Walter Sutton, *American Free Verse: The Modern Revolution in Poetry* (New York, 1973), p. 202.

8. "Author's Note," in *The Geography of Lograire* (New York, 1969), p. 1; hereafter cited as *GL.*

9. "Paradise Bugged," *Critic* 25 (February–March 1967):69–71. Review of Louis Zukofsky's *All the Collected Short Poems: 1956–1964.*

10. Some of the discussion of *The Geography of Lograire* which follows is based upon my article in *Exploration* 5 (December 1977):15–27.

11. Further details about how Merton incorporated his reading into *Lograire* can be observed in the "Notes on Sources," pp. 139–53.

12. James York Glimm's "Thomas Merton's Last Poem: *The Geography of Lograire, Renascence,* 26 (Winter 1974), pp. 95–104 provides an overview of the poem.

13. Schmidt, "The Poetry of Thomas Merton," pp. 130–83.

Chapter Nine

1. Ralph Waldo Emerson, *The Selected Writings of Ralph Waldo Emerson* (New York, 1940), p. 153.

2. *The Asian Journal of Thomas Merton,* p. 4.

3. *Contemplation in a World of Action* (New York, 1973), p. 343.

4. *Love and Living* (New York, 1979), p. 76.

5. *Contemplative Prayer* (New York, 1969), p. 27.

6. "Inner Experience"; manuscript at the Thomas Merton Studies Center, Bellarmine College. This manuscript has been carefully studied by scholars and parts of it have been published. See, for example, passages in Raymond Bailey's *Thomas Merton on Mysticism,* pp. 134–58.

Chapter Ten

1. Edited from notebooks by Naomi Burton, Brother Patrick Hart, and James Laughlin; consulting editor, Amiya Chakravarty, (New York: New Directions, 1973). This book includes selections from travel journals, diaries, and reading notes. Appendixes, including letters, and an extensive glossary of terms. All the books by, and about, Merton surveyed in this afterword are listed immediately below with subsequent citations noted within the text:

Thomas Merton. *The Collected Poems of Thomas Merton.* Paperback edition. New York: New Directions, 1980. 1048 pp.

Thomas Merton. *Eighteen Poems.* New York: New Directions, 1985. Unpaged.

Thomas Merton. *The Hidden Ground of Love,* The Letters of Thomas Merton on Religious and Social Concerns. Selected and Edited by William H. Shannon. New York: Farrar, Straus, Giroux, 1985. xiv + 669 pp.

Thomas Merton. *The Literary Essays of Thomas Merton.* Edited by Brother Patrick Hart. New York: New Directions, 1981. 549 pp.

Thomas Merton. *Thomas Merton on Saint Bernard.* Kalamazoo: Cistercian Publications, 1980. 242 pp.

Thomas Merton. *Love and Living.* Naomi Burton Stone and Brother Patrick Hart, eds. New York: Farrar, Straus, Giroux, 1979. 232 pp.

Thomas Merton. *Day of a Stranger.* Introduction by Robert E. Daggy. Salt Lake City: Gibbs M. Smith, Inc., 1981, 63 pp.

Thomas Merton. *Woods, Shore, Desert.* Introduction and Notes by Joel Weishaus. Santa Fe: Museum of New Mexico Press, 1982, 58 pp.

Thomas Merton. *The Alaskan Journal of Thomas Merton.* Edited by Robert E.

Daggy. New York: New Directions, 1987; and Isla Vista, California: Turkey Press, 1987 (projected date of publication).

Thomas Merton and Robert Lax. *A Catch of Anti-Letters*. Kansas City: Sheed, Andrews and McMeel, Inc., 1978. xiii, 128 pp.

Deba Patnaik, ed. *Geography of Holiness, The Photography of Thomas Merton*. New York: The Pilgrim Press, 1980. xii, 128 unnumbered pp.

William H. Shannon. *Thomas Merton's Dark Path, The Inner Experience of a Contemplative*. New York: Farrar, Straus, Giroux, 1981, 222 pp.

Thomas Merton. "The Inner Experience" manuscript has been edited by Brother Patrick Hart and published in installments in successive issues of *Cistercian Studies*, Vols. 18 & 19 (1983, 1984).

Donald Grayston. *Thomas Merton: The Development of a Spiritual Theologian*, New York and Toronto: Edwin Mellen Press, 1985.

Monica Furlong. *Merton, A Biography*. San Francisco: Harper & Row, 1980. xx. 342 pp.

John Howard Griffin. *Follow the Ecstasy*. Fort Worth: JHG Editions/Latitudes Press; 1983. ix + 208 pp. plus index.

Michael Mott. *The Seven Mountains of Thomas Merton*. Boston: Houghton Mifflin, 1984. xxvi + 690 pp. (including index).

Paul Wilkes, ed. *Merton: By Those Who Knew Him Best*. San Francisco, Harper, 1984, xi + 171 pp.

James Forest. *Thomas Merton, A Pictorial Biography*. New York: Paulist Press, 1980. 102 pp.

George Woodcock. *Thomas Merton, Monk and Poet: A Critical Study*. New York: Farrar, Straus, Giroux, 1978. 200 pp.

Ross Labrie, *The Art of Thomas Merton*. Fort Worth: Texas Christian University Press, 1979. xiii, 188 pp.

Padovano, Anthony T. *The Human Journey, Thomas Merton: Symbol of a Century*. New York: Doubleday, 1982. 193 pp.

Sister Thérèse Lentfoehr. *Words and Silence: On the Poetry of Thomas Merton.* New York: New Directions, 1979. ix, 166 pp.

James Finley. *Merton's Palace of Nowhere: A Search for God Through Awareness of the True Self*. Notre Dame: Ave Maria Press, 1978. 158 pp.

Daniel J. Adams. *Thomas Merton's Shared Contemplation, A Protestant Perspective*. Kalamazoo: Cistercian Publications, 1979. 361 pp.

Elena Malits. *The Solitary Explorer, Thomas Merton's Transforming Journey*. San Francisco: Harper & Row, 1980. xiii, 197 pp.

Cashen, Richard Anthony. *Solitude in the Writings of Thomas Merton*. Kalamazoo: Cistercian Publications, 1982. 168 pp.

Lipski, Alexander. *Thomas Merton and Asia: His Quest for Utopia*. Kalamazoo: Cistercian Publications, 1983. iv + 92 pp.

Gerald Twomey, ed. *Thomas Merton: Prophet in the Belly of Paradox*. New York: Paulist Press, 1978. xiii, 237 pp.

Brother Patrick Hart, ed. *The Message of Thomas Merton*. Kalamazoo: Cistercian Publications, 1981. xvi, 231 pp.

Brother Patrick Hart, ed. *The Legacy of Thomas Merton*. Kalamazoo: Cistercian Publications, 1986. 241 pp.

Marquita E. Breit and Robert Daggy. *Thomas Merton: A Comprehensive Bibliography;* New Edition. New York: Garland Publishing, 1986. 736 pp.

2. Marquita Breit, *Thomas Merton: A Biography* (Metuchen, N.J.: The Scarecrow Press, 1974); and Frank Dell 'Isola, *Thomas Merton: A Bibliography* (New York: Farrar, Straus, & Cudahy, 1956); and *Thomas Merton, A Bibliography;* 1st revised edition (Kent State: Kent State University Press, 1975); and finally, the comprehensive bibliography by Marquita E. Breit and Robert E. Daggy, which is reviewed in this afterword (See note 1). Dell 'Isola's is a systematic bibliographic description of Merton's book as well as a listing of periodical contributions, translations, miscellanea, poetry, translations, and juvenalia. Breit's 1974 bibliography includes a listing of secondary sources about Merton.

3. These books include *Contemplative Prayer* (New York: Herder and Herder, 1969); *The Collected Poems of Thomas Merton* (New York: New Directions, 1977) hardback edition; *My Argument With the Gestapo* (Garden City: Doubleday, 1969); *Contemplation in a World of Action* (Garden City: Doubleday, 1971); *The Monastic Journey* (Kansas City: Sheed, Andrews and McMeel, Inc., 1977); *A Hidden Wholeness, The Visual World of Thomas Merton*, photographs by Thomas Merton and John Howard Griffin. Text by Griffin. (Boston: Houghton Mifflin Co., 1970).

Other books not reviewed in this afterword include the collections edited by Gordon Zahn called *Thomas Merton on Peace* (New York: McCall Publishing, 1971) republished under the title *The Non-Violent Alternative* (New York: Farrar, Straus, and Giroux, 1981); and *Ishi Means Man, Essays on Native Americans*, with a foreward by Dorothy Day (Greensboro: Unicorn, 1976). Also of value are the appointment calendars for 1979 and 1980 (Sheed, Andrews, and McMeel) which include texts and original drawings by Merton. The 1981 calendar, issued by the same publisher includes photographs by Merton. Much of the material in these appointment calendars had not been published before.

4. The major repository for Merton manuscripts, tapes, books, photographs, etc. is The Thomas Merton Studies Center at Bellarmine College in Louisville. A second large collection is at the Merton Center at Columbia University in New York City. The Thomas Merton Studies Center at Bellarmine publishes *The Merton Seasonal of Bellarmine College* which includes a listing of publications by and about Merton. An example of the continuing work being done at The Thomas Merton Studies Center is the publication of the selected foreign prefaces to editions of Merton's books: Edited by Robert E. Daggy, this collection is called *Introductions East and West: The Foreign Prefaces of Thomas Merton* (Greensboro: Unicorn Press, 1981).

5. *Thomas Merton/Monk* A Monastic Tribute (New York: Sheed and Ward, 1974). See note 17.

6. *Merton's Theology of Prayer* (Spencer: Cistercian Publications, 1971), p. ix.

7. *Thomas Merton-Social Critic* (Lexington: The University Press of Kentucky, 1971).

8. *Man Before God, Thomas Merton on Social Responsibility* (Garden City: Doubleday, 1974).

9. *Thomas Merton on Mysticism* (Garden City: Doubleday, 1975).

10. Reviews of *The Collected Poetry* have ranged from disapprobation to enthusiasm. See, for example, Daniel Berrigan's comments in "the seventy times seven storey mountain," *Cross Currents.* 26, No. 4 (Winter 1977–78), pp. 385–393.

11. See pp. 79ff, 240ff, 408–409 of *The Seven Storey Mountain* (New York: Harcourt, Brace, 1948) for evidence of their friendship.

12. *The Geography of Lograire* (New York: New Directions, 1969) contains an author's note and notes compiled by editors (included in *The Collected Poems of Thomas Merton*) which this posthumous material qualifies.

13. *The Man in the Sycamore Tree, An Entertainment.* (Garden City: Doubleday, 1970), p. 80.

14. The "Thomas Merton Oral History" project under the direction of Victor A. Kramer has completed 19 interviews of persons close to Merton. Transcribed, edited, and bound copies of these interviews are on deposit at Merton research centers. An article, "Thomas Merton Oral History: A Beginning — A Report On Nineteen Archival Interviews," which describes this project is in Vol. 11, No. 2 of *The Merton Seasonal,* pp. 8–9.

15. See, for example, Merton's review of *All The Collected Short Poems, 1956–1964,* by Louis Zukofsky, in *The Critic* (February-March 1968), pp. 69–71, and "Zukofsky: The Paradise Ear" *Peace News* (London) (28 July 1967), p. 8ff.

16. From "We Were Poor Poor Poor" and "Strip Mining" in *Prison Poems* (New York: Viking, 1973), pp. 87, 109.

17. This book (Kalamazoo: Cistercian Publications, 1983) has been expanded and revised, and now includes pieces by Father Daniel Berrigan, various Latin American writers, the Canadian Father Armand Veilleux, now Abbot at the Monastery of the Holy Spirit, Conyers, Georgia, and Rosemary Houghton. The international flavor of the first edition is thereby expanded and thus the growing world-wide interest in Merton is reflected.

Selected Bibliography

PRIMARY SOURCES

1. Autobiography

The Seven Storey Mountain. New York: Harcourt, Brace, 1948.

The Sign of Jonas. New York: Harcourt, Brace, 1953.

The Secular Journal of Thomas Merton. New York: Farrar, Straus & Cudahy, 1959.

Conjectures of a Guilty Bystander. Garden City: Doubleday, 1966.

The Asian Journal of Thomas Merton. Edited from notebooks by Naomi Burton, Brother Patrick Hart, and James Laughlin. New York: New Directions, 1973.

Day of a Stranger. Introduction by Robert E. Daggy. Salt Lake City: Gibbs M. Smith, 1981.

2. Devotional

Exile Ends in Glory. Milwaukee: Bruce, 1948.

What Is Contemplation? Notre Dame: Holy Cross, 1948.

Seeds of Contemplation. New York: New Directions, 1949.

What Are These Wounds? Milwaukee: Bruce, 1950.

No Man Is an Island. New York: Harcourt, Brace, 1955.

Praying the Psalms. Collegeville: Liturgical Press, 1956.

Thoughts in Solitude. New York: Farrar, Straus & Cudahy, 1958.

New Seeds of Contemplation. New York: New Directions, 1961.

Contemplative Prayer. New York: Herder & Herder, 1969. Also published as *The Climate of Monastic Prayer,* Cistercian Studies Series, no. 1.

Opening the Bible. Collegeville, Minn.: Liturgical Press, 1970.

He Is Risen. Niles, Ill.: Argus Communications, 1975.

3. Essays

Bread in the Wilderness. New York: New Directions, 1953.

Disputed Questions. New York: Farrar, Straus & Cudahy, 1960.

The Behavior of Titans. New York: New Directions, 1961.

The New Man. New York: Farrar, Straus & Cudahy, 1961.

Life and Holiness. New York: Herder & Herder, 1963.

Seeds of Destruction. New York: Farrar, Straus & Giroux, 1964.

Seasons of Celebration. New York: Farrar, Straus & Giroux, 1965.

Raids on the Unspeakable. New York: New Directions, 1966.
Mystics and Zen Masters. New York: Farrar, Straus & Giroux, 1967.
Zen and the Birds of Appetite. New York: New Directions, 1968.
Faith and Violence. Notre Dame, Ind.: University of Notre Dame Press, 1968.
Contemplation in a World of Action. Garden City, N.Y.: Doubleday, 1971.
Ishe Means Man. Greensboro, N.C.: Unicorn Press, 1976.
The Monastic Journey. Edited by Brother Patrick Hart. Kansas City: Sheed, Andrews, & McMeel, 1977.
Love and Living. New York: Farrar, Straus & Giroux, 1979.
Thomas Merton on St. Bernard. Kalamazoo, Mich.: Cistercian Publications, 1980.
The Literary Essays of Thomas Merton. New York: New Directions, 1981.

4. Fiction
My Argument with the Gestapo: A Macaronic Journal. Garden City, N.Y.: Doubleday, 1969.

5. Poetry
Thirty Poems. New York: New Directions, 1944.
A Man in the Divided Sea. New York: New Directions, 1946.
Figures for an Apocalypse. New York: New Directions, 1948.
The Tears of the Blind Lions. New York: New Directions, 1949.
Selected Poems. London: Hollis & Carter, 1950. First English edition.
The Strange Islands. New York: New Directions, 1957.
The Tower of Babel. Hamburg, West Germany: Laughlin, 1957.
Selected Poems of Thomas Merton. New York: New Directions, 1959.
Original Child Bomb. New York: New Directions, 1962.
Emblems of a Season of Fury. New York: New Directions, 1963.
Cables to the Ace. New York: New Directions, 1968.
The Geography of Lograire. New York: New Directions, 1969.
The Collected Poems of Thomas Merton. New York: New Directions, 1977.

6. Other work
The Waters of Siloe. New York: Harcourt, Brace, 1949.
The Ascent to Truth. New York: Harcourt, Brace, 1951.
The Last of the Fathers. New York: Harcourt, Brace, 1954.
The Living Bread. New York: Farrar, Straus & Cudahy, 1956.
The Silent Life. New York: Farrar, Straus & Cudahy, 1957.
Spiritual Direction and Meditation. Collegeville, Minn.: Liturgical Press, 1960.
A Thomas Merton Reader. Edited by Thomas P. McDonnell. New York: Harcourt, Brace, 1962.

Thomas Merton on Peace. Edited by Gordon C. Zahn. New York: McCall, 1971. Republished as *The Non-Violent Alternative* (New York: Farrar, Straus & Giroux, 1980).

A Catch of Anti-Letters. Kansas City: Sheed, Andrews, & McMeel, 1978. Letters by Merton and Robert Lax.

Geography of Holiness: The Photography of Thomas Merton. Edited by Deba Prasad Patnaik. New York: Pilgrim Press, 1980.

7. Collections edited by Merton

Breakthrough to Peace. New York: New Directions, 1963.

Gandhi on Non-Violence. New York: New Directions, 1965.

8. Translations

The Wisdom of the Desert. New York: New Directions, 1960.

Clement of Alexandria. Verona, Italy: Stamperia, Valdonega, 1962.

The Way of Chuang Tzu. New York: New Directions, 1965.

9. Tapes and film

Commercial Merton audio tapes are available. Electronic Paperbacks, Chappaqua, New York, has issued twenty-four hour-long cassettes, material recorded during informal conferences for novices. A film and video tape of Merton's Bangkok talk, *Last Day of Thomas Merton,* is available through Ikonographics, Louisville, Kentucky.

10. Selected pamphlets, translations of monastic materials, limited editions, and edited journal

The Soul of the Apostolate. Trappist, Ky.: Gethsemani, 1946. Translation.

Cistercian Contemplatives. Trappist, Ky.: Gethsemani, 1948.

The Spirit of Simplicity. Trappist, Ky.: Gethsemani, 1948.

Gethsemani Magnificat. Trappist, Ky.: Gethsemani, 1949. 200 photographs.

A Balanced Life of Prayer. Trappist, Ky.: Gethsemani, 1951.

Devotions to St. John of the Cross. Trappist, Ky.: Gethsemani, 1953.

Basic Principles of Monastic Spirituality. Trappist, Ky.: Gethsemani, 1957.

Monastic Peace. Trappist, Ky.: Gethsemani, 1958.

Prometheus, A Meditation. Lexington: University of Kentucky, 1958.

Nativity Kerygma. St. Paul, Minn.: North Central Publishing, 1958.

The Christmas Sermons of Bl. Guerric of Igny. Trappist, Ky.: Gethsemani, 1959.

Hagia Sophia. Lexington, Ky.: Stamperia del Santuccio, 1962.

The Solitary Life: Guigo the Carthusian. Worcester, Mass.: Stanbrook, 1963. Translation.

Monastic Life at Gethsemani. Trappist, Ky.: Gethsemani, 1966.

Monk's Pond, nos. 1–4 (Spring-Winter 1968). Published at Gethsemani; quarterly; edited by Merton.

The True Solitude. N.p.: Hallmark editions, 1969. Selections.

Pasternak/Merton: Six Letters. Lexington: University of Kentucky Press, 1973.

11. Note about research materials

The major collection of Thomas Merton research material is located at the Thomas Merton Studies Center of Bellarmine College, Louisville, Kentucky. Included in this extensive collection are manuscripts and correspondence, galleys, books with marginalia, photographs, and tapes made from Merton's conferences at the Abbey of Gethsemani. Additional Merton research materials of major interest are in the collection of Sister Thérèse Lentfoehr, at the Merton Center of Columbia University. Other sources of research materials are at St. Bonaventure University; Columbia University Library; the Humanities Research Center of the University of Texas; and the University of Rochester.

SECONDARY SOURCES

1. Bibliographies

Breit, Marquita. *Thomas Merton: A Bibliography.* Metuchen, N.J.: Scarecrow Press, 1974. Lists over 1,800 items by and about Thomas Merton published between the years 1957 and 1973.

Dell I'Sola, Frank. *Thomas Merton: A Bibliography.* New York: Farrar, Straus & Cudahy, 1956. Expanded edition published as no. 31 in the Serif Series of Bibliographies (Kent State, Ohio: Kent State University Press, 1975). Includes sections on books and pamphlets by Merton; books with contributions by Merton; contributions by Merton to newspapers and periodicals; translations; miscellaneous poetry in periodicals, newspapers, and books; translations of Merton; and juvenilia, as well as various indices.

2. Books about Merton

Adams, Daniel J. *Thomas Merton's Shared Contemplation, A Protestant Perspective.* Kalamazoo, Mich.: Cistercian Studies Press, 1979. Study of the development of Merton's thought which stresses the interrelationship of solitude and sharing.

Bailey, Raymond. *Thomas Merton on Mysticism.* New York: Doubleday, 1975. Thorough consideration of Merton's development of thought concerning mysticism.

Baker, James. *Thomas Merton—Social Critic.* Lexington: University of Kentucky Press, 1971. Study of Merton's major writings, with emphasis upon questions about the world, race, war, and implications of contemplation in relation to the world.

Cashen, Richard Anthony. *Solitude in the Thought of Thomas Merton.* Kalamazoo, Mich.: Cistercian Publications, 1981. Study of the theme of solitude within Merton's major writing in relation to the progression of his life and traditions of solitude within the church.

Finley, James. *Merton's Palace of Nowhere: A Search for God through Awareness of the True Self.* Notre Dame, Ind.: Ava Maria Press, 1978. Valuable application of Merton's ideas about the false and the true self.

Forest, James H. *Thomas Merton: A Pictorial Biography.* New York: Paulist Press, 1980. A popular retelling of the life of Merton accompanied by many previously unpublished documentary photographs.

Furlong, Monica. *Merton, A Biography.* New York: Harper & Row, 1980. An overview of Merton's life and career with new information especially about his European years.

Griffin, John Howard. *A Hidden Wholeness/The Visual World of Thomas Merton.* Photographs by Merton and John Howard Griffin. Text by Griffin. Boston: Houghton Mifflin, 1970. Photographs by, and of, Merton which reflect his interests especially during the final years of his life.

Hart, Patrick, Br. ed. *Thomas Merton/Monk.* New York: Sheed & Ward, 1974. Valuable essays by commentators who were in most cases extremely close to Merton during his life.

―――. *The Message of Thomas Merton.* Kalamazoo, Mich.: Cistercian Publications, 1981. Twelve essays about the most significant aspects of the thought and life, selected from several symposia held in 1978 to commemorate the tenth anniversary of Merton's death with a helpful introduction about Merton's spirituality by the editor.

Higgins, John J. *Merton's Theology of Prayer.* Kalamazoo, Mich.: Cistercian Studies, 1971. Republished as *Thomas Merton on Prayer* (New York: Doubleday, 1974). A comprehensive study of Merton's thoughts on prayer, sometimes difficult to follow because chronological development is not stressed.

Kelly, Frederic Joseph. *Man Before God: Thomas Merton on Social Responsibility.* New York: Doubleday, 1974. Systematic overview of Merton's life and writings in relation to the development of his social awareness.

Labrie, Ross. *The Art of Thomas Merton.* Fort Worth: Texas Christian University Press, 1979. An assessment of Merton's skill in various forms—novel, diary, essay, and poem—in relation to how he used art to emphasize the contemplative.

Lentfoehr, Thérèse, Sr. *Words and Silence: On the Poetry of Thomas Merton.* New York: New Directions, 1979. A careful reading of Merton's poetry qualified by a thorough knowledge of all his work and access to unpublished manuscript materials.

McInerny, Dennis Q. *Thomas Merton: The Man and His Work.* Kalamazoo, Mich.: Cistercian Publications, 1974. An overview of Merton's accomplishment, sometimes narrow in its estimation of the final works, but nevertheless valuable.

Malits, Elena. *The Solitary Explorer: Thomas Merton's Transforming Journey.* New York: Harper & Row, 1980. Systematic study of Merton's use of image and metaphor to relate his own continuing conversion.

Nouwen, Henri J. M. *Pray to Live, Thomas Merton: Contemplative Critic.* Notre Dame: Fides/Claretian, 1972. An introduction to the life and thought of Merton as a way for modern man to understand his need for a contemplative foundation in life.

Rice, Edward. *The Man in the Sycamore Tree, The Good Times and Hard Life of Thomas Merton: An Entertainment.* Garden City, N.Y.: Doubleday, 1970. An informal biography which includes many photographs, and while sometimes opinionated, full of good insights.

Shannon, William H. *Thomas Merton's Dark Path: The Inner Experience of a Contemplative.* New York: Farrar, Straus & Giroux, 1981. Close examination of Merton's books which treat the contemplative experience along with a twenty-eight page section from the manuscript "The Inner Experience."

Twomey, Gerald, ed. *Thomas Merton: Prophet in the Belly of a Paradox.* New York: Paulist Press, 1978. Collection of essays which surveys varied aspects of Merton's life, art, and commitment.

Woodcock, George. *Thomas Merton: Monk and Poet.* New York: Farrar, Straus, Giroux, 1978. Insightful study of Merton's major writing, valuable as introduction to the poetry, and to Merton's later interest in the East.

3. Dissertations

Campbell, Susan Margaret, Sr. "The Poetry of Thomas Merton: A Study in Theory, Influences and Form." Ph.D. dissertation, Stanford University, 1954. Valuable as a systematic attack on Merton's flaws as poet.

Higgins, Michael. "Thomas Merton: the silent-seeking poet." Ph.D. dissertation, York University, Toronto, 1979. Valuable examination of all of the poetry.

Kilcourse, George A. "Incarnation as the Integrating Principle in Thomas Merton's Poetry and Spirituality." Ph.D. dissertation, Fordham University, 1974. Valuable as overview, this includes a detailed review of Merton criticism; it stands as one of the best comprehensive overviews of Merton's poetry.

Schmidt, Gail Ramshaw. "The Poetry of Thomas Merton: An Introduction." Ph.D. dissertation, University of Wisconsin, 1976. Valuable as explication and especially for final poetry because of manuscript study.

4. Articles

Berrigan, Daniel. "The seventy times seventy seven storey mountain." *Cross Currents* 27 (Winter 1977–78):385–93. Enthusiastic review of *The Collected Poems* with many insights and speculations about this "whale" of a book.

Bigane, John E. "Mysticism, Merton and Solitude." *American Benedictine Review* 33 (June 1982):204–13. Investigation of Merton's spirituality and questions of solitude not as monastic escape, but involvement with others, not solitary existence, but existence as solidarity.

Boyd, John D., S.J. "Christian Imaginative Patterns and the Poetry of Thomas Merton." *Greyfriar-Siena Studies in Literature* 13 (1972):3–14. Insightful study of the relationship of Merton's poetic themes to traditional Christian thought.

Flaherty, Luke. "Thomas Merton's *Cables to the Ace:* A Critical Study." *Renascence* 24 (Fall 1971):3–32. Early insightful analysis of basic themes, images, and influences in *Cables.*

Gavin, Rosemarie Julie, Sr. "Influences Shaping the Poetic Imagery of Merton." *Renascence* 9 (Summer 1957):188–97, 222. Study of the influence of symbolist and surrealist techniques, as well as particular poets such as Crashaw, Traherne, Hopkins, and St. John of the Cross on Merton.

Glimm, James York. "Thomas Merton's Last Poem: *The Geography of Lograire.*" *Renascence* 26 (Winter 1974):95–104. Careful study of *Lograire* as Merton's myth-dream which leads western man into the myth-dreams of other cultures.

Johnson, Carol. "The Vision and the Poem." *Poetry* 96 (September 1960):387–91. Evaluation of Merton's poetic accomplishment through the publication of *Selected Poems.*

Kelly, Richard. "Thomas Merton and Poetic Vitality." *Renascence* 12 (Spring 1960):139–42, 148. Demonstration that the poetry shares points with Robert Lowell and Lawrence Ferlinghetti and that the influence of Lorca is also evident.

Kramer, Victor A. "Thomas Merton's Published Journals: The Paradox of Writing as a Step Toward Contemplation." *Studia Mystica* 3 (1980):3–20. Investigation of major published journals as works of art which reveal the writer's movement toward a more contemplative attitude.

Lentfoehr, Thérèse, Sr. "Thomas Merton: The Dimensions of Solitude." *American Benedictine Review* 23 (September 1972):337–52. Study of the development of the theme of solitude in significant writings of Merton.

Malits, Elena. "Thomas Merton: Symbol and Synthesis of Contemporary Catholicism." *Critic* 35 (Spring 1977):26–33. Valuable explanation of Merton's chief themes and of his appeal for today's audience.

Merton Seasonal of Bellarmine College. An occasional publication of the Thomas Merton Studies Center, Bellarmine College, Louisville, Kentucky, which includes articles, information about Merton scholarship, and a regular listing of bibliographical items by and about Merton.

Randall, Virginia F. "Contrapuntal Irony and Theme in Thomas Merton's *The Geography of Lograire.*" *Renascence* 28 (Summer 1976):191–202. Study of *The Geography of Lograire* as epic and meditation, and explanation of how opposed themes such as the "struggle of love and death" support each other throughout the poem.

Sturm, Ralph. "Thomas Merton: Poet." *American Benedictine Review* 22 (March 1971):1–20. Survey of Merton's accomplishment which maintains there is little change in technique; not helpful for final poetry, but useful as assessment of Merton as "minor" poet.

Suther, Judith D. "Thomas Merton Translates Raïssa Maritain." *Renascence* 28 (Summer 1976):181–90. Useful study of Merton's ability as translator and indirectly as indication of his aesthetic.

Sutton, Walter. *American Free Verse: The modern revolution in poetry.* New York: New Directions, 1973, pp. 198–203. Helpful analysis of Merton's last books of poetry in relation to the American epic tradition and developments in free verse.

Index

CISTERCIAN PUBLICATIONS INC.

Kalamazoo, Michigan

TITLES LISTING

THE CISTERCIAN FATHERS SERIES

Texts and Studies
in the
Monastic Tradition

* Temporarily out of print   *† Forthcoming*

THE CISTERCIAN STUDIES SERIES

MONASTIC TEXTS

CHRISTIAN SPIRITUALITY

MONASTIC STUDIES

CISTERCIAN STUDIES

* *Temporarily out of print*

† *Forthcoming*

THE CISTERCIAN LITURGICAL
DOCUMENTS SERIES

STUDIA PATRISTICA

Papers of the Oxford Patristics Conference 1983
(Elizabeth A. Livingstone, ed.)

1. Historica-Gnostica-Biblica
2. Critica-Classica-Ascetica-Liturgica
3. The Second Century-Clement and Origen-The
   Cappodocian Fathers †
4. Augustine-Post Nicene Latin Fathers-Oriental
   Texts-*Nachleben* of the Fathers †

FAIRACRES PRESS, OXFORD

The Wisdom of the Desert Fathers

The World of the Desert Fathers

The Letters of St Antony the Great

The Letters of Ammonas, Successor of
St Antony

A Study of Wisdom. Three Tracts by the author
of *The Cloud of Unknowing*

The Power of the Name. The Jesus Prayer in
Orthodox Spirituality (Kallistos Ware)

Contemporary Monasticism

The Influence of St Bernard

Theology and Spirituality (Andrew Louth)

Prayer and Holiness (Dumitru Staniloae)

Saint Gregory Nazianzen: Selected Poems

Eight Chapters on Perfection and Angel's Song
(Walter Hilton)

Creative Suffering (Iulia de Beausobre)

Bringing Forth Christ. Five Feasts of the Child
Jesus (St Bonaventure)

Gentleness in St John of the Cross

Distributed in North America only for Fairacres Press.

DISTRIBUTED BOOKS

St Benedict: Man with An Idea (Melbourne Studies)

The Spirit of Simplicity

Benedict's Disciples (David Hugh Farmer)

The Emperor's Monk: A Contemporary Life of
Benedict of Aniane

A Guide to Cistercian Scholarship (2nd ed.)

*North American customers may order
through booksellers or directly
from the publisher:*

Cistercian Publications
WMU Station
Kalamazoo, Michigan 49008
(616) 383-4985

*Cistercian Publications are available in
Britain, Europe and the Common-
wealth through A. R. Mowbray &
Co Ltd   St Thomas House   Oxford
OX1 1SJ.
For a sterling price list, please consult
Mowbray's General Catalogue.*

*A complete catalogue of texts-in-
translation and studies on early,
medieval, and modern Christian
monasticism is available at no cost
from Cistercian Publications.*

*Cistercian monks and nuns have been
living lives of prayer & praise, meditation &
manual labor since the twelfth century.
They are part of an unbroken tradition
which extends back to the fourth century
and which continues today in the Catholic
church, the Orthodox churches, the
Anglican communion, and, most recently,
in the Protestant churches.*

*Share their way of life and their search for
God by reading Cistercian Publications.*